AF560086

DYNAMICS OF THE RITUAL GIFT SYSTEM

Dynamics of the Ritual Gift System

Some Unexplored Dimensions

VIJAY NATH

MANOHAR
2012

First published 2012

© Kamaleshwar Nath, 2012

All rights reserved. No part of this publication may be reproduced or transmitted, in any form or by any means, without the prior permission of the publisher

ISBN 978-81-7304-926-2

Published by
Ajay Kumar Jain *for*
Manohar Publishers & Distributors
4753/23 Ansari Road, Daryaganj
New Delhi 110 002

Printed at
Salasar Imaging Systems
Delhi 110 032

To

Prof. R.S. Sharma

Contents

Acknowledgements

Like my previous book titled *Purāṇic World*, this book too owes its inception to rather unusual circumstances, the most crucial being my failing mobility and indifferent health, which has lately instilled in me a certain sense of urgency. The subject of *dāna* on which I had been working for the past twenty years and in normal circumstances might have continued doing so for some more, became suddenly the object of my feverish attention with the sole purpose of getting it published. That it could get published in such short a time the credit goes entirely to my publisher, Shri Ramesh Jain and my editor, Shri Siddharth Chowdhury, without whose cooperation the book might not have materialized. I am equally indebted to Prof. D.N Jha for continually extending to me his moral support, just as my guru and mentor Prof. R.S. Sharma has been my constant source of inspiration. The support supplied by my entire family, particularly my husband and my elder daughter Nidhi, has been chiefly responsible for giving me the necessary incentive to steadfastly work on the book. I will be missing in my duty if I do not mention some other cardinal members of this fantastic support group, namely my friends who have always been so encouraging and Sabrina, the girl from Jharkhand, with whose constant help and care I could manage to finish the book so speedily.

VIJAY NATH

Introduction

The present book is an eclectic collection of articles written over a period of almost twenty years and dealing with a religious institution that is unique to Indian culture, namely *dāna* or ritual gift-making. The institution has engaged the attention of Brāhmaṇical lawgivers from the earliest times and, by the end of the first millennium AD, had even become the thematic focus of innumerable *nibandhas* or digests. It was, however, only in the later half of the twentieth century when, in the context of feudal formations during the early medieval period, the practice of issuing land grants as a form of ritual gift-making became the subject of extensive research, that *dāna* came to evoke a lot of historical interest.

Moreover, in the wake of Darwin's famous theory of mutual aid,[1] furbished further by Kessler[2] and Petr Kropotkin,[3] gift-making in its other aspects of exchange and redistribution, especially in a pre-literate social context, became the subject of anthropological field studies undertaken by some well-known scholars such as Emile Durkheim,[4] B. Malinowski,[5] Raymond Firth,[6] Evans Pritchard,[7] and has continued to figure prominently in the works of more recent sociologists such as Erich Fromm,[8] Max Gluckman,[9] and Erik Schwimmer.[10] However, it was Marcel Mauss's famous work, *Essai sur le don, forme archaique de l'e change*,[11] in which sociological dimensions of the practice were probed with special reference to some great civilizations of the past, including that of India, that brought *dāna* within the ambit of other forms of gift-making. It inevitably aroused the interest of some noted historians such as J. Gonda[12] and Romila Thapar,[13] though a major section devoted to the topic of *dāna* as delineated in the Dharmaśāstras already figured in P.V. Kane's *magnum opus*, the *History of Dharmaśāstra*. The subject also constituted the main theme of K.V.R. Aiyangar's commentary on Lakṣmīdhara's work, *The Dāna Kāṇḍa of Kṛtyakalpataru*. *Dāna* finds brief mention even in the *Encyclopedia of Religion and Ethics* edited by James Hastings, though it is essentially in a limited context of the practice of charity in early societies.

Despite these early writings on *dāna*, since no exclusive work on the subject had been attempted and considering its potential as a social institution that could have dialectical linkages not only with other social and religious formations but even with developments related to polity and economy, I made it the subject of my PhD research under the guidance of Prof. R.S. Sharma, the chief proponent of the Indian feudalism theory. My findings were published in 1987 under the title *Dāna: Gift-system in Ancient India*. Being the first book on the subject, the work was well-received by scholars of ancient Indian history. In this book, in order to make an in-depth study of all available original sources which could throw light on the subject, I deliberately limited the field of my research to a smaller period of history beginning with the age of the Buddha to the end of the Kuṣāṇa-Sātavāhana period, i.e. from *c.* 600 BC to *c.* AD 300.

I analysed various components of ritual *dāna* such as different categories of donors, recipients, gift-items and the procedural mode of its performance, and put them in a historical perspective. I also undertook a semantic study of the changing connotations and hidden nuances of the two terms *dāna* and *dakṣiṇā*, besides extensively probing the symbiotic relationship between gift-objects and the growth of property-right, as well as the scope in a patriarchal society of making close kin, mainly wife and children, the object of gift. However, such discussions remained essentially confined to the limited time-frame adopted for this book. Nevertheless, it is significant that ever since its publication, no other book on *dāna* has come out so far and it continues to be the chief reference book on the subject.

However, as the author of the book, I soon came to realize that due to its limited purview as far as the period of history surveyed was concerned, there was no scope for analysing the changing trends in the institution from one period of history to another. The institution, as it evolved during the early Vedic phase, is found to undergo a complete transformation by post-Vedic times. Similarly, the institution as reflected in the Purāṇas had developed a ritual format that was different from that propounded in the Dharmaśāstra texts. This was equally true of certain donor and recipient categories as well, for they are found to undergo major variations from one period of history to another. Thus, whereas the position of women as donors remained almost unchanged during the post-Vedic phase when, due to developments in the field of commercial enterprise and urbanization, a certain section of urban-based women drawn mainly from the mercantile background figured as a prominent donor category, the sources pertaining to the Vedic as well as the Gupta/post-Gupta periods reflect a completely different scenario about women as donors.

Similarly, in the case of brāhmaṇas as a dominant category of recipients, I find that the basic qualifications that entitled them to receive *dāna* underwent significant modifications from one age to another, largely subject to the changing material milieu. In the case of gift-items, too, the impact of the changing material culture is directly perceptible in the variations found in the quantum and range of articles that were both recommended as well as actually bestowed as ritual offerings. However, in the case of gift-objects, along with the changes, a certain amount of continuity is equally noticeable.

Consequently, to correctly assess the importance of the institution of *dāna* in changing historical contexts it became necessary to study these variations not only in a broader time-frame but also from a dialectical perspective. The period of history surveyed in the present book covers over two millennia of cultural growth and development and broadly spans the Vedic, post-Vedic, and the Gupta/post-Gupta periods, though each of these phases of history needs to be further divided into smaller time segments. Thus, just as the two successive stages of cultural development evident during the Vedic period evince significant changes in the general tenor of the institution of *dāna*, a similar phenomenon is perceptible during the post-Vedic phase when, with the help of NBPW archaeological data, it is possible to discern two distinct stages of development in material culture, pre-Mauryan/Mauryan and Kuṣāṇa/Sātavāhana. The subsequent period beginning with the age of the Guptas and covering the entire early medieval period reveals more than two successive stages of socio-economic development, along with corresponding changes in the institution of *dāna*.

Each of these periods of history was characterized by sharp cultural changes. Thus, if the early Vedic cultural phase was predominantly pastoral, the later period showed signs of a more settled economy with significant developments in the field of agriculture and craft production. During the post-Vedic period, while the earlier half corresponding to the pre-Mauryan/Mauryan period represented a preliminary phase of developments in the field of trade, urbanization and monetary economy, the later half or the Kuṣāṇa/Sātavāhana period was marked by a flourishing economy in which all these three spheres showed remarkable growth and advancement. For a brief period under the Kuṣāṇas, India, taking centre-stage even in the field of Central Asian polity is known to have radiated and received cultural influences to and from other region. By the time of the Guptas, however, a reverse trend becomes perceptible. Not only there was a certain amount of regression in trade and commerce but the cultural focus now shifted to agricultural production. The trend became even more accentuated by the early medieval period when, in the wake of commercial decline, there followed not only urban decay but the monetary system also languished, thus paving the way for a closed landed economy. The latter, in its turn, was responsible for giving rise to a feudal social order. What is significant is that throughout this long period of cultural variations the institution of *dāna* never lost its relevance.

In keeping with the widening time-range, I had to not only marshal more extensive data but also contend with more variety of source material. Thus, in the case of the Vedic period, besides archaeological data in the form of PGW remains, our sources mainly comprise the Vedas and Vedāṅgas, primarily consisting of the four Saṁhitās and the large number of Brāhmaṇical texts based on them in the form of the Brāhmaṇas, Āraṇyakas and Upaniṣads. However, the sources tend to become more prolific and varied in the case of the subsequent post-Vedic period, when Brāhmaṇical sources in the form of the Dharmasūtras and the early Smṛtis are supplemented not only by a large compendium of Pāli literature but also by a new genre of writings in the form of texts having a more secular base and orientation such as those dealing with linguistics, statecraft and other disciplines. Forthcoming for the first time in this period are, besides foreign accounts, coins as well as inscriptions recording royal proclamations and votive donations. But it is for the Gupta/post-Gupta phase that we come across a huge amount of Brāhmaṇical and non-Brāhmaṇical literature, as well as archaeological data. The latter, especially in the form of architectural remains and inscriptions recording royal *praśastis* and land grants, have proved to be an indispensable source of information on *dāna*. As far as Brāhmaṇical texts including the vast compendium of Purāṇic literature are concerned, without which a reconstruction of the institution of *dāna* is inconceivable, any effort to fully utilize them gets thwarted by difficulties faced in fixing their exact date of composition. Consequently, in view of the rather large period of history covered in the book, I have generally accepted the dates suggested by P.V. Kane for various Brāhmaṇical texts.

Besides looking into variations in the different components of *dāna* as manifested in different periods of history, there are numerous other dimensions of the institution that have also required probing, especially in the light of more recent researches conducted worldwide. For instance, there was a need to investigate the ritual symbolism of *dāna* in order to understand the rationale for the continued popularity of the institution through almost three millennia of Indian history. For any social institution to retain its relevance and viability for over three thousand years speaks volumes for it and it has to be credited with an extraordinary potential to adapt to the varying needs of a continually changing society.

Similarly, it was equally necessary to look into its ideological dimensions for assessing the degree of impact it exercised on contemporary life. The use of an institution as an ideological mechanism by ideologues can be, to some extent, responsible for bringing about a shift in the belief-system and even prove conducive to cultural transition. The role played by the institution of *dāna* not only in endorsing and popularizing the principle of non-violence or *ahiṁsā*, as opposed to sacrificial ideology during the post-Vedic period, but also in facilitating and promoting a feudal ethos during the early medieval period is undeniable. Both ritual symbolism as well as the ideological dimension of *dāna* had a significant bearing on the contemporary polity and economy, and have been made the subject of two separate chapters in the present book.

Moreover, it was equally necessary to situate the institution in the wider framework of Brāhmaṇical ritualism in order to assess its centrality and importance as a ritual construct. In the first chapter of the book, an attempt has been made to achieve this with large inputs derived from my other published articles dealing with varied aspects of Brāhmaṇical ritualism. Some Brāhmaṇical rituals that gained popularity mainly in the Gupta/post-Gupta period were temple-worship (*pūjā*), *vratas* and *tīrthas* which are found to have a close affinity with the institution of *dāna*; though the latter's centrality in the sacrificial as well as sacramental ritualism of Vedic and post-Vedic times was equally undeniable.

In the backdrop of recent urban studies and, more especially, in the light of the contentious debate[14] triggered by Mauss's statement that brāhmaṇas who lived by soliciting and receiving gifts, that is solely by religious service, refused 'to have anything to do with a national economy dominated by towns, money and markets' and remained 'faithful to the economy and morality of the old Indo-Iranian shepherds',[15] it has become imperative to analyse the dialectics of the institution with processes of urban development. My study reveals that the new commerce and urban-dominated social order of the Kuṣāṇa/Sātavāhana times not only gave rise to a totally new form of gift-system but the latter itself proved to be a phenomenon integral to the urbanization process witnessed during post-Vedic centuries. The subject has been discussed at length in the last chapter of the book.

Another area that needed to be scrutinized was the impact exercised on the dynamics of ritual gift-system by the peasantry, which, from post-Vedic times, constituted an overwhelmingly large proportion of the Indian population, even though there is hardly any forthcoming evidence that sheds light on their role as donors. Nevertheless, since food in the form of agricultural produce had begun to figure as an important gift-item right from the later Vedic times, the role of peasantry *vis-à-vis* the institution of *dāna*, even if it remained mostly indirect and passive, can hardly be disputed. Similarly, as widely acknowledged, the growing practice of making land grants as part of ritual gift offering, during the Gupta/post-Gupta period, exercised a crucial impact on the condition of the peasantry. It not only reduced a large segment within it virtually to the position of serfs but also delegated them to the lowest order in the social scale, that of śūdras. The dialectics between the peasantry and the ritual gift system, therefore, forms the subject of another important chapter in the book.

In the larger context of ritual gift-making in ancient India, I felt it was necessary to not only fix the exact connotation of the term *kanyā-dāna*, which came to be popularly used for the marriage of a daughter, but also determine how far it came within the purview of ritual gift-making. In a separate chapter of the book, and in the light of available data, I have tried to arrive at certain conclusions with regard to both these issues.

I have also tried to investigate how far it would be appropriate to regard almsgiving, a practice that has a ubiquitous presence in all class-divided societies, in the early Indian context figured more as a distended form of *dāna*. Almsgiving in early India like *dāna* had represented a unilateral form of gift-making, which sustained not only the practice of beggary but had also been vital for the foundation of the heterodox monastic systems, their members, i.e. the *bhikkhus* being solely dependent for their food and other essential requirements on *bhikkhā* or alms. By highlighting some of the common features that characterized the two modes of unilateral gift making I have tried to show how the gap between the two often got blurred and sometimes even became completely obliterated.

There was also the need to find the rationale for the introduction of some innovative forms of ritual gift-making such as *mahādāna* and *parvata* or *meru-dāna* which are not heard of before the time of the Purāṇas but which not only gained immense popularity thenceforth but were soon to become also the thematic focus of innumerable digests composed from the end of first millennium AD, some more noted works being Lakṣmīdhara's *Dānakalpataru*, Ballālasena's *Dānasāgara*, Hemādri's *Dāna-khaṇḍa*, Caṇḍeśvara's *Dānaratnākara*, Viśvabhaṭṭa's *Dānasāra*, Govindānanda's *Dānakriyākaumudī*, Bhaṭṭa Nīlakaṇṭha's *Dānamayūkha*. A significant fact that emerges in this context is the close conjunction between the time when land grants had already played a major role in the emergence of a feudal society and the period when an extensive literature in the form of *nibandhas* on *dāna* began to be composed. As pointed out by K.V.R. Aiyangar[16] the fact that these texts were meant chiefly for the edification of the feudal elite is more than evident from the kind of thrust that was generally laid in them on *mahādānas*, which considering their ostentatious character and the inscriptional testimony that is forthcoming, could have been performed mainly by members of an affluent feudal aristocracy. This is recognized even by one of the early writers on *dāna* Govindānanda Kavikaṅkaṇācārya[17] who lived in the sixteenth century, and claims to have deliberately omitted the sixteen *mahādānas*, the ten *acaladānas* and the *dhenudānas* on the ground that these were within the capacity of only ruling princes and noblemen, and that they could turn for information about the omitted great gifts to treatises on *dāna*. The fact that by the end of the millennium the institution of *dāna* gave rise to a whole new genre of literature clearly shows that its centrality to society and economy of the early medieval period was undisputed and cannot be overemphasized.

Since the publication of my earlier book on *dāna* I have been consistently engaged in working on many of these unexplored dimensions of the institution and articles dealing with some of them have also been published. Because these were written at different points of time spanning almost twenty years it was inevitable that many factual details and even certain basic conceptual thrusts recur in more than one article. This inevitably accounts for some amount of overlapping of factual details in the present book, though some of it is also caused by the articles having a common thematic focus. Readers' indulgence is, therefore, sought in this regard.

Moreover, in view of the very long period of history that has been surveyed in the book and the abundance of source material available for the subject, I cannot claim to have scanned and utilized the entire corpus of the available data. Instead on the basis of direct evidence derived mainly from inscriptions and Brāhmaṇical texts, I have tried to delineate certain broad trends that characterized the institution of *dāna* during different periods of history leaving ample scope for a more in-depth study on the subject.

NOTES

1. *Descent of Man*, p. 63.
2. *The Law of Mutual Aid.*
3. *Mutual Aid: A Factor of Evolution*, New York, 1904.
4. *The Elementary Forms of the Religious Life*, London, 1915.
5. *Argonauts of the Western Pacific*, London, 1922.

6. *Primitive Polynesian Economy*, London, 1939.
7. *The Nuer.*
8. *The Anatomy of Human Destructiveness.*
9. *Politics, Law and Religion in Tribal Society*, Oxford, 1977.
10. 'Reciprocity and Structure', *Man*, XIV, no. II, 1979, pp. 271-85.
11. Originally published in Paris, 1950; translated into English by I.A.N. Cunnison with an Introduction by Evans Pritchard and published under the title *The Gift: Forms and Functions of Exchange in Archaic Societies*, London, 1970.
12. 'Gifts and Giving in the Ṛgveda', *Selected Studies*, vol. IV, pp. 122ff.
13. '*Dāna* and *Dākṣiṇā* as Forms of Exchange'.
14. R.N. Nandi, *Social Roots of Religion*, p. 11.
15. M. Mauss, *The Gift*, p. 57.
16. K.V.R. Aiyangar, ed., *Kṛtyakalpataru of Bhaṭṭa Lakṣmīdhara*, vol. V, Dānakāṇḍa, Baroda, 1941, p. 103.
17. Idid., p. 57.

1

Situating *Dāna* in Brāhmaṇical Ritualism

Dāna or ritual gift-making has been integral to Brāhmaṇical ritualism right from Vedic times. The very inception and subsequent growth of the latter was directly linked with the way the gift system was conceptualized and developed by its ideologues. The concept of *dāna* not only provided the basic framework on which the superstructure of Brāhmaṇical ritualism was raised but also the chief source of livelihood of its proponents. In fact, the very emergence and ascendancy of the brāhmaṇa stratum as well as its continued hegemonic hold over society through the ages depended upon the way *dāna* ritualism was formulated, and the manner in which it successfully retained its viability and vibrancy. The latter was mainly due to several mutations and variations perceptible in its continually changing aspect, even though the basic format of *dāna* ritualism remained more or less constant.

The chief constituent elements (*aṅgas*) of ritual *dāna*, without which its fruition was considered incomplete, were the donor (*dātā*), recipient (*pratigrahīta*), gift-item (*deya*), attitude of devotion and faith (*śraddhā*), as well as a proper time and place for making the gift.[1] Another constant feature of ritual *dāna* which distinguished it from other reciprocal forms of gift-making was its unilateral character. According to the section on *dāna* in the *Kṛtyakalpataru* of Lakṣmīdhara, 'reciprocal gifts are not gifts; they are sinful' (*parasparasya dānāni lokayātrānadharmavat*).[2] The only return expected through *dāna* was in the form of spiritual merit (*puṇya/adṛṣṭa*). Similarly, although initially *dāna*, especially when made at the time of sacrificial performances, sported a voluntary aspect, as it was increasingly incorporated into sacramental and expiatory ritualism it tended to become almost obligatory.

Moreover, while in other forms of gift exchange, parity in social status between the donor and donee is a prerequisite, and even ordinary almsgiving requires the donor to wield better economic competence and social esteem, in the case of *dāna*, it was the brāhmaṇa recipient who inevitably held a superior ritual status compared to the donor, even if the latter was both economically and politically much better-off. Consequently, instead of the donor simply gratifying the donee as in any ordinary almsgiving, in the case of *dāna*, the latter was also supposed to do a favour to the benefactor by accepting it. Though acquiring some amount of prestige through ordinary gift-making is a commonly acknowledged fact, yet the donor expected to beget through *dāna* something more. Besides prestige, *dāna* was expected to yield spiritual merit as well as religious sanction and validation for the donor's power and social status.

Much of the efficacy of *dāna* ritualism thus directly depended upon the spiritual authority commanded by the brāhmaṇa recipients. But it is equally true that the exalted social status and religious authority they enjoyed was made possible by the financial support received in the form of *dāna*, which enabled them to devote all their time and energy in acquiring and disseminating spiritual knowledge and developing and practising their priestly craft. The two, namely the brāhmaṇa stratum and the institution of *dāna*, were, therefore, quintessentially interdependent; the continued growth and ascendancy of the one without the other was almost unthinkable. In fact, the Buddhist *saṁgha* and its active votaries, the *bhikṣus*, had an almost similar kind of symbiotic relationship with almsgiving or *bhikṣā*.

I

The genesis of *dāna* ritualism can be traced back to the practice of gift-making by Vedic tribal chiefs at the time of *soma* sacrifices. We learn about them from the laudatory verses in the form of *dāna-stutis* contained in the *Ṛgveda*, which bestow lavish praise upon munificent donors, both celestial and human. Regarding the role of tituals in early societies, anthropologists maintain that early religions had no dogmas or creeds but consisted entirely of ritual acts, which were primarily social in nature. These fulfilled two compelling needs, namely, tribal or group integration and instilling in its members a sense of unity with nature. In the case of gift-making, however, an ostensible function performed by it was of a magico-religious nature where the gift was symbolic of communion with the supernatural and promoted group integrity and well-being. In a slightly less egalitarian social context in which some stratification was already visible, it could also become instrumental in the donor and recipient conferring status upon each other, although the source of their respective status was bound to be different.

Some of these primary functions served by gift-making would also hold true of *dāna* during the early Ṛgvedic tribal phase when it was centred mainly in sacrificial ritualism. If sacrificial offerings to gods helped to reaffirm group solidarity and well-being, the ritual offering of *dāna* and *dakṣiṇā* to hymnodists and priests officiating at sacrifices was instrumental in conferring status and prestige on the donor. This is especially manifest from the *dāna-stutis*.[3] Thus, kings Sudās Paijavana, Svanaya, Prasṭoka Sarañjaya, Ṛṇañcaya, Purumiha, Rathaviti and many others have been described as munificent donors. The latter received encomiums and attendant fame by giving away, at times, as many as sixty thousand cows, ten four-horsed chariots, two thousand camels, etc.[4] The statistical figures furnished in the *dāna-stutis* cannot be expected to be exact but would seem to be more notional, and meant to emphasize the sheer quantum of the largesse. Wealth being an important criterion of social status in any society, such munificence, by reflecting the affluence of the donor, automatically added to his prestige within the group. According to a verse of the *Ṛgveda* (X.107.8), 'The liberal die not: never are they ruined: the liberal suffer neither harm nor trouble'.[5]

In the *Ṛgveda*, two terms occur in the sense of ritual gift-making, namely *dāna* and *dakṣiṇā*, both having entirely different connotations. The latter have been discussed at length in the chapter dealing with brāhmaṇas as recipients. Nevertheless, in order to situate *dāna* and *dakṣiṇā vis-à-vis* Brāhmaṇical ritualism, it becomes necessary to bring out the finer differentiation between them. Thus, we find that though in post-Vedic times, *dakṣiṇā* came to be understood more as sacrificial fee or remuneration for priestly services, yet as J.C. Heesterman points out,[6] in the Ṛgvedic context it not only fortified sacrifices performed by the tribal chieftains but seems to have also formed part of a bigger sphere of gift-exchange as it was given both to the officiating priests as well as to others present at the sacrifice. Thus, even brāhmaṇas who attended the sacrifice more as observers are said to receive such offerings. *Dakṣiṇā* according to Heesterman, could not, therefore, have merely constituted a sacrificial fee or remuneration for priestly services. Even J. Gonda considers such gift-making to have been undertaken not solely 'in order to pay for services, but also to maintain a profitable alliance'. Elaborating further on the theme, Gonda maintains that 'sacrifice is divided between these two (the gods and the human gods, i.e. the brāhmaṇas), the oblations going to the gods and the *dakṣiṇā*—which is a special form of gift—offering to the brāhmaṇas. Both kinds of gods when gratified, place (the sacrificer) in a state of bliss'.[7] However, as Romila Thapar rightly points out, though *dakṣiṇā* could not have been a 'sacrificial fee to begin with' but with the passage of time, especially by the time of the Dharmaśāstras, it definitely came to acquire that aspect.[8] However, it needs to be noted that even during the later period, the donor was invariably enjoined to pay *dakṣiṇā* over and above the stipulated amount of *dāna*. Whether this was done to pay for the priestly services of the brāhmaṇas who also acting as ministrant priests or was given mainly to boost the spiritual efficacy of *dāna* itself is not very clear. From statements contained in the Purāṇas, the latter would appear to be more apt. Thus, according to the *Agni Purāṇa* (209.63), a bit of gold by way of *dakṣiṇā* should be given to the brāhmaṇa in order to further augment the efficacy of the act of *dāna* (*etaddānapratiṣṭhārtham suvarṇam dakṣiṇam dade*). At another place, it is stated that 'gold should be given by way of *dakṣiṇā* in connection with all other gifts'.[9]

In the Ṛgvedic context, gift-making, therefore, whether in the form of *dāna* or *dakṣiṇā*, formed part of sacrificial ritualism. Just as without munificent gift-making to priests and others associated with the performance of the sacrifice, the latter's efficacy could not be vouchsafed, similarly, receiving lavish gifts must have served as a strong incentive for the former to actively participate in the group spectacle connected with *yajña* offerings. Consequently, *dāna* ritualism *per se* could not have wielded much significance. Its importance lay more in the deep ramifications that sacrificial ritualism had in a tribal order. The purpose of these *yajña* performances in a slightly earlier phase was chiefly to uphold the social order and to renew and reinforce the sense of belonging to the group, although begetting prestige and validation for the chieftain's power soon became some of the more important ends served by them.

II

By the time the later Vedas, Brāhmaṇas and Upaniṣads were composed, a relatively more stratified social order is attested by our sources and *dāna* ritualism, though not completely dissociated from *yajña* ritualism, nevertheless came to acquire a distinctive format. The *dāna* was no longer confined to sacrificial ceremonialism alone is quite apparent from the distinction that came to be made between the *iṣṭa* and *pūrtta* forms of gift-making. Though the two terms occur together as one word in as early a text as the *Ṛgveda* (X.14.8), it has been used more in the sense of 'cumulative spiritual merit due to a man's performance of sacrifices and charitable act'. Even in several later Vedic texts such as the *Atharvaveda* (II.12.4), the *Taittirīya Saṁhitā* (V.7.7.1-3) and the *Kaṭhopaniṣad* (I.1.8), the term is found to carry a similar connotation.[10] Gradually, though, *iṣṭa* came to be differentiated from *pūrtta* as a distinct form of gift-making, though proper definitions of the two terms are forthcoming only in the Dharmaśāstras, especially in the later Smṛti texts and digests dealing with *dāna*. Thus, whereas *iṣṭa* was understood in the sense of offerings made inside the sacrificial altar (*vedī*), *pūrtta* was considered to have a wider purview that covered even charitable works such as distribution of food. The charitable activities of Janaśruti Pautrāyaṇa may be cited as an example of the *pūrtta* category of gift-making. Described in the *Chāndogya Upaniṣad* (IV.1-2) as a man of faith and very charitable, he is said to have erected shelters in order to feed at all times people that came from all quarters.[11] An important distinction between *iṣṭa* and *pūrtta* that became manifest in the period of the later Smṛtis was that considerations of ritual purity and status so stringently upheld in the case of the former were done away with in the case of the latter, for even śūdras were permitted to undertake such gift-making.[12]

The changing contours of the institution of *dāna* were directly linked to the emergence of brāhmaṇas as a dominant social category and their appropriation of the role of lawgivers. They succeeded in exercising such a stronghold over the emergent *varṇa*-stratified society, which was fast replacing the Vedic tribal order, that whatever they dictated tended to gain the efficacy of law. In fact, the claim that the brāhmaṇas are gods on earth already occurs in the *Atharvaveda* (V.11.11). According to the *Śatapatha Brāhmaṇa* (II.2.10.6), 'verily there are two kinds of *devas*, the gods (heavenly) and the human gods, viz., brāhmaṇas who have studies the Veda and mastered it'. Brāhmaṇas came to even appropriate many privileges, judicial and social. The *Śatapatha Brāhmaṇa* (XI.v.71) mentions 'honour, gifts, freedom from oppression and security against capital punishment' amongst the prerogatives which brāhmaṇas had come to enjoy.[13] But as Gonda points out, the ascendancy of the brāhmaṇas had the consensual though latent backing of the entire society, for 'if the other classes of society had not themselves more or less shared these ideas, no amount of iteration on the part of the brāhmaṇas would have succeeded in inculcating them so firmly'.[14]

In fact, the superiority claimed by the brāhmaṇas was not wholly undeserved, at least in the initial phase when the latter had still not crystallized into a closed grouping.[15] They must have striven hard during that early phase to live up to the high moral and intellectual standards they were associated with. During this period, besides being looked upon as repositories of religious knowledge, their austere lifestyle and high moral stature, as epitomized in the concept of an ideal brāhmaṇa, came to beget universal respect and veneration for them.

Brāhmaṇas as a social entity, therefore, came to be associated with certain superordinate and other-worldly qualities. They were imbued with a religious dignity which inspired spontaneous respect and made their well-being the direct concern of the society. Offering *dāna* to them was, thus, a mode of showing solicitude and reverence and seeking their blessings. Yet if the blessings of the brāhmaṇas were solicited, their ire was equally feared. Being cursed by a brāhmaṇa could spell disaster. *Dāna* to the brāhmaṇas, therefore, turned out to be an effective means of not just winning them over but also of placating them and earning spiritual merit. Consequently, by the end of the later Vedic phase, *dāna* had come to be imbued with a mystical efficacy, which, while adding to its popularity, also emphasized the need to treat it with circumspection and caution. This was rendered especially necessary by the fact that, even during this early phase, not all brāhmaṇas lived up to the high moral and intellectual standards set for them, as clearly suggested by some of the early Pāli texts. In the *Dīgha Nikāya* (XIX, Mahāgovinda Suttanta, II.247), we come across the caustic comment, 'Leaving the world means little power and little gain, to be a brāhmaṇa brings great power and great gain.' This 'great power' and 'great gain' with which brāhmaṇas came to be associated in popular perception, in fact, had less to do with their intellectual and spiritual prowess and more with a number of other socio-economic factors that augmented their position in society.

An important factor that led to the dominance of brāhmaṇas during this period was the monopolistic hold they were able to exercise over sacrificial ritual. The beginnings of intensive agriculture, by making available a small surplus and giving rise to numerous fertility rites, further emphasized the potential of sacrificial ritualism. It also provided greater scope for the latter to acquire a more complex and ostentatious aspect. The priestly class capitalized on the development and played a seminal role in promoting it. We learn from later Vedic literature, especially the Brāhmaṇa texts, that there was an unprecedented increase in the number of occasions sacrificial offerings that came to be recommended. What really added to the dominance of the brāhmaṇas was that they were able to gradually arrogate to themselves the supreme position of superintending priests, enjoyed earlier by the *hotā*. By the end of the later Vedic period when the Śrautasūtras began to be composed, all members of the priestly order were drawn exclusively from the brāhmaṇa *varṇa*. Thus, according to the *Kātyāyana Śrautasūtra* (I.2.8), only brāhmaṇas were eligible to officiate and eat at sacrifices. The *Sāṅkhyāyana Śrautasūtra* (18.14.8) similarly stipulates that nobody should serve as a priest without proving their descent from three or ten generations of *ṛṣis*. The fact that we do not come across any reference to a non-brāhmaṇa officiating as a priest at a sacrifice even in early Pāli literature would indirectly prove that brāhmaṇas had already established exclusive control over priestcraft.

III

In the subsequent post-Vedic phase when a large compendium of Brāhmaṇical law-books in the form of Dharmasūtras and Dharmaśāstras was being composed, the practice of the *pūrtta* form of gift-making gained wider proportions. Its distended base inevitably presumes a changed social ethos marked by growing agricultural expansion, occupational specialization, beginnings of urbanization and the complete breakdown of the tribal order. The latter development in its wake not only aggravated the condition of the poor and the destitute with no kin-based group support to fall back upon but also emphasized the need to meet certain emergent agriculture and urban-related challenges by adopting more innovative forms of gift-making. Besides catering to the needs of orphans and the impoverished, as well as of wandering ascetics and monks, *pūrtta* category of *dāna* reveals wide variations. For instance, it could even take the form of sponsoring works of public utility such as constructing wells, tanks, alms halls, etc., and formally dedicating them by performing certain duly prescribed rituals, which entailed payment of *dāna* and *dakṣiṇā* to the ministrant priests. Some idea about the wide variations possible in the *pūrtta* form of gift-making can be had from the Karle and Nasik inscriptions[16] belonging to Uśāvadata, the son-in-law of the Śaka king Nahapāṇa who ruled during the first century AD. Uśāvadata is said to have given away three lakh of cows, sixteen villages to gods and brāhamaṇas, fed one lakh of brāhmaṇas every year, got eight brāhmaṇas married at his own expense at Prabhāsa, built flights of steps on the river Barnasa, constructed quadrangles, houses and halting places (*pratiśraya*) at Bharukaccha, Daśapura, Govardhana and Sorparaga; constructed wells and tanks; kept free ferry boats over the rivers, established meeting halls and shelters for the gratuitous distribution of water; and conferred 32,000 coconut trees in Nanangola on the assembly of brāhamaṇas in Sorparaga and three other places.

Another extension of the *pūrtta* form of gift-making was its becoming integral to sacramental (*saṁskāra*) ritualism. The latter was directly linked with the changing material milieu, marked by a growing spirit of individualism. In the preceding Vedic tribal order where the individual was subservient to the collectivity, all ritualism, especially of a sacrificial nature, had been group-oriented. However, with rapid developments in the field of iron technology that promoted agricultural and craft specialization and the growth of private property, the tribal order could not survive very long and the individual automatically gained in importance against the collectivity. It was natural, therefore, for newly-framed rituals to be more individual-centric.

For defining the social and ritual status of the individual within the family and society, it became necessary to undergo a series of sacramental rites starting from the time of conception and birth of a child (*jāta-karma*) to initiation to educational career (*upanayana/yajñopavīta*) to acquiring through marriage the status of a householder (*vivāha*) to the final journey marked by death (*mṛtyu/antyeṣṭi*). Though *rites de passage* is equally important in early tribal societies, there is one major difference between the latter and those performed in a stratified society. Whereas, in the case of the former, the group remains the chief focus and the individual through performance of these rites gets formal recognition as its member, in the latter, it is the individual who takes centrestage and his status and role in the family and society are duly defined and acknowledged.

If the emergent spirit of individualism and social stratification resulting from occupational specialization made it incumbent for the lawgivers to frame rules related to sacramental ritualism, developments related to the growth of private property and monetization rendered it possible to incorporate gift-making into it. Any form of unilateral giving involves the transfer of property rights on a permanent basis to the donee. Lawgivers belonging to the early medieval period were fully cognizant of this fact and categorically maintained that one can make a gift only of what one owns.[17] The *Nārada Smṛti*[18] forbids eight kinds of gifts. Some of the important excluded categories were property jointly owned with others, one's entire property when one has children, and what has already been promised to another man. To independently own property, it was necessary for the donor to have some independent source of income over which he could exercise full discretionary rights of alienation in whatever way he wished, without having to seek the consent of other claimants. Such a situation could arise only when, in the wake of occupational specialization, both in the field of craft, trade and other vocations, there was a tremendous increase in the size of individually-owned wealth with growing monetization further making its accumulation and expenditure possible. Brāhmaṇical lawgivers such as *Āpastamba Gṛhyasūtra* (VI.16.4), *Āśvalāyana Gṛhyasūtra* (IV.7.17) and *Sāṅkhyāyana* (III.11.16; IV.16.5), taking advantage of these developments, began to draft elaborate rules making ritual *dāna* on sacramental occasions compulsory. The performance of sacramental (*saṁskāra*) rites was not considered consummated unless adequate *dāna* was offered to a minimum number of well-qualified brāhmaṇas, besides the officiating priests, who had to be properly invited, fed and honoured with gifts on the occasion. According to the *Manusmṛti* (III.233), 'Delighted, one should please brāhmaṇas, and cause them to eat by degrees and entice them frequently by the cooked rice and by the curries.'

Closely connected with sacramental rites was the concept of offering *śrāddha* oblations to ancestors. The beginnings of such ritualism undoubtedly lay, as in the case of sacramental ritualism, in the growing importance of the institution of family, extended or otherwise, as compared to the tribal group. But the deepening patriarchal character of Brāhmaṇical society combined with the growth of private property, especially of an immovable kind, were some other developments which brought into sharper focus the problems of patrilineal inheritance. It provided the lawgivers not only the scope for framing laws of inheritance but also the excuse to introduce new rituals, which could make the issue of succession appear less equivocal and more consensual in nature. Thus, the right to perform *śrāddha* rites was exclusively restricted to the legitimate heirs of deceased ancestors. With the entire family property at stake, these rituals must have naturally acquired great importance for its members. Brāhmaṇical lawgivers, therefore, in order to transform the *śrāddha* rites into a lucrative source of income, made the giving the *dāna* to brāhmaṇas mandatory on such occasions. In fact, during the *śrāddha* rite, it was the specially invited brāhmaṇas who were considered to substitute for the manes and had to be, therefore, accorded the utmost respect or *śrāddha*. According to Manu (III.237) 'As long as the cooked rice is hot, as long as (a brāhmaṇa) eats in silence, so long he manes eat (it).' The brāhmaṇas invited to a *śrāddha* rite had to be duly worshipped and honoured with food is made amply clear by Manu (III.251). 'After having asked, "Have you eaten well?" one should cause (those who are) satisfied to rinse their mouths and say to them when they have done so, "rest!".' A similar injunction occurs in later Brāhmaṇical texts such as the *Mārkaṇḍeya Purāṇa* (28.49-51). According to a verse of the *Viṣṇu Purāṇa* (III.13.12), 'as long as the mourner wishes he should feed the brāhmaṇas, for the soul of the dead derives pleasure inasmuch as his kinsmen are satisfied with their entertainment'. Such a dictum tended to encourage the belief that the more gratified brāhmaṇas were during the performance of the *śrāddha* rite, the better pleased the ancestors would be. The belief finds candid expression during the subsequent period when the Purāṇas began to be composed. Thus, whereas, according to the *Vāmana Purāṇa* (15.105), 'one should donate land, etc., for the purpose of *pitara* so that they could enjoy pleasure above', the *Viṣṇu Purāṇa* (III.14.23-4) stipulates that 'he should, if he is rich, give to brāhmaṇas jewels, clothes, land, conveyances, wealth and various other eatables'. If 'he has not got so much wealth he should feed with faith and humility excellent brāhmaṇas according to his means'. According to the *Mārkaṇḍeya Purāṇa* (29.38), 'when the ancestral manes are pleased with *śrāddha*, they confer longevity, wisdom, riches, learning, heaven, liberation and happiness as well as kingdom'. It may, however, be noted that references to *dāna* accompanying sacramental and *śrāddha* rites are not as forthcoming in the early Dharamaśāstras as in the literature of the early medieval period, especially in the Purāṇas. This could be largely due to the fact that most ritual formations of the post-Vedic period were still in an early formative stage and elaborate procedural rules could not have been duly ratified.

Another form of ritualism to which ritual *dāna* became central was expiatory in nature. Revolving around the concept of sin and ritual pollution, their conception was directly connected with developments related to social stratification. The *varṇa* social order as it crystallized and struck roots during the later Vedic and post-Vedic times could be sustained largely through certain ideological constructs and ritual tenets articulated in the Dharmasūtras and the Dharmaśāstras. This was to justify and augment its hierarchical structure as much as to condone its many anomalies. If the doctrine of action or *karma* provided the much needed *raison d'être* for glaring social and economic disparities prevailing within the society, sacramental rites helped to include or exclude from the *varṇa* order, as well as define the duties and ritual status of members of both genders belonging to different *varṇas*. The concept of sin (*pāpa*) as opposed to spiritual merit (*puṇya*) similarly became instrumental in rationalizing some of the structural deviations that, with the passage of time, became inevitable and threatened to erode the very stability of the *varṇa* system. Thus, according to Dharmaśāstric dictates, any transgression of *varṇa* rules, particularly those related to inter- and intra-*varṇa* marriages, was to be treated as a sin for which expiation was possible only through the performance of penance or certain difficult rites of a punitive nature which find detailed exposition in the law-books. These expiatory rites could range from various forms of abstinence to undergoing severe physical ordeals and penance to making liberal gifts to brāhmaṇas. According to a Dharmaśāstric dictum, 'A sinner is freed from sin by proclaiming (it), by repenting, by austerity, by perusing (the Vedas), and also in time of need by gifts'.[19] The last form of expiation derived its efficacy from the belief that, by giving gifts to brāhmaṇas, the person who had committed sin could ritually transfer it along with the gift to the recipient and, thus, become absolved from it. The brāhmaṇa recipients, in turn, were expected to counteract the adverse effects of such sin transference by their spiritual powers gained through diligent ascetic and intellectual pursuits. According to *Manu* (XI.247), 'as fire by its heat burns up in a moment the wood it has laid hold of, so a Veda-wise man by the fire of knowledge consumes all sin'. The belief is reiterated in the *Agni Purāṇa* (209.54). The brāhmaṇas are said to be 'like the burning fire, incapable of sin and pollution'. In course of time, however, *dāna*, being the easiest of expiatory measures, gained greater currency as compared to other more difficult methods of expiation. This naturally buttressed the economic interests of the brāhmaṇas who must have encouraged their clients to resort to this simpler and, for them, decidedly more lucrative mode of expiation as much as possible. According to the *Matsya Purāṇa* (92.33), 'One, who himself cannot perform, but merely touches, hears or even advises others to give these gifts, is liberated from sins and goes to the region of Viṣṇu.' Similarly, according to the *Vāmana Purāṇa* (36.2), 'the people who feed brāhmaṇas on a cuisine of *śyāmaka* rice cooked in milk and added *ghee*, become free from the clutches of sins'. Even in the case of such grievous sins (*mahāpātaka*) as the killing of a brāhmaṇa, if a person is unable to atone through more rigorous forms of penance that have been prescribed in law-books, then, as a final resort he could, according to the *Agni Purāṇa* (169.4), 'make over all his household goods and cattle and whatever else he might be possessed of to a brāhmaṇa well-versed in the Vedas'. In the case of accidentally killing a cow, even after performing penance a person was required 'to make over eleven bullocks and two cows to a brāhmaṇa'.[20]

Another concept endemic to *varṇa* ideology was that of ritual pollution. The segregation and transformation of *varṇas* into watertight segments could be possible largely through emphasizing the need to maintain ritual purity by strictly adhering to connubial and behavioural norms laid down in the Dharmaśāstras for members of different *varṇas*. Thus, if an attempt to overstep these rules made it incumbent for the defaulter to perform expiatory rites, the person who lost ritual purity on its account was likewise required to undergo certain purificatory rites for regaining his original ritual status. The concept of ritual purity was centred in the belief in the essential dichotomy between sacred and profane; a belief held in common by almost all early societies. This was utilized to utmost advantage by Brāhmaṇical lawgivers who made it mandatory for all polluted objects, person and places to be sanctified once again through the performance of various purificatory rites. Some common sources of pollution could be through touch and commensality, i.e. sharing or partaking food cooked by a member of the lower *varṇa* stratum. Even occasions like birth and death were considered to have a polluting effect on members of the family.[21] Such forms of ritual pollution are dealt with in a more elaborate manner in the Purāṇas. The *Vāmana Purāṇa* (15.82) very clearly enjoins that 'one should not take food in the residences of Sūtikas, Saṇḍa, Mārjāra, Kukkuṭa, *Patita*, Apavidha, Nagna and Cāṇḍāla'. According to the *Mārkaṇḍeya Purāṇa* (32.91), after the expiry of the mandatory period of ritual pollution following death, 'the wise should make presents of whatever object is held in highest esteem in this world and whatever agreeable object is in the house to accomplished brāhmaṇas'. With the passage of time, as *varṇa* norms tended to become more stringent, even the sight of a tabooed object or person could result in transmitting ritual impurity, and therefore needed to be expunged through the performance of purificatory rites, which could include making gifts to brāhmaṇas. Manu's (V.107) stipulation in this regard is quite clear: 'The learned become pure by tranquility; those doing what is not to be done by gifts; those with concealed sin by muttering (sacred texts); the most learned in the Vedas by austerity'. As in the case of expiatory rites, for heightening the efficacy of purificatory rites, some ritual offering to the brāhmaṇas was also recommended.

By the opening centuries of the Christian era, if there was an enormous increase in the volume of Brāhmaṇical ritualism, there was an almost proportionate extention of *dāna* ritualism, which was already becoming if not completely intrinsic to the former than, at least, its necessary addendum. Even fertility-related rites with strong magical overtones were considered to be efficacious only when accompanied with the gift of food and other items to the brāhmaṇas. However, as can be seen from sources belonging to the later half of the first millennium BC the institution of *dāna*, especially in the Brāhmaṇical context, had still not developed any independent ritual format. In fact, in the earliest Dharmasūtra works of Āpastamba, Gautama and Baudhāyana, no complete section is exclusively devoted to gift-making.[22] Similarly, in earlier Smṛti works like those of Manu and Yājñavalkya, limited space seems to be allotted to the discussion of *dāna*, with more space being taken up by subjects such as *śrāddha*, ritual purification, penance, etc.[23] Even aspects of the *dāna*-making procedure, which are touched upon in these texts, are not of a very comprehensive nature. They chiefly deal with subjects such as the general praise and advocacy of *dāna*.[24] There is no reference to any distinct procedural code connected with the *pūrtta* form of gift-making as in subsequent Brāhmaṇical texts. Consequently, the ritual procedure adopted in making *dāna* during this period was inevitably conditioned by the dominant ritual formation to which it was affiliated at the time. Thus, gift-making rules are known to differ when made on the occasion of a sacrifice from those followed at a sacramental ceremony. The difference is especially conspicuous in the case of *dāna* connected with those *saṁskāras* that were performed at the time of birth or death for, in such situations, it was natural to attach more importance to those rites that were meant to rid the donor of ritual pollution. Similarly, in the case of *śrāddha* rites, besides preserving the solemnity of the occasion, the brāhmaṇa recipients representing the manes were to be offered the same reverence that one was supposed to accord to one's ancestors. The Purāṇas are known to further elaborate on the nature of gifts to be offered. Thus, according to the *Vāmana Purāṇa* (15.106), 'the things preferred by the person when he was living' should be offered to meritorious brāhmaṇas 'with a wish of their being abundantly available to him after death'. We do not come across in contemporary texts, as we do in subsequent literature, any elaborate ritual procedure specifically connected with the dedication of wells and tanks and the consecration of images, a form of *dāna* which gained great popularity during this period.

IV

Though the ubiquitous aspect acquired by ritual gift-making through its affiliation to dominant ritual formations of the time[25] became even more emphasized during the Gupta and post-Gupta centuries, yet it was also during this period that, for the first time, *dāna per se* began to receive detailed exposition in contemporary literature. Besides the *Mahābhārata* and the numerous Purāṇas in which entire sections are devoted to expounding *dāna*-related rules and regulations, a large number of digests dealing with the topic of ritual gift-making also began to be composed. Some of the more well-known works focusing on the subject are Dānakhaṇḍa (of the *Caturvargacintāmaṇi*) by Hemādri, Dānakhaṇḍa (of *Kṛtyakalpataru*) by Lakṣmīdhara, *Dānakriyākaumudī* by Govindānanda, *Dānamyūkha* by Nīlakaṇṭha and *Dānasāgara* by Ballālasena. Not only there is evident a proliferation in the various types of *dāna* that came to be recommended such as *bhūmi-dāna* and the sixteen forms of *mahādānas*[26] but there also developed an elaborate set of procedural rules pertaining to all its six constituent elements, namely the donor or *dātā*, recipient or *pratigrahītā*, gift-item or *deya*, faith or *śraddhā*, right time or *kāla* and right place or *sthāna*, disregarding which could render the gift void. There is a very clear injunction contained in the *Viṣṇu Smṛti* (57.8) in this regard: 'He, who accepts the gift of an article, of the mode of accepting which he is ignorant, is drowned with the giver in hell'.

With its expanding purview, the parameters of ritual *dāna* came to be defined in a more precise manner. In the *Agni Purāṇa* (209), there occurs a whole section called, '*dāna paribhāsaka*' devoted to the delineation of gift-making rules pertaining to both the *iṣṭa* and *pūrtta* categories of *dāna*. If the performance of an *agnihotra* sacrifice, practice of austerities and offering of oblations known as the *viśva-devapiṇḍas* were considered to be *iṣṭa* acts (209.3), 'the endowments of tanks, wells, divine edifices, gratuitous feeding-houses, gardens of fruits and caravansarais are known as *pūrtta*, and their endowers enjoy an immunity from the cycles of rebirth' (209.2). According to the *Purāṇa* (209.4), the *pūrtta* category also included 'gifts made on the occasions of the eclipses of the planets, on the passing of the sun to a new zodiacal sign, or on the day of the twelfth phase of the moon's wane or increase'. According to another stipulation, the 'gift made on the occasion of a *śrāddha* ceremony of one's ancestors carries four or eight times the merit of making gifts on any other occasion' (209.8).

Dāna had also come to be differentiated on the basis of the qualitative nature of the items gifted (*deya*) or the purpose which it was meant to serve. Thus, if *dāna* of an *uttama* (highest), *madhyama* (middling) and *kanīyasa* (lowest) order based on the kind of gift-items that were given away finds mention in the Purāṇas,[27] we also come across another classification of *dāna* into three categories, namely *nitya* or which was given daily such as food after performing the *vaiśvadeva* rite, *kāmya* or which was given with a certain desire such as for securing progeny or prosperity, and *naimittika* or which was given on certain occasions like at the time of an eclipse. Numerous references to the latter category of *dāna* are forthcoming from contemporary stone and copper-plate inscriptions recording the grant of land at the time of a particular planetary conjunction or a solar or lunar eclipse.[28] The *Kūrma Purāṇa* (II.26.4-8) adds a fourth category of *dāna* described as *vimala* or which was pure and given without any desire or occasion.

A significant development that characterized the institution of *dāna* during the early medieval period was the formal inclusion of śūdras within the donor categories. It is stated in the *Agni Purāṇa* (209.28) that 'a brāhmaṇa should accept only the gifts made by a brāhmaṇa, a kṣatriya and a vaiśya, and out of compassion only, a gift made by a śūdra'. According to the same Purāṇa (209.53), 'even an anchorite who has renounced the world and its concerns, can safely take such articles as the juice of sweet trees and canes from the hands of a śūdra, without any fear of being polluted by such contamination'. Further amplifying on the subject, the Purāṇa enunciates that 'a brāhmaṇa who does not live by receiving gifts, can take them from people of all castes and colour'. However, a certain differentiation in the mode of receiving a gift from a śūdra had to be necessarily made. Thus, whereas while accepting a gift from a person who was a twice-born (*dvija*), the benediction had to be pronounced openly, it had to be recited only 'mentally when the giver is a śūdra' (209.39).

There is also a certain lowering in the intellectual and moral standards of brāhmaṇa recipients. This is candidly acknowledged in the Purāṇas. According to the *Agni Purāṇa* (209.55), 'it was the custom in the *kṛta* age to make a gift to a person by calling at his house. In the *tretā* age, a brāhmaṇa was invited to the house of the giver and sent back honoured with a gift. In the *dvāpara yuga* it was the custom to make a gift to a person who had asked for it, while in the present *kali yuga* gifts are made to persons who actually run after the giver'. It is further stated that 'a gift made to a brāhmaṇa who does not practice penances and austerities and lives by begging alone tends to lower the status of the giver in the next existence'.[29]

Perhaps the most significant change which came to characterize the institution of *dāna* was with regard to the growing popularity of land as a gift-item. This is borne out not only by the Purāṇas and other contemporary literature but also by extensive epigraphic data.[30] Whereas, according to the *Mahābhārata* (Anuśāsana Parva, 59.5), 'gifts of gold, cows and land save even the wicked', the *Agni Purāṇa* (211.33) stipulates that 'by making over the proprietary right in a plot of land to a brāhmaṇa, a man is said to propitiate the gods and the souls of his departed manes'. The elasticity in the concept of land as an item of gift becomes quite manifest from the following verse of the same *Purāṇa* (211.34-5; 213.9), 'By making the gift of a town or a village, hamlet, a field in full harvest, or even a plot of land to the extent of the hyde of a cow (*gocarma*), a man attains everything'. In fact, the gift of land had come to be lauded and recommended as early as the period of the Dharmaśāstras[31] and even certain procedural rules attending *bhūmidāna* were postulated as evident from the injunction contained in the *Yājñavalkya Smṛti* (I.318-20). It was, however, only from the opening centuries of the Christian era that the practice of making land grants actually gained momentum. The development was largely the fallout of changes occurring in the contemporary politico-economic field. By the fifth century AD, a flourishing market system had been effectively replaced by an agriculture-based economy, which automatically catapulted land into a position of being the most valued and coveted item not only of wealth but also of ritual gift-making.

As in the case of any other social formation, our sources reveal a dialectical relationship between the institution of *dāna* and the changing material milieu, which was marked by certain salient developments resulting in the emergence of a feudal ethos. If commercial decline was responsible for augmenting the position of land as the chief means of production, it was the issue of land grants in large numbers which became partly instrumental in heralding a closed agrarian economic system. It was this changed cultural scenario which not only affected Brāhmaṇical ritualism but also gave rise to a new genre of literature, namely the Purāṇas.[32] Substitution of a commercially vibrant economic order by a land-dominated economy caused civilizational influences to penetrate cultural backwaters inhabited by indigenous groups. This, in turn, triggered off a series of cultural vicissitudes that impacted the fundamental moorings of the Brāhmaṇical belief system. It not only eroded its elitist base but also invested it with a wholly new aspect having a strong folk orientation.

Maximum change is perceptible in the domain of ritual formation, which underwent unprecedented growth. If some earlier forms of ritual beliefs such as sacrifices involving killing of animals on a large scale now existed more in a residual form,[33] a whole range of new ones gained wider currency and prominence. Amongst the latter, besides the institution of *dāna*, the practice of visiting *tīrthas*, offering worship in temples and shrines, and observing *vratas* received maximum importance and space in contemporary literature. This is especially evident from the Purāṇas in which whole sections are devoted to the exposition of themes related to a whole new range of ritual *dāna*, consecration of idols and offering of worship (*pūjā*), architectural details and mode of temple building, long lists of *tīrthas* dispersed all over the subcontinent along with tales about their mythical origins and importance, as well as innumerable types of *vratas* meant for a wide cross-section of society. In the very opening verses of the *Vāmana Purāṇa* (1.8), Nārada queries sage Pulastya about 'the importance of holy places (*tīrtha*) and the magnificence of donations (*dāna*) as well as the procedure for observing the number of fasts (*vrata*) as contemplated in the scriptures'.

In the *Agni Purāṇa* (chapter 38), temple-building and the installation of images have been lauded as extremely meritorious acts.

According to the *Purāṇa* (38.6), by building a temple 'one acquires the fruits of bathing at all the sacred shrines' and 'reaps the fruit which he does not even by celebrating a sacrifice'. In another verse of the same *Purāṇa* (38.31), it is stated that by building temples for Śiva, Brahmā, the Sun, Caṇḍī and Lakṣmī, 'one acquires religious merit. Greater merit is acquired by installing images'. At another place[34] we come across a rhetorical observation, 'Useless is the acquisition of his riches, who, with hard earned money, does not have a temple built for Kṛṣṇa, whose wealth is not enjoyed by the *pitṛs*, brāhmaṇas, the celestials and friends'. The *Agni Purāṇa* also contains entire sections dealing with architectural details and the mode of constructing a temple (chapter 42) as well as the installation and consecration of idols, along with the procedure to be followed in offering worship (*pūjā*) to the latter (chapters 33-4, 36, 43-55, 62).

The Purāṇas contain long lists of *vratas* which were meant to promote and safeguard specific interests of different segments of society, including unmarried and married women as well as prostitutes. In the *Matsya Purāṇa* (chapter 61), we get a reference to *saptalokādhipatyaprāpti vrata*, which was performed for obtaining mastery over the seven regions as well as for gaining prosperity, beauty and long life. The same *Purāṇa* (62.31) proclaims *Gaurī-tṛtīyā vrata* to be the 'giver of endless merit' and 'worthy of being followed by men and women'. On its completion, 'a bedstead along with a golden lotus' should be given to a brāhmaṇa. The *Agni Purāṇa* (178.25) stipulates that at the conclusion of another *vrata* called *saubhāgyaśayana*, 'beds and rooms with furniture should be given to a brāhmaṇa and a married brāhmaṇa couple should be feasted with sumptuous repasts'. In the *Vāmana Purāṇa* (chapter 16), we get a reference to a detailed procedure attending various *vratas*, and the nature and volume of gifts (*dakṣiṇā*) to be paid to brāhmaṇas at the time of particular planetary conjunctions. The *Agni Purāṇa* (176.60), while listing the various fasts, ceremonies and penances to be observed on the passing over of the sun to new zodiacal signs, or under the auspices of benignant asterisms and phases of the moon and the exact procedural code to be followed in the case of each one of them, makes a general stipulation that 'gifts should be made at the close of all *vratas*. Twenty-four, twelve, five or a single brāhmaṇa in the alternative, should be feasted in such a connection'.

Various other forms of ritual performances entailing *dāna* to brāhmaṇas also find mention in the Purāṇas. In the *Matsya Purāṇa* (chapter 93), we get a reference to elaborate rites to be performed and the specific kind of gifts to be made to brāhmaṇas for propitiating the nine planets (*graha-śānti*). That at the end of most ritual observances some form of gift-making to brāhmaṇas, even if it was just a sumptuous repast, was considered almost mandatory by the *Purāṇa* composers becomes quite apparent from the *Agni Purāṇa* (208.6-9). It narrates the precise manner and special words to be spoken at the time of giving away to brāhmaṇas gifts, including all the *pūjā*-articles which had been used in the course of offering any kind of worship.

Besides the collective ethos that they tended to project, a feature that is common to most ritual formations of this period is their non-elitist popular base. The latter is especially revealed by the generally modest form of ritual gift-making that came to be associated with most of the emergent forms of ritualism, particularly with *tīrtha*, *vratas* and temple worship, though the construction of magnificent religious monuments on a grandiose scale did provide an ample opportunity to scions of royal dynasties to engage in ostentatious gift-making. The *Skanda Purāṇa* (V.1.14.25-8) enjoins the gift of a *kusumāṇḍa* (red pumpkin) at Catuhsamudrarāja at Avanti. It (V.3.158.6) further recommends the gift of a bell, a flag and a canopy (*chatra*) at various *tīrthas*.[35] According to the *Matsya Purāṇa* (101.17-18), 'the devotee who maintains the vow of silence in the evenings for a year and at the end of it gives a jar of clarified butter, a pair of clothes, sesamum, and a bell to a brāhmaṇa, goes to the domain of Sarasvatī'. The same is also reiterated in the *Agni Purāṇa* (199.2). In the case of *nakṣatra-puruṣa vrata*, the *Vāmana Purāṇa* (80.28) stipulates that 'the wise man should give in donation an umbrella, a pair of white shoes, seven cereals, gold and vessel of *ghee* to the brāhmaṇa'. In the case of a ceremony called *Vaiṣṇava Yajña*, the *Agni Purāṇa* (204.11) enjoins that 'gifts of a pair of clothes, a metal pot, a seat, an umbrella, a prepared holy thread, a pair of shoes and a *yogapaṭṭa* should be made to each of the thirteen brāhmaṇas invited on the occasion'.

A significant development which marked ritual growth during this period is the overarching of the institution of *tīrtha* over most other ritual formations of the time. The Purāṇas, besides emphasizing the spiritual merit accruing from visits to *tīrthas per se*, also widely recommend the performance of religious rites connected with *dāna*, *saṁskāra*, *śrāddha* and even *prāyaścitta* (expiatory) at pilgrimage sites in order to heighten their efficacy. According to the *Agni Purāṇa* (209.20), 'a man should not wait to be asked for anything at the holy places such as the city of Gayā or Prayāga, the banks of the Ganges or at the holy shrines, but voluntarily give alms and dole out charities'. According to the *Vāmana Purāṇa* (36.41), 'At the holy place Sutīrthaka the *pitṛs* with gods reside'. Hence, a bath and the worship of the gods and *pitṛs* there endows the man with the fruit of an *Aśvamedha* sacrifice. Another verse of the same *Purāṇa* (36.53) mentions that a man receives the fruits of the *Rājasūya Yajña*, Sāṁkhya and Yoga when he takes a bath in the Panikhata-*tīrtha* and performs *tarpaṇa* for *pitṛs*.

Tīrthas also came to be closely associated with temple worship (*deva pūjā*) and numerous other ritual performances such as bathing in holy rivers and tanks, especially at the time of the solar and lunar eclipses and particular planetary conjunctions (*snāna*),[36] tonsure (*muṇḍana*), circumambulation (*pradakṣiṇā*),[37] recital of Purāṇic tales (*kathā-vācana*),[38] religious suicide, as well as taking around the idol of the presiding deity kept on a chariot on special ceremonial occasions (*ratha-yātrā*) and celebrating other *tīrtha*-related festivals (*yātrotsava* or *parb*). The *Agni Purāṇa* (chapter 68) contains a detailed exposition of *yātrotsava* which could last for as many as eight consequtive nights. It further stipulates that 'consecration (of image) without the celebration of such a feast is to be deemed as bereft of all merit'. A common feature of all these rituals was the offering of *dāna* and *dakṣiṇā* to brāhmaṇas, both for their priestly services as well as for earning spiritual merit for themselves.

Considering the unexpected proliferation in the number of *tīrthas*[39] as well as the huge crowds from all parts of the country that congregated there, *dāna* made to brāhmaṇas at these sites, though expectedly modest in nature, not only widened and diversified its ritual purview but also greatly added to the latters' source of income. Some idea about how the sphere of *dāna* ritualism was constantly widening can be had from a verse of the *Vāmana Purāṇa* (80.29), which categorically lays down that 'brāhmaṇas should be worshipped/honoured at the conjoining of each and every constellation'.

By the time of the Purāṇas, ritual *dāna* had come to permeate almost all forms of Brāhmaṇical ritualism performed both in private and public and, unlike the Vedic phase, certain fixed procedural norms such as pouring water on the hand of the donee, the chanting of certain *mantras* and offering *dakṣiṇā* along with the gift had come to be diligently observed to add to the efficacy of the ritual act. Nevertheless, there existed wide variations in the manner in which actual *dāna*-rites were performed in different ritual contexts. Some variation in them was inevitable due to the nature of gift-items. The ritual observed in the case of a gift of land or that of a number of cows or the dedication of a well or tank was bound to differ from one another. Thus, a chapter of the *Matsya Purāṇa* (chapter 58) is wholly devoted to expounding different forms of ritual procedure to be followed in dedicating tanks, wells, groves, etc. (*taḍāgārāmakūpādinām pratiṣṭhāvidhivarṇanam*), though, in all of them, feasting and offering various kinds of gifts to brāhmaṇas are uniformly recommended. Similarly, the *Agni Purāṇa* (chapter 64) carries an entire chapter that deals with the procedure of consecrating wells, tanks and ponds (*kūpavāpitaḍāgādipratiṣṭhākathanam*). But even this *Purāṇa* makes it mandatory for such consecration rites to be accompanied by gifts of money and cows to brāhmaṇas (64.39, 41).

Thus, our sources reveal that *dāna*, besides being central to Brāhmaṇical ritualism through the ages, also exercised a deep conditioning effect over it. It was, to a certain extent, not only instrumental in giving rise to some of the prominent ritual formations of the time as well as in determining their elitist/non-elitist base and orientation, but also their subsequent proliferation, widening purview, escalating popularity and ritual importance. The institution of *dāna*, moreover, provided the sinews for upholding the *varṇāśrama dharma*, the mainstay of Brahmanism. But, most importantly, it served as an excellent gauge for assessing the vicissitudes which the economy during the ancient and early medieval periods of Indian history underwent. In fact, the varations overtaking the constituent elements of *dāna*, especially the undulating popularity graph of gift-items, provide a fairly accurate picture of the changes besetting the contemporary economy.

NOTES

1. P.V. Kane, *History of Dharmaśāstra*, vol. II, pt. ii, p. 843.
2. *Kṛtyakalpataru of Bhaṭṭa Lakṣmīdhara*, Dāna Khaṇḍa, ed. K.V. Rangaswami Aiyangar, Baroda, 1941.
3. *Ṛgveda*, I.125. 5-7; I.126.1-5; V. 61; VI. 47.22-5; VII.18.22-5; VIII.5.37-9; VIII.6.46-8; VIII.46.21-4; VIII.68.8-11, Kane, op. cit., p. 837.
4. Ibid., pp. 837-8.
5. *The Hymns of the Ṛgveda*, tr. R.T.H. Griffith, Delhi, rev. edn., 1976, p. 619.
6. *The Ancient Indian Royal Consecration*, p. 164; Heesterman, 'Reflections on the Significance of the Dakṣiṇā', *Indo-Iranian Journal*, 1959, no. III, pp. 241-58
7. 'Gifts', *Change and Continuity in Indian Religion*, Delhi, p. 212; 'Gifts and Giving in the *Ṛgveda*', *Vishveshvaranand Indological Journal*, II, Hoshiarpur, 1964, pp. 9ff.
8. '*Dāna* and *Dakṣiṇā* as forms of Exchange', *Ancient Indian Social History*, New Delhi, 1978, p. 106.
9. *Agni Purāṇa*, 211.30.
10. Kane, op. cit., p. 843.
11. Ibid., p. 838.
12. Ibid., p. 845.
13. J. Gonda, *Change and Continuity in Indian Religion*, rpt., New Delhi, 1985, p. 203.
14. Ibid., p. 204.
15. *Chāndogyopaniṣad*, 4.4.1.
16. *Epigraphia Indica*, vol. VII, p. 57; vol. VIII, p. 78.
17. Jaimini, VI.7, 1-7. Kane, op. cit., p. 849.
18. *Dattapradānika*, 4-5. Kane, op. cit., p. 850.
19. *Manusmṛti*, XI.228.
20. *Agni Purāṇa*, 169.7.
21. *Manusmṛti*, V.61.
22. G. Bühler, *The Sacred Books of the Aryas*, SBE, vol. II, pt. I, pp. vii-viii; vol. XIV, pt. II, pp. vii-ix.
23. Vijay Nath, *Dāna: Gift System in Ancient India*, op. cit., p. 192.
24. Ibid.
25. S.A. Dange, *Encyclopaedia of Puranic Beliefs and Practices*, vol. II, New Delhi, 1987, p. 632.
26. *Matsya Purāṇa*, chapters 271-89; Vijay Nath, '*Mahādāna*: The Dynamics of Gift-economy and the Feudal Milieu' *The Feudal Order: State, Society and Ideology in Early Medieval India*, ed. D.N. Jha, New Delhi, 2000, pp. 441-54.
27. Dange, op. cit., p. 635.

28. Kane, op. cit., p. 853.
29. *Agni Purāṇa*, 209.37.
30. Kane, op. cit., pp. 858-69.
31. *Vasiṣṭha Dharmasūtra*, 29.16.
32. Vijay Nath, *Purāṇas and Acculturation*, Delhi, 2001.
33. *Agni Purāṇa*, 32.6-8.
34. *Agni Purāṇa*, 38.22-3.
35. Dange, op. cit., p. 648.
36. *Vāmana Purāṇa*, 36.52; 79.
37. *Vāmana Purāṇa*, 43.9.
38. *Agni Purāṇa*, 174.12, 'A perusal of this present work (*Agni Purāṇa*), as well as hearing it recited by a brāhmaṇa reader, destroys all sins.'
39. Vijay Nath, 'Puranic *Tīrthas*: A Study of Their Indigenous Origins', *Indian Historical Review*, vol. XXXIV, no. 1, 2007, pp. 1-46.

2

Ideological Dimensions of *Dāna*

A broader definition of the term *dāna* as used in early Sanskrit and Pāli texts would comprehend, within its purview, not only Brāhmaṇical ritual gift-making but also other forms of unilateral gifts to members of monastic orders and to the poor. In order to discern the ideological dimensions of the institution of *dāna* as it developed in ancient India, we will need to take into account this more inclusive definition. The exercise, moreover, would entail utilizing the two methods of investigation, namely the Marxian and the functionalist modes of analysing ritual formations. The first one considers all religious developments to be the product of material culture, though, once developed, these religious beliefs become an effective ideological tool for affecting other socio-economic changes. The functionalist approach, on the other hand, lays greater emphasis on the purposive aspect of a ritual act and its essentially symbolic character. We find both the methods complementary and intend to use them *in tandem* to assess the ideological undercurrents that characterized the institution of ritual gift-making through both the first millennia BC and AD.

A close scrutiny of the data related to the ritual gift system in ancient India reveals two salient features: (i) the centrality of the concept of *dāna* to all three successive stages of socio-economic development, namely the tribal subsistence economy of the Vedic times (*c.* 1500-700 BC), the urban-based market economy of the post-Vedic times (*c.* 600 BC-AD 300) and the feudal economy of the Gupta and post-Gupta period (*c.* AD 400 onwards); (ii) despite the continually changing aspect and functional role performed by the institution in the three varying cultural contexts,[1] *dāna* ideology served as a mechanism of social control, besides facilitating the transition from one cultural phase to another by providing a conducive ideological base and environment. To assess these ideological dimensions, we would need to look at the changes that beset the institution and the functional role it performed in the three successive stages of cultural development.

I

During the first stage of socio-economic development, a scrutiny of the text of the Ṛgvedic content shows that the subject of gift, in some form or the other, constituted its chief theme. It led R.S. Sharma to suggest that the social fabric during the Ṛgvedic period was 'based on some kind of gift economy, respected by custom in the beginning and sanctioned by force at a later stage'.[2] *Dāna* in the *Ṛgveda* is generally found to be connected with munificent gifts made mostly by tribal chiefs to hymnodists and priests at *yajña* performances to promote the group well-being.

The repeated use of the terms *aṁśa* and *bhāga* in the *Ṛgveda*, however, may suggest, according to Sharma, that gift-distribution was not confined to hymnodist priests alone and that the *yajña*-based gift system served the purpose of redistribution of tribal wealth more.[3] Since the 'lion's share went to priests in lieu of the prayers they offered to gods on behalf of their patrons', such a distribution could not be expected to be equal and must have 'benefitted the higher segments of society'.[4] Incidentally, we do come across another term *draviṇaṣaḥ* in the *Ṛgveda* (I.15.7), which denoted a person who sat down to distribute wealth. S.A. Dange has also interpreted *dāna* in the Ṛgvedic context chiefly in the sense of distribution.[5]

However, as Romila Thapar pointed out, by the time the *Ṛgveda* was composed, 'both redistribution as well as participation of the tribe in the *yajña* was more limited'.[6] It could have been, therefore, only in a relatively earlier phase, when 'a successful battle or cattle raid resulted in an enforced acquisition of wealth on the part of the victorious tribe', and when all members must have participated in the *yajña*, that some of the wealth may have been redistributed among a wider group. However, by the time the Ṛgvedic hymns were composed, some sort of private ownership, at least of moveable property, as well as a distinction between those who possessed wealth and the rest of the tribe (*viṣ*), is clearly affirmed.[7] Nevertheless, in both these early Vedic phases, it is the *yajña* format of *dāna* which comes out foremost and even though its redistributive function is not well-established, *dāna* as a source of begetting prestige and status for the donor is evident, especially from the *dāna-stutis*.[8] Incidentally, two very common terms which occur in the *Ṛgveda* are *māgham* (bounty) and *Māghavan* (generous giver).[9] The word *māgham* is derived from the root √ *mahma*, meaning to give.[10] Giving a gift is described as *māgha-dāya*.[11] This shows that *dāna* in the Vedic context not only presupposed the possession of an excessive bounty by the donor but was also expected to win fame and prestige for him.[12]

The evidence furnished by the later Vedas and the Brāhmaṇas testifies to *dāna* generally continuing to be an integral component of all sacrificial ritualism. A certain distinction between the *iṣṭa* and *pūrtta* categories of gift-offerings had already begun to be recognized, the latter being ritual gift-offerings made outside the pale of the sacrificial altar.[13] *Yajña* ceremonialism by this time, however, had acquired a more elaborate and complex hue. The dimensions and occasions for performing them became more varied, as the purpose was no longer augmenting group identity. Instead, *yajñas* were now meant to beget not merely prestige and power for the individual donor, though it continued to be the foremost purpose, but also magical ends such as increasing fertility, promoting material well-being, eradicating epidemics or annihilating enemies. Whatever the purpose, the making of *dāna* to religious beneficiaries remained a constant feature of such ceremonialism. There is also some diversification evident in the kind of gifts offered at *yajña* performances. Cattle continued to be a much sought-after and munificently bestowed gift-item.[14] Along with this, horses,[15] precious metals, finished goods and even grain[16] came to be added to the list of coveted articles of gift, the change very definitely reflecting a transition from a pastoral to a more settled stage of economic development.

The suggestion made by Marcel Mauss that gift-making in early societies was an important mode of goods exchange might hold true, in the later Vedic context, only to a limited degree.[17] The concept perhaps finds an echo in the assertion contained in the *Taittirīya Saṁhitā* (I.8.4.1, *dehi me dadāmi te, ni me dehi ni te dadhe*). The functional value of gift-exchange exists chiefly in a pre-monetary, if not exactly a pre-market economy. To serve the purpose of exchange, gift-making must be bilateral and take place between people specializing in the manufacture of different goods whose economic status is more or less at par with one another.[18] Judging by these parameters, we find that while presence of metallic currency in the Vedic period is not attested by archaeology, a few instances of a bilateral exchange of gifts by princes and chiefs are recorded in the *Mahābhārata*, a text essentially reflecting the later Vedic ethos. We learn from the epic[19] how, on the occasion of the *rājasūya* sacrifice performed by Yudhiṣṭhira, rare and opulent objects were brought as gifts by his close and distant princely neighbours. These gifts, however, were returned manifold by Yudhiṣṭhira. The account not only brings out the bilateral character of sacrificial gifts but also shows shades of the institution of 'potlatch', involving ostentatious wealth display through gift-distribution.[20] The gift-exchange purpose of *dāna* during this phase is also indicated by some kind of linkage that can be discerned between popular gift-items such as the cow and grain (*dhānya*) and the dominant media of exchange in vogue, especially during the early half of the first millennia BC when developed metallic currency did not exist on an extensive scale. Thus, we get copious references to the cow and grain being used as standard units of measuring the value of a commodity. It may be presumed, therefore, that the institution of *dāna* during the Vedic period, to some extent, served the same purpose which was fulfilled by an incipient non-metal or metal currency under a regular market system.

II

Gift-exchange as one of the purposes of *dāna* must have become incongruous in the market economy of the post-Vedic period, when ritual gift-making not only became confined to parties holding an unequal economic and ritual status but also became unilateral. In fact, in the emergent surplus-based economic order revealed by NBPW archaeology, both the *iṣṭa* and *pūrtta* categories of *dāna* made by ruling chiefs and princes would appear to be aimed mainly towards diverting a part of the surplus from the producers to the priestly class. It was done chiefly to win over the brāhmaṇas who, in their self-appropriated role of lawgivers and the chief validating authority, became collaborators of the ruling stratum in controlling and organizing production. Ritual gift-making in its new aspect, thus, became axial to the brāhmaṇa-kṣatriya nexus.[21]

In fact, the post-Vedic economic order besides being marked by remarkable technological growth and surplus production was also characterized by a widening gap between the producers and consumers. Between both now stood a new class: the organizers of production and distribution. The latter comprised ruling kṣatriyas and trading merchants. While transmitting commodity goods from peasants and artisanal manufacturers to consumers, they also managed to appropriate a large surplus in the shape of wide margins of profit[22] or by way of compulsory taxes. In the *Mahāsudassana Sutta*, a king boastfully claims: 'I have enough wealth, my friends, laid up for myself, the produce of righteous taxation'.[23] This resulted in much capital becoming permanently blocked, especially since the spirit of enterprise was not yet so strong as to induce wealth-owners to disregard commercial hazards and re-invest their wealth in risky but lucrative business ventures, to keep social wealth in circulation. Our data is full of notices of wealth being hidden underground in large pitchers and jars.[24] That the hoarding of wealth was a widespread evil at this time is apparent from a number of *Jātaka* stories.[25] The accumulation of wealth was, therefore, decried not only by the Dharmaśāstra writers[26] but also as a matter of state policy, as is evident from Aśoka's Rock Edict III which upholds non-accumulation (*apbhāṇḍata*) as a necessary virtue.[27]

Under the circumstances, gift-making came to be popularly conceived as a corrective to the evil of hoarding. The practice of *dāna*, therefore, must have been considered instrumental in bringing back some of this hoarded wealth into circulation. That *dāna* very often constituted a link in a circular chain of give and take becomes evident from a statement contained in the *Majjhima Nikāya* (XCIV, Ghoṭamukha Sutta, II.163): 'Moreover Udena, the king of the Anga country, gives me a regular daily allowance out of which I will give you a regular allowance.' From contemporary sources, we learn how wealthy *seṭṭhis* and merchants, out of their religious zeal, vied with one another in lavishing, on religious orders as well as on the infirm and destitute, much wealth, which otherwise might have remained blocked in their coffers.[28] It was in consonance with this development that Brāhmaṇical lawgivers are known to recommend the practice of *dāna* as a compulsory virtue for all those possessing wealth, especially the king. While the *Gautama Dharmasūtra* (18.24.27) stipulates stern action against those who persisted with non-giving, Manu (XI.15) unambiguously maintains: 'He may take it by force or fraud from one who always takes but never gives and who refuses to give it.' Hence, redistribution of wealth through *dāna* cannot be understood in the limited egalitarian tribal context alone, for even in the context of a class-divided society with a developed market apparatus, as existed during the post-Vedic times, gift-making may still have served as an instrument of the redistribution of social wealth.[29] As pointed out by N.K. Bose, 'If the class differences brought about a growing inequality of income, as they were likely to do, the evils of increasing polarization could be offset by the custom of conspicuous expenditure. Anyone who spent lavishly in beneficent acts, or even in sheer exhibitionism, was applauded more than one who hoarded.'[30] Such a distribution could scarcely be expected to be either equitable or comprehensive, i.e. covering all the varied segments of society. Nevertheless, by preventing or lessening the concentration of wealth in the hands of a few, viz., the landed *gahapatis*, the *khattiya* nobility and the commercial entrepreneurs or *seṭṭhis*, and diverting it towards those who otherwise possessed no means by which they could lay claim to a share in the social wealth adequate for their survival, such gift-making may be regarded to have performed a distinct redistributive function, even though its benefits remained confined mainly to sections which rendered religious services. It can, therefore, hardly be gainsaid that the prevention of maldistribution of social wealth was one of the important economic functions performed by the institution of *dāna* in the post-Vedic material milieu.

Moreover, the growth of a surplus economy and a class-stratified social structure, combined with other developments in the field of economic production and urbanization, led not only to the breakdown of the kin-based tribal order but also gave rise to a spirit of individualism. Consequently, *yajñas*, which, in the tribal context, served to reinforce the collective spirit and group solidarity, lost their functional viability and could no longer remain the basis of gift-ritualism. The new agricultural techniques based on animal husbandry further eroded the very basis of *yajña* ideology. The latter could not find favour with emergent categories of potential donors, namely the urban-based mercantile and artisanal groups. They lacked both the time and resources needed for the performance of elaborate *yajñas*, particularly those involving the destruction of cattle on a large scale. The new economic scenario led to *dāna* becoming an appendage to the *gṛhya* rituals, which were performed essentially for the individual and projected the spirit of individualism.[31] Consequently, *dāna* at this time is found to be more closely associated with *saṁskāras* such as those performed on the occasion of birth, initiation, marriage and death of a person, rather than with *yajña* ceremonialism.[32]

The post-Vedic period also witnessed considerable activity in the field of social legislation, for it was during this period that brāhmaṇa lawgivers, in the form of Dharmasūtras and Dharmaśāstras, began framing rules and regulations, prescribing the detailed code of conduct to be strictly observed by members of different *varṇas*. Transgression of these rules was regarded tantamount to committing a grave sin, which could partly be atoned for through offering gifts to brāhmaṇas. The concept of ritual pollution was yet another development directly related to the tightening of *varṇa* restrictions and *dāna* to brāhmaṇas became the chief means of regaining purity. Thus, *dāna* during this period became central to most expiatory and penitentiary rites, and was, to a large extent, instrumental in augmenting *varṇa* differ-entiation.

Developments in the field of intensive agriculture and commercial enterprise brought about further changes in the institution of *dāna*. Its purview extended considerably to include several other *pūrtta* categories of *dāna* such as the dedication of wells, tanks and hospices, as also alms to mendicants and the poor. *Dāna*, in its newer aspect of unilateral alms and monetary endowments to monastic orders and charitable establishments, helped not only to sustain heterodox religious movements but also to meet the challenges thrown by new socio-economic developments, particularly those related to urbanization and class stratification. Our sources reveal that the ever-increasing number of orphans and destitutes, who were left impoverished and homeless by frequent wars and economic upheavals and could no longer fall back on the care and support of their kin-group, now relied mainly on alms for their subsistence.[33]

Moreover, the mode of undertaking such benefactions also underwent a drastic change. We learn from contemporary records about the practice of creating monetary trusts (*akṣaya-nivī*) with corporate-guilds (*śreṇī*) for getting works of public utility and buildings and establishments of a religious or charitable nature constructed, as well as maintained by the latter on a permanent basis.

A significant change perceptible in the list of gift-items during the post-Vedic period was the inclusion of villages and land. Though references to the latter are extremely rare in contemporary literature, notices of the gift of villages are fairly common. Thus, a rare instance of the gift of land is furnished by the *Cullavagga* (VI.4.9) in the form of a reference to the gift of Jetavana to the Buddhist *saṁgha* by the householder, Anāthapiṇḍika. Of the numerous allusions to the gift of villages to brāhmaṇa beneficiaries, the one that occurs in the *Mahāummaga Jātaka*[34] may be cited. It relates how King Culāni once gifted as many as eighty villages in Kāśī. While the joint ownership of land by large families and clans would seem to account for land, agricultural or otherwise, not figuring in the list of common gift-items, village grants made in fairly large numbers during the centuries preceding the Christian era can be understood chiefly in the light of some crucial gains that must have accrued from them, both for the beneficiaries as well as the royal donors. If reclamation of forest and waste land was the chief benefit sought by the latter, the former by gaining the right to collect revenue from the village as well as ownership over the forest and marsh land falling within the village boundaries, must have been able to muster the requisite means for undertaking this reclamation. The grant must also have given authority and influence over the village residents to the recipient, making it possible for the latter to utilize the former's labour and services for getting the adjacent forest areas cleared. During the post-Vedic cultural phase, the importance of ritual gift-making in general and the role of village grants in making the forest and waste land cultivable, therefore, cannot be overemphasized.

III

During the subsequent Gupta and post-Gupta centuries, which were marked by developments such as the decline of the market economy and urban decay, religious gift-making, especially in the form of land grants, were chiefly instrumental in giving rise to a politico-economic situation that bordered on the feudal. The fall of large empires and the decline of long-distance trade and craft-production had considerably eroded the fiscal and military base of nascent political powers. The problem posed by these developments could be partly met through the issue of land grants on an extensive scale. In the absence of ready liquidity, the top rung of bureaucratic functionaries could now be remunerated by the state in the form of land grants. Although land granted to non-religious beneficiaries is not commonly attested by our sources, some indication of the existence of such a practice have been noted by scholars such as R.S. Sharma.[35] Even in the case of religious beneficiaries, the two major administrative responsibilities of collecting revenue and maintaining law and order could, henceforth, partly devolve upon the recipient of the grant; the latter acting as an intermediary between the ruler and the class of producers, who were virtually reduced to a semi-serf status.[36] The latter were not only permanently attached to the land but were subjected to exploitation through coercive measures such as corvee (*viṣṭi*), which came to be legally sanctioned by contemporary lawgivers. The specially framed rules pertaining to land grants were chiefly meant to secure the interests of brāhmaṇa beneficiaries, transforming them into a permanent and influential category of landowners.[37] Thus, in the emergent feudal context, the role of the *dāna* ideology as a mechanism of social control gained in importance. In a feudal ethos, *dāna* ritualism, besides offering an extra economic sanction to the ruling class for surplus extraction, also became one of the forms of exploitation of the producing classes. The inclusion of *viṣṭi* or forced labour amongst additional privileges granted along with the land to the beneficiary invested the latter with the right to exact labour from sharecroppers or tillers attached to the soil, reducing them to a state of servility.[38]

Land grants also became instrumental in reclaiming virgin and waste land, especially in the peripheral zones, thereby adding to the overall productivity of land. Moreover, our sources reveal that the practice of land grants, besides unleashing the forces of acculturation in the outlying regions, was also responsible for bringing about salient changes in the structural framework of the brāhmaṇa *varṇa* stratum.[39] The practice would seem to be chiefly responsible for grading the brāhmaṇas on the basis of their intellectual proficiency as also their status as landowners and the region to which they belonged. Thus, we hear of the Kānyakubja, Gauḍa, Gayawāl and many other categories of brāhmaṇas. In fact, we hear of five distinct categories of brāhmaṇas dwelling in south India during this period called *pañca-draviḍa*.[40]

Besides developments related to land grants, other changes also occurred in the institution of *dāna* during this period. Our chief Brāhmaṇical source for this period, namely the Purāṇic texts supplemented by other genres of contemporary literature and epigraphic records, testify to the institution undergoing unprecedented elaboration and change. Besides the practice of making land grants in favour of religious beneficiaries, more innovative forms of *dāna* such as *mahādāna*, *merudāna*, *dhenudāna*, etc., that bore an opulent aspect, also came to be introduced by the Purāṇa composers. That these newer forms of gift-making gained wide currency during the post-Gupta centuries is affirmed by contemporary epigraphic records, which also testify to *dāna* continuing to be integral to whatever vestiges remained of sacrificial ceremonialism, in which some of the aspirant rulers were known to indulge.[41]

However, the most remarkable change which characterized *dāna* during this period was the dilution of its elitist ritual format. It is found to acquire, in the Purāṇas, a more popular base and a strong folk orientation. *Dāna* now came to be associated with most of the ritual formations that gained popularity at this time, such as temple worship and the act of visiting *tīrthas*. The development brought about a sea change in the categories of donors, recipients and gift-items, as well as the ritual format of making *dāna*. As far as the donor categories are concerned, we find that the making of *dāna* was no longer confined to the affluent, for even people with extremely limited resources came to undertake it. There was a corresponding change, therefore, in the gift-items, which now ranged from the very opulent to others that were extremely modest in nature. Whereas offerings at temples could consist of flowers, leaves, fruits, roasted gram, common items of cooked food, pieces of cloth and utensils to animal meat and liquor, ritual *dāna* made to brāhmaṇas also became equally unpretentious and even petty goods, small cash or a handful of grain could suffice as an offering. The ritual procedure accompanying the act of *dāna* became less complicated, often not needing the assistance of an officiating priest. As for the categories of donees receiving *dāna*, we find that under Tāntric influences that assailed most existent religious systems of the time, an unprecedented flexibility came to be shown by the Purāṇa composers, who came to recognize even *dāna* made to very young girls as well as to the infirm and destitutes as yielding great spiritual merit.

IV

Corresponding to the changing material milieu, the variations besetting *dāna* in the form of its ever-widening purview and continually changing aspect from *yajña* to *saṁskāra* to land grants to modest forms of offerings at temples and *tīrthas*, definitely underscore its role as an adaptive mechanism. It shows how the institution served as a most potent ideological device, which helped to create a favourable environment and the right outlook necessary for such a cultural transition. The role of rituals in affecting social change has been especially highlighted by Clifford Geertz.[42] The Dharmasūtra and Smṛti texts reveal that it was by advocating *saṁskāra*-based *dāna* and other religious and charitable forms of gift-making that the principle of *ahiṁsā* emphasizing the non-killing of animals could be put across and popularized. The changing tenor of Brāhmaṇical ideology as expressed through emergent *dāna* ritualism was instrumental in not only substituting *yajña* religiosity with ritual gift-making but also in completely eroding the *yajña* basis of the Vedic society. Gift-making at the time of sacrificial performances was now substituted by charity and mandatory *dāna* on sacramental occasions. The two forms of gift-making came to be prescribed as the obligatory duties of all householders. It was, thus, a clear case of one religious ideology being replaced by another for the sake of promoting economic production.

The dual principles of charity and *ahiṁsā*, in fact, provided a broad ideological framework to the emergent heterodox movement during 600 BC. Moreover, if the advocacy of *dāna* and almsgiving during the inaugural post-Vedic phase helped to overcome the vicissitudes of a tribal order that was getting replaced by a class differentiated society, the practice of land grants during the Gupta/post-Gupta centuries became instrumental in effecting a transition from the urban-based market economy of the Kuṣāṇa-Sātavāhana times to the feudalistic developments of the subsequent period. In fact, had it not been for the immense ideological potential and pliancy exhibited by the institution of *dāna*, which was exploited to the fullest by lawgivers, such cultural transitions might have proved more catastrophic.

More than anything else, the practice of ritual gift-making remained, throughout this period, a very powerful ideological tool in the hands of the sacredotal class. The latter used it to safeguard and promote their self-interests. Thus, as revealed by the *dāna-stutis*, in the Ṛgvedic tribal order, *dāna*, at the time of *yajñas*, was mainly aimed at ensuring a large share in the tribal wealth for the priests and hymn-composers. This had its source mainly in the inter- and intra-tribal wars waged for cattle. Once the tribal order broke down and the subsequent developments effectively discredited *yajña* religiosity, as during the post-Vedic cultural phase, the interests of the priestly class were directly affected. In the newly emergent social order, the ritual gift-system became subject to some cardinal changes, primarily to create fresh sources of income for the brāhmaṇas. Since the urban-based mercantile and artisanal clientele was ill-equipped and even ill-disposed towards undertaking elaborate sacrifices, which had served chiefly to augment group identity or used as instruments of gaining validation for political power, ritual *dāna* on the occasion of *saṁskāras* began to be favoured instead and widely recommended by the lawgivers. Juxtaposed to sacrifices, *dāna* on sacramental occasions served the totally different purpose of defining the ritual and social status of a person in both his family and society. As the chief accrediting device, *dāna* continued to be an important validating mechanism as well as a lucrative source of income for members of the sacredotal class.

The ritual gift-system, by supporting and sustaining the top *varṇa* stratum, would seem to have had a significant bearing, at least during the early formative stages, on the emergence and growth of a unique social structure based on the *varṇa* division. It was mainly the institution of *dāna* which enabled the members of the highest *varṇa* to adopt an economically unproductive mode of living and it also provided them with a powerful ideological tool that could be used for appropriating both power and wealth. The concept of *dāna* is found to constitute, in fact, one of the important bases of the *varṇa* ideology.

Similarly, in its other aspect of almsgiving, *dāna* to mendicants provided the sole means of subsistence to the heterodox monks who depended entirely on alms or *bhikṣā*. In fact, the heterodox religious movement which dominated the intellectual scene during the post-Vedic phase was sustained wholly through the institution of *dāna*. But for the munificent benefactions made in favour of monastic orders by ruling chiefs and wealthy merchants, as also the alms and gifts liberally bestowed by lay followers, the rise of heterodox sects and the ideology based on *ahiṁsā* and renunciation propagated by them might have never made much headway or swayed the popular mind to such an extent.

In fact, the institution of *dāna*, by creating an alternate form of subsistence for religious mendicants, might have been instrumental in inducing a fairly large section of the population to give up the task of actual production, agricultural or otherwise, and take to alms-seeking, which was tantamount to adopting a parasitical mode of living. In the *Therigāthā* (LXVII, Rohini), the recluse's life is thus denounced: 'Not fain to work are they, the lazy crew. They make their living off what others give.' According to the Jaina text, *Sūtrakṛtāṅga* (I.3.1): 'Common people say that men become monks because they will not work.' Similarly, in the *Theragāthā* (canto I, pts. V-XVIII), a field labourer about to don a monk's robes thus exclaims: 'Well rid am I from these crooked tasks and tools, rid of my reaping with your sickles, rid of my trudging after ploughs.' That adoption of a mendicant's life proved generally detrimental to economic growth is evident from the *Khadirāṅga Jātaka* (vol. I, no. 4, p. 100). It relates how the merchant, Anāthapiṇḍika, due to his preoccupation with gift-making, 'engaged in no traffic and undertook no business, so that his income diminished and his estate grew less and less'. From the *Mahāvagga* (VI.24.2), we learn how a brāhmaṇa followed the fraternity of *bhikkhus* with the Buddha at its head continuously for two months in the hope of making a meal for them, so that many of his household affairs suffered badly.

The parasitical tendency encouraged by gift-making in general is also apparent from the following remark contained in the *Illīsa Jātaka* (vol. I, no. 78, p. 199): 'What you have done for me today will enable me to live without doing another stroke of work.' The adoption of such a parasitical mode of living by a large section of the population might have, therefore, put an unnecessary burden upon the rest of the producers and even exerted some pressure on the contemporary economy. Thus, the *Vinaya* (Nissagīya, XXII.i) records how a 'potter making many bowls for the monks, could not make other goods for sale, and he could not keep himself going and his wife and children suffered'. Some idea about the pressure on the economy caused by such a phenomenon can be had from the fact that Kauṭilya in the *Arthaśāstra* (II.1.29) not only prescribed a fine for all those who renounced their home to become ascetics, without providing for their sons and wives, but also forbade ascetic sects other than forest hermits from settling in the countryside. Perhaps it was the same fear of causing economic instability which led Jaina leaders to exhort monks not to seek alms in newly-occupied villages (*gāma*), settlements (*sannivesa*) and habitations (*niveṣa*).

During the post-Gupta centuries, the decline of trade and craft production led to urban decay.[43] The development seriously affected the economic competence of those *jajamānī* brāhmaṇas who lived in the decaying towns. According to a theory proposed by R.N. Nandi, the institution of *tīrthas* developed and gained popularity mainly to arrest the process of urban decay. He has cited evidence to show that a large number of places such as Mathura, Varanasi (Rājghāṭ), Prayāga (Bhita) and Dwarka (Prabhāsa), which had once been thriving market centres, later came to be proclaimed as *tīrthas* to which people from all parts of the country thronged and made ritual *dāna* to brāhmaṇas.[44] Though the suggestion may carry some historical truth, especially in the context of the Brāhmaṇical heartland confined mostly to north India, our own study of contemporary data, particularly the Purāṇic texts, reveals that the rise of *tīrthas* was, in fact, a pan-Indian phenomenon.[45] It would seem to be linked less with urban decay and more with the processes of the Brahmanization of autochthonous groups residing in outlying regions, as well as some amount of tribalization of Purāṇic Brāhmanism.[46] The forces of acculturation had been triggered off chiefly by the issue of land grants to brāhmaṇas by aspirant ruling chiefs and princes in regions lying on the outskirts of the core civilizational zone. The unprecedented increase in the numerical size and popularity of *tīrthas* throughout the subcontinent during the post-Gupta centuries is attested both by the Purāṇas as well as contemporary epigraphic records. The development has to be attributed largely to the Brāhmanization and assimilation of popular indigenous deities into the continually expanding Purāṇic pantheon, and the categorization of local shrines and popular cultic centres patronized chiefly by tribal folks as sacred *tīrthas* in the Purāṇas.[47] Since the performance of *dāna* at *tīrthas* was declared to be an obligatory rite without which the act of pilgrimage was devoid of all spiritual merit, the unprecedented popularity gained by the institution of *tīrthas* would bear testimony not only to the generally expanding purview of Brāhmaṇical ritualism but also to that of ritual gift-making *per se*. In fact, all ritual acts performed at the *tīrtha* site such as *snāna* or ritual bathing, *parikramā* or circumambulation of the sacred region, listening to Purāṇic *kathā*, and offering *pūjā* or worship at the temple had to be customarily attended by ritual *dāna* made to brāhmaṇa priests. Thus, throughout the ancient period and in all its variable forms and aspects, *dāna* remained an effective adaptive mechanism and a lucrative source of income for brāhmaṇas.

V

For assessing the true social import of *dāna* ritualism, we would, however, need to also apply the functionalist technique of analysis as expounded by Radcliffe Brown[48] and V.W. Turner.[49] According to it, all religious rituals are symbolic acts and expressive of some social value or concern of a group. Rituals serve both as referential and condensational symbols, and are pregnant with more than one meaning. For fixing the symbolic content of a particular ritual, therefore, we need to analyse the widely different structural contexts in which it occurs. With reference to ritual *dāna*, we find that whether made at the time of *yajña* or *saṁskāra* it was meant to confer a higher ritual and social status on the donor.[50] Even in the context of *dāna* made at a more modest level, such as those at the time of visits to *tīrthas* and temples, the expectancy of spiritual merit could have undercurrents of the hope of scaling higher in the esteem of the dominant cultural group.

In the early and later Vedic context, the large-scale distribution of gifts to officiating priests and brāhmaṇas by ruling chiefs at the time of *yajñas* were clearly meant to beget validation of power as well as prestige within and outside the tribal group for them. The *Dānastutis* in the *Ṛgveda* are entirely devoted to singing paeans to such liberal donors. Even in the subsequent phases of cultural development, especially under the Sātavāhanas and Imperial Guptas, ostentatious gift-making at the time of sacrificial performances continued to be undertaken by kings and their kinsmen for proclaiming sovereignty, as well as for reviving their power or augmenting hold over their kingdoms, particularly in the wake of some internal crisis or external threat.

Similarly, *saṁskāras* attended by liberal *dāna* to brāhmaṇas during the post-Vedic phase, became the chief determinants of *varṇa* status. Without their performance, a person was considered ritually impure and unfit to be formally recognized as a member of the *varṇa* stratum to which he otherwise belonged by birth. The injunction contained in the Dharmaśāstras was quite explicit in this regard. According to it, a person by birth is born a śūdra. It is only through the performance of the initiatory rite or *upanayana saṁskāra* that he gains the status of a twice-born. Likewise, other *saṁskāras* performed to mark life-crises situations signified the progress of a person from one stage of life to another, and the acquisition by him of a new social status, both *vis-à-vis* the family and society, as well as its attendant set of duties and responsibilities. *Dāna* at the time of *saṁskāras*, therefore, is found to bequeath a higher social status to the donor by affecting ritual purification.

In the context of sacramental ritualism, the dual purpose served by *dāna*, namely ritual purification and status elevation, continued to be equally manifest during the early medieval period, when ritual gift-making became the chief mechanism of affecting social mobility and cultural assimilation of foreign and indigenous groups into the traditional caste order, as well as for providing the chief meeting ground for collaboration between the sacredotal class and the ruling stratum, irrespective of the latter's social antecedents.[51] Thus ostentatious gift-making that accompanied the performance of *mahādānas* such as the *hiraṇyagarbha*, *mahābhūtaghaṭa*, *brahmāṇḍa* and *tulāpuruṣa*, and the issue of land grants to brāhmaṇas and other religious beneficiaries by aspirant ruling chiefs lacking a *bona fide* dynastic background, became a recognized mode of securing religious sanction and support for the latter's newly acquired political power. Members of lower social orders, as also people of foreign and indigenous extraction, could aspire to achieve a modicum of upward mobility by offering *dāna* to brāhmaṇas for rendering priestly services, as well as by adopting Brāhmaṇical practices such as undertaking ritual gift-making at *tīrthas* or making *dāna* in the course of observing *vratas* that entailed practising body cleanliness, along with various kinds of abstinence such as from killing of animals and the consumption of meat and liquor. The latter practices had been integral throughout to popular tribal mores but were not favoured by brāhmaṇa lawgivers who were advocating stricter ethical norms. No wonder there is evident, during this period, a phenomenal increase in the size of both the ruling stratum as well as the śūdra substratum, comprising largely tillers of soil, a development that might be attributed to the process of cultural assimilation facilitated by the institution of *dāna*, be it in the form of land grants, *mahādānas*, benefactions made in favour of temples and monasteries, and ritual gifts made to brāhmaṇas at *tīrthas*, on sacramental occasions, at the time of performing sacrifices, observing *vratas*, performing expiatory rites or offering *pūjā*, etc. In fact, *dāna* was central to all ritual acts performed to better one's status, both political and social.

Thus, despite the continually changing configuration of its form, purpose and context, the manifest ideological framework and status conferring role of *dāna* largely accounts for its continued relevance and viability throughout the ancient period.

NOTES

1. Vijay Nath, 'Continuity and Change in the Institution of Dāna', *Journal of the Asiatic Society of Bombay*, NS, LIV-LV, 1979-80, pp. 95-102.
2. R.S. Sharma, 'Conflict, Distribution and Differentiation in Ṛgvedic Society', *PIHC*, 1977.
3. Ibid.; Vijay Nath, *Dāna: Gift System in Ancient India*, Delhi, 1987, p. 170.
4. R.S. Sharma, 'Forms of Property', *EHS*, p. 101.
5. S.A. Dange, *India from Primitive Communism to Slavery: A Marxist Study of Ancient History in Outline*, Delhi, 1979.
6. Romila Thapar, *Ancient Indian Social History*, New Delhi, 1978, p. 111.
7. *Ṛgveda*, I.162; IV.41.10.
8. Ibid., I.125; I.126.1-5; V.61; VI.47.22-5; VII.18.22-5; VIII.5.37-9; VIII.6.46-8; VIII.46.21-4.
9. *Vedic Index*, II, p. 118, *Māghavan* is the regular name for the generous giver of bounties to priests.
10. Brajdeo Prasad Rao, *The Later Vedic Economy*, p. 52.

11. *Ṛgveda*, VII.67.9; X.156.2.
12. Nath, *Dāna: Gift System in Ancient India*, p. 14.
13. Aparārka (p. 290), quoting the *Mahābhārata* thus defines *iṣṭa* and *pūrtta*: 'whatever is offered inside the *vedī* (in *śrauta* sacrifices) are called *iṣṭa*; while dedication of deep wells, tanks, temples, distribution of food, and maintaining public gardens . . . these are called *pūrtta*'. P.V. Kane, *History of Dharmaśāstras*, vol. II, pt. ii, p. 844.
14. *Ṛgveda*, I.126.3.
15. Ibid., V.18.5.
16. Ibid., X.117.6.
17. Marcel Mauss, *The Gift*, tr. I.A.N. Cunnison, London, 1954, pp. 45ff.
18. Ibid.
19. *Mahābhārata*, Sabhā Parva, tr. K.M. Ganguly, 3rd edn., Delhi, 1975, p. 48.
20. John Beattie, *Other Cultures*, New York, 1964, p. 199.
21. R.S. Sharma, 'Class Formation and its Material Basis in the upper Gangetic Basin (*c.* 1000-500)', *Indian Historical Review*, vol. II, 1975, pp. 1-13.
22. Bhaskar Chatterjee, 'Religion and Polity in Kuṣāṇa Age', *JIH*, LIV, 1976, p. 515.
23. *Mahā Sudassana Sutta*: *The Great King of Glory,* 6.4, Sacred Books of the East, p. 264.
24. *Manu*, VIII.37; *Jaruḍapāna Jātaka*, vol. II, no. 256, p. 205; *Nanda Jātaka*, vol. I, no. 39, p. 98.
25. M.M. Singh, 'The *Dhamma* of Jātakas', *Journal of Bihar Research Society*, 1976, p. 47.
26. *Manusmṛti*, IV.7.
27. D.C. Sircar, *Select Inscriptions Bearing on Indian History and Civilization*, vol. I, Calcutta, 1965.
28. Nath, *Dāna: Gift System in Ancient India*, Delhi, p. 177.
29. Karl Polanyi, *The Great Transformation*, New York, 1975, pp. 50-2.
30. 'Class and Caste', *Man in India*, XI, 1965, p. 272.
31. Nath, op. cit., pp. 32-5.
32. R.N. Nandi, 'Client, Ritual and Conflict in Early Brāhmaṇical Order', *Indian Historical Review*, vol. VI, nos. i-ii, p. 68.
33. G.S.P. Mishra, 'A Study of Philanthropy in Early Buddhist Ethics', *Indica*, vol. XVIII, no. ii, 1981, pp. 73-81.
34. *Jātakas*, vol. VI, no. 546, p. 237.
35. *Indian Feudalism*.
36. B.N.S. Yadava, 'The Problem of Emergence of Feudal Relations', in D.N. Jha, ed., *The Feudal Order: State, Society and Ideology in Early Medieval India*, Delhi, 2000, p. 254.
37. R.S. Sharma, *Indian Feudalism*, p. 38; Raghavendra Vajpeyi, 'Bṛhaspati on the Emergence of Land-owning Brāhmaṇa Community', *ABORI*, LVII, 1976, pp. 181-7.

38. Yadava, 'The Problem of Emergence of Feudal Relations in Early India', in D.N. Jha, ed., *The Feudal Order*, p. 275.
39. Vijay Nath, *Purāṇas and Acculturation: A Historico-Anthropological Perspective*, Delhi, 2001, pp. 56-8.
40. D.C. Sircar, *Studies in Geography of Ancient and Medieval India*, Delhi, 1960, p. 16.
41. V.S. Pathak, 'Vedic Rituals in Early Medieval Period: An Epigraphic Study', *ABORI*, XI, 1959, p. 222.
42. Clifford Geertz, 'Ritual and Social Change', *Religion, Culture and Society*, ed. Louis Schneider, 1964; K.S. Mathur, ed., *Studies in Social Change*, Lucknow, 1973.
43. R.S. Sharma, *Urban Decay in India*, Delhi, 1987.
44. R.N. Nandi, *Social Roots of Religion in India*, Calcutta, 1986, p. 7.
45. Vijay Nath, '*Tīrthas* and Acculturation'.
46. Vijay Nath, 'From "Brahmanism" to "Hinduism": Negotiating the Myth of the Great Tradition', Presidential Address, Ancient India Section , 61st Session of the *Indian History Congress*, Calcutta, 2001.
47. Vijay Nath, 'Indigenous *Tirthas* and Their Puranic Transformation'.
48. A.R. Radcliff Brown, 'Religion and Society', *Journal of the Royal Anthropological Institute*, 1945.
49. V.W. Turner, 'Symbols in Ndembu Ritual', *Closed Systems and Open Minds*, ed. Max Gluckman, 1964.
50. See Chapter on 'Symbolism and Status-Conferring Role of Dāna'.
51. R. Thapar, 'Social Mobility in Ancient India', *Ancient Indian Social History*, 1978, p. 147.

3

Ritual Symbolism and Status-conferring Role of *Dāna*

The functionalist mode of analysing ritual makes it out to be a symbolic act expressive of some social value or concern of a group. Religious rituals serve both as referential and condensational symbols, and are pregnant with more than one meaning. For fixing the symbolic content of a particular ritual, we, therefore, need to analyse the widely different cultural and structural contexts in which it occurs. In the case of *dāna* ritualism as it evolved and developed during the early period, such a study would entail tracing its growth through three successive stages of socio-economic development (tribal/ pastoral, commerce-dominated urban and feudal) that marked the Vedic (*c*. 1500 BC-600 BC), post-Vedic (*c*. 600 BC-AD 300), and the Gupta and post-Gupta (*c*. AD 400 onwards) periods, respectively. The study will also have to take cognizance of two important features that marked ritual gift-system throughout this long period spanning two millennia, namely, its continued relevance to all three stages of socio-economic development, and its constantly changing aspect and functional role in the three varying cultural contexts.[1]

On the basis of Ṛgvedic evidence, the early Vedic economy can easily be described as a gift economy[2]; the *yajña*-based gift-system, especially in the more initial phase, serving the purpose of redistribution of tribal wealth.[3] It is the *yajña* format of *dāna* which is foremost in the early Vedic tribal context. With the growth of a surplus agrarian economy and a class-stratified social structure, which replaced the pastoral tribal order during the subsequent period marked by the NBPW phase of cultural development, the redistributory role of *dāna* became more or less redundant. The new agricultural techniques based on animal husbandry eroded the very basis of *yajña* ideology. The latter could also not find favour with the new category of potential donors, the urban-based mercantile and artisanal groups. They apparently lacked both the time and the resources needed for the performance of these elaborate sacrifices.

Dāna, at this time, is found to be more closely associated with *gṛhya* rituals (*saṁskāras*)[4] such as those performed on the occasion of birth, initiation, marriage or death of a person, rather than with *yajña* ceremonialism. The change is clearly linked with the developments in the field of economic production and urbanization, which were directly responsible for giving rise to a spirit of individualism. Consequently, the *yajña* which in the tribal context may have served to reinforce the collective spirit and group solidarity, lost into functional viability and could no longer remain the basis of gift-ritualism. The new economic scenario led to *dāna* becoming an appendage to *gṛhya* rituals, especially initiatory rites, which were performed essentially for the individual and projected the spirit of individualism.[5]

Against the background of post-Gupta developments such as the decline of the market economy and de-urbanization,[6] religious gift-making in the shape of land grants became chiefly instrumental in giving rise to a politico-economic situation which bordered on the feudal pattern.[7] Consequent to the fall of empires and the decline of long-distance trade and craft-production, the fiscal and military base of political powers grew weak. The practice of land grants served as a possible means of diffusing this crisis. The two major responsibilities of collecting revenue and maintaining law and order henceforth partly devolved upon the beneficiaries, who now stood as landed intermediaries between the king and the class of producers. The latter were reduced to a semi-serf status. Not only were they permanently attached to the land but they were also subjected to exploitation through coercive measures such as *viṣṭi* that were legally sanctioned by the lawgivers of this period.[8] The changing aspect of *dāna* from *yajña* to *saṁskāra* to land grant in response to the changing modes of production demonstrated its adaptive nature.

In order to assess the true social import of *dāna*, we need to apply the functionalist technique of analysis as developed by Radcliffe-Brown[9] and V.W. Turner,[10] though for fixing the symbolic content of a particular ritual we have to depend on more than one method of analysis and then cross-check our findings in order to discern its more obscure meanings. Thus, one way of inferring ritual symbolism could be through adopting the semantic method and analysing the change apparent in the meaning of the word *dāna* at different stages of cultural development. Two texts, though widely divided in time, may be made the basis of such a study. Both the *Nighaṇṭu*, assigned to *c.* seventh century BC[11] and the *Amarakoṣa*,[12] believed to be composed during sixth-seventh century AD the furnish a number of equivalent terms for *dāna*. A comparative study of the two groups of synonyms may help us to fix the exact connotative inflexion of the term at a particular point of time.

The substitutes for *dāna* suggested by the author of the *Nighaṇṭu* are *rati*, *dāsati*, *tuṁjhati*, *maṁhati*, and *prīṇāti*.[13] The word *rati* means to be liberal.[14] Significantly, *rayi* another derivative from the same root although used in the sense of wealth, literally means 'the object to be given away'. The idea which is sought to be conveyed through the use of this synonym is that wealth is meant to be given away or constitutes the object of gift. *Dātī*, on the other hand, literally means to give or distribute and would seem to focus upon the distributory role of *dāna*. But *dātī* has two other lexical meanings as well, to cut and to destroy. The latter are not totally inapplicable to *dāna*, for they would seem to imbue it with the aspect of a potlatch. According to anthropologists, potlatch is a characteristic of tribal societies. It is aimed at gaining prestige through an ostentatious distribution or destruction of wealth.[15] *Dāsati*, on the other hand, means to offer an oblation, while *prīṇāti* is used in the sense of 'to please' or 'to propitiate'. Since Vedic *yajñas* had a propitiatory character, *dāna* made on the occasion of these sacrifices can also be understood in this special sense. However, propitiation was only one of the purposes served by *dāna*. Sacrificial offerings were also meant to augment the powers of the deity so that the latter may bestow munificent gifts in return. According to J. Gonda,[16] the idea of reciprocity is clearly implied in the saying *dehi me dadāmi te* (give me, I give thee) that occurs in the *Śatapatha Brāhmaṇa* (II.5.3.19). *Dāna*, therefore, initiated a flow of wealth which created a two-way link between the donor and the recipient, both divine and human. Another synonym of *dāna*, *tuṁjhati*, also has dual shades of meaning: to guard, protect or cherish and to reach out or flow forth. The latter meaning clearly underlines the function of *dāna* noted above, that of forging close ties between the donor and the receiver of gifts. However, the use of *tuṁjhati* in the sense of protection can be appreciated only in the context of gifts made by the Vedic tribal chiefs, whose main duties were the redistribution of tribal wealth and the protection of the tribal group.

Another alternate meaning of *dāna* suggested in the *Nighaṇṭu* is *maṁhati*, which, in the *Ṛgveda*, is used in the sense of 'to grow' or 'to increase'. The use of the word *dāna* in this particular sense would very obviously convey the meaning that wealth tends to multiply through giving. Since more wealth means more prestige, it logically follows that *dāna* is a source of prestige for the donor. Incidentally, *maṁhati* like *dātī* has another connotation: that of an aggressive act against a rival. *Dāna*, in this context, would come very close to the concept of potlatch, to which the notion of prestige is central. Thus, besides its redistributory role, the one common idea reinforced through the various synonyms suggested for *dāna* in the *Nighaṇṭu* is that liberal gift-making is an important mechanism for gaining prestige, a fact which is adequately substantiated by the *Dānastutis* contained in the *Ṛgveda*.

As compared to the shades of meaning of *dāna* hinted at in the *Nighaṇṭu*, those suggested by Amarasiṁha offer a sharp contrast. Amongst the synonyms mentioned in the *Amarakoṣa* (II.7.29) are *nirvapanam*, *utsarjanam*, *tyāga*, *visarjanam*, *vitarṇam*, *pratipādanam*, *sparśaṇam*, and *apavarjanam*. The lexical meaning of *nirvapanam* is 'to sprinkle' or 'to pour out', and may hint at the ritual overgrowth connected with *dāna*, which is amply attested by the Purāṇas. The two other terms, *utsarjanam* and *tyāga*, when used as synonyms of *dāna*, underline one of its more latent aspects. Apparently it is the idea of sacrifice and loss implied in the relinquishment of one's claim over the gift-article in favour of the recipient which is emphasized through the use of such words. Significantly, Kauṭilya, in the *Arthaśāstra* (I.3.9; 13.17), has also used the term *tyāga* in the sense of gift-making. As compared to the gift-distribution of tribal wealth, gifts made out of private holdings must have naturally entailed some amount of sacrifice. Such a meaning of *dāna* therefore, can be appreciated mainly in a cultural milieu characterized by developments in the field of private property. The same idea is further reinforced by the other synonym *visarjanam*, which literally means cessation. As an equivalent term for *dāna*, it makes sense only when interpreted to mean the termination of the donor's right of ownership over the gift-item. Even *vitarṇam*, which literally means transference, will be coherent only if understood in the context of the transfer of property entailed in the act of *dāna*. *Sparśaṇam* as a synonym, however, reaffirms the idea already contained in the *Nighaṇṭu* that gift-making helps to create a close bond between the donor and donee. But the other term, *apavarjanam*, which literally means to discharge a debt, casts *dāna* more in an obligatory mould.

The two groups of synonyms contained in the *Nighaṇṭu* and the *Amarakoṣa* provide an interesting insight into the changing aspect of *dāna*. If, in the former, the thrust appears to be more on the distribution and gift of wealth as a source of gaining prestige, in the latter, *dāna* seems to have acquired not only a more prominent ritual tenor and obligatory character but also an extremely pronounced property-based connotation. Such a marked difference in focus corresponds largely to the changes taking place in the mode and social relations of production. If, in the Vedic tribal milieu, it was understood more in the sense of distribution of tribal wealth, in the feudal economic order of the Gupta and post-Gupta times, the legal inflexion of *dāna*, involving transference of property, became more conspicuous.

Despite the change in its more manifest meaning, a closer scrutiny of these two sets of synonyms show that the idea which remained central to the concept of *dāna* was that gift-making, in some subtle indefinable manner, added to the worth and social consequence of the donor. Although this notion, or the specific criterion of assessing the social worth of a person, may have differed from one cultural stage of development to another, yet the causal connection between *dāna* and improved status remained undeniable. Thus, if in the Vedic ethos, the ruling chief hoped to gain prestige and power through ostentatious gift-making, in the market-based urban ethos of the Mauryan and post-Mauryan times, *dāna* was believed to beget for the donor both ritual purity and spiritual merit (*puṇya* or *iṣṭa/pūrtta*). Since in the *varṇa*-differentiated society, ritual purity was regarded as the chief determinant of *varṇa* status, *dāna* came to be acknowledged as one of the more dependable means of securing a better ritual status. However, during the subsequent period marked by feudal formations, property, especially in the shape of landholdings, became the most important yardstick for measuring social status. In the emergent social ethos, property assumed a special significance. It is in this new cultural context that we need to view and assess the property-laden meaning of *dāna* as projected in the *Amarakoṣa*. Status elevation or acquisition of prestige, therefore, appears to be one of the more manifest purposes of *dāna*, regardless of the fact that it was undertaken in a predominantly tribal or feudal setting.

Another method by which *dāna* symbolism may be delineated is through analysing the structural contexts in which it is predominantly known to occur. Our analysis shows that in the later Vedic context, *dāna* figures primarily as an adjunct to sacrificial ceremonialism. In the *Ṛgveda*, however, gifts are known to be made mostly to the hymn-composers and officiating priests, both by divine and human donors. The latter were mostly tribal chiefs and warriors. Although not explicitly stated, the event was generally a successful battle or cattle-raid. The gift would have been made, therefore, not so much in the spirit of charity but to commemorate military success and as an investment towards further success on future occasions.[17] As suggested by Thapar the association with *soma* implies that it was made on the occasion of the *soma*-pressing ceremony.[18]

Even the quantum of gifts seems to have lent them an ostentatious character.[19] The most prized gift and object of wealth was cattle, with figures ranging from 100 to 60,000 heads of cattle. Other items of gift included horses, chariots, wagons, slave-girls, garments and gold. The listing of wealth was evidently an indication of status. Those who gave large gifts such as Divodāsa, Pṛthuśravas or the Yādavas were acknowledged as being more powerful and wealthy than those who made lesser gifts such as Āsaṅga or Saṇḍa.[20] Making a gift, therefore, was a visible sign of prosperity. Anthropological studies show that the power of wealth and generosity are quite often synonymous, so that in a predominantly tribal context, *dāna* was made either for distributing tribal wealth or for gaining prestige and a dominant status amongst tribal chiefs. To some extent, it must have borne the aspect of a potlatch, a form of scoring over one's rivals and equals. This is especially evident from the *Mahābhārata*.

Once the tribal economy had been effectively replaced by a surplus economy with a strong urban base, *dāna* is known to be made more on life-crises situations, marked by the performance of *saṁskāras* or *rites de passage*. The important occasions in the life of a person when *dāna* was required to be made was at the time of birth, initiation,[21] marriage and death. *Dāna* was recommended also on the occasion of the *śrāddha* ceremony. Even though the detailed rituals to be observed on these occasions as prescribed in the Dharmaśāstras did not explicitly include *dāna*, feasting brāhmaṇas constituted an integral part of all *saṁskāra* ritualism.[22] Moreover, both Brāhmaṇical and Buddhist sources very definitely vouch for gift-making being widely practised on these occasions. We come across scores of references to large-scale gift distribution at the time of birth, marriage and death of a person. Gifts were also known to be made at the time of embarking on a new economic venture. The association of *dāna* with life-crises situations is significant and can be explained only if we assume that *dāna*, in some way, symbolized a change in status, be it ritual, social or even political. So if the *rite de passage* or *saṁskāra* rituals marked the transition from one stage of life to another, the act of *dāna* evidently put a stamp to such a change. The inference is clear: *dāna* symbolized change even if the change was related to personality development and status in life.

Significantly, another idea which came to be closely linked with *dāna* at this time was that of ritual purity. The expiatory efficacy of *dāna* ritualism was acknowledged and stressed in the Dharmaśāstras. It was considered an effective means of sin-expiation as well as for regaining ritual purity. The gravest of moral lapses could be atoned for through *dāna*. This clearly reveals a causal link between *dāna* and improvement of ritual status. This is especially evident in the case of the common practice of feeding brāhmaṇas as a part of ritual gift-making on the occasion of *saṁskāras*. Commensality in most cultural contexts is regarded as a very powerful symbol only amongst equals. Acceptance of food from a member of a non-kin group, especially from those belonging to a lower social strata, would, therefore, be generally construed as conferring upon the latter a better if not equal status. Restrictions on commensality have, thus, always been a very effective tool of maintaining and preserving social differentiation. Inversely, the rejection of food taboos would amount to recognition of social parity. Hence, *dāna* in general and the gift of food in particular made in favour of the brāhmaṇas was considered to represent a change in the status of a person.

In the feudal setting of the post-Gupta times, one of the important forms of *dāna* practised was land grants, though many other more innovative forms of gift-making such as *mahādānas* were also recommended in the Purāṇas and gaining considerable popularity.[23] As is now generally conceded on the basis of large epigraphic data, gifts of land were primarily aimed at securing a better footing in the traditional social order, and at gaining validation for not-so-well entrenched political power.[24] That the performance of *mahādānas* by ruling aspirants lacking illustrious dynastic backgrounds were meant to gain for them a political foothold is amply attested by our sources. Epigraphic evidence testifies that the scions, especially founders, of dynasties that had risen from relative obscurity to political eminence, such as the Viṣṇukuṇḍin, Kacchapaghāta, Rāṣṭrakūṭa, Sena, Kalacuri and Candella, have resorted to the performance of one or the other *mahādānas* such as the *tulāpuruṣa*, *hiraṇyagarbha*, or *brahmāṇḍa*, for staking claim as well as augmenting political power. If land grants and *mahādānas* were performed by donors possessing considerable economic means and political influence, other more modest forms of gift-making were made by members of ethnic groups who might have been swayed by an urge to enter the cultural mainstream. *Dāna*, and more especially land grants from the Gupta period onwards, was greatly instrumental in effecting both cultural expansion in peripheral areas and assimilation of new ethnic groups into the traditional caste order.[25] The inflated size of the śūdra substratum as attested by Alberuni was undoubtedly the result of this assimilation, largely made possible through *dāna* ritualism.

Thus, the idea of upgrading social status is clearly implied not only in the practice of land grants but by ritual gift-making in general and, hence, reinforces our contention that the efficacy of gift ritualism throughout the period under study lay in the belief that *dāna* was capable of conferring higher status. *Dāna* as a symbol of better social and ritual status must have been a major factor in effecting social mobility.

NOTES

1. Vijay Nath, 'Continuity and Change in the Institution of Dāna', *JASB* (Bombay), 1979-80, pp. 95-102.

2. R.S. Sharma, 'Conflict, Distribution and Differentiation in Ṛgvedic Society', *PIHC*, 1977.
3. Ibid.; Vijay Nath, *Dāna: Gift System in Ancient India*, Delhi, 1987, p. 170; S.A. Dange, *India from Primitive Communism to Slavery*, p. 93.
4. R.N. Nandi, 'Client, Ritual and Conflict in Early Brahmanical Order, *IHR*, vol. VI, nos. i & ii, p. 68.
5. Nath, op. cit., 1987, pp. 32-5.
6. R.S. Sharma, *Urban Decay in India*, Delhi, 1987.
7. R.S. Sharma, *Indian Feudalism*, Delhi, 1980.
8. D.N. Jha, ed., *Feudal-Social Formation in Ancient India*, Delhi, 1987.
9. A.R. Radcliff Brown, 'Religion and Society', *Journal of the Royal Anthropological Institute*, 1945.
10. V.W. Turner, 'Symbols in Ndembu Ritual', in Max Gluckman, ed., *Closed System and Open Minds*, 1964.
11. Winternitz, *History of Indian Literature*, vol. I.
12. A.B. Keith, *History of Sanskrit Literature*, p. 413.
13. *Nighaṇṭu.*
14. For our present discussion, we have adopted the literal meaning of these terms as given by Monier-Williams in the *Sanskrit-English Dictionary*. However, the need for a more detailed analysis of the actual meaning of these terms with reference to the precise textual context in which they occur cannot be over-emphasized.
15. A Chinook term defined in *Webster's Third International Dictionary* as an ostentatious distribution of gifts that entails elaborate reciprocation.
16. J. Gonda, 'Gifts and Giving', *Selected Studies*, vol. IV, pp. 122ff.
17. R. Thapar, 'Dāna and Dakṣiṇā as Forms of Exchange', *Ancient Indian Social History*, p. 108.
18. Ibid.
19. *Ṛgveda*, I.126; VI.47.
20. R. Thapar, '*Dāna* and *Dakṣiṇā* as Forms of Gift Exchange', p. 109.
21. J. Gonda, 'Dīkṣā', *Change and Continuity in Indian Religion*, New Delhi, 1985.
22. P.V. Kane, *History of Dharmaśāstra*, vol. II, pt. I, p. 192.
23. See Chapter on *Mahādāna.*
24. Vijay Nath, *Gift System in Ancient India*, p. 45; R.S. Sharma, *Indian Feudalism*, Delhi, 1980; D.N. Jha, ed., *Feudal-Social Fomation in Ancient India*, Delhi, 1987.
25. R. Thapar, 'Social Mobility in Ancient India', *Ancient Indian Social History*, 1978, p. 143; K.S. Mathur, ed., *Studies in Social Change*, Lucknow, 1973; Clifford Geertz, 'Ritual and Social Change' in Louis Schneider, ed., *Religion, Culture and Society*, 1964.

4

Women Donors in Ancient India

References to women donors are forthcoming as early as the Vedic period. The fifth book of the *Ṛgveda* alludes to 'bounteous ladies' but such adjectives have been used mostly to extol goddesses, whose munificence is eagerly sought. If, in one of the verses, Earth is described as a 'bounteous lady, liberal of her gifts',[1] another verse of the same book[2] contains an invocation to the goddess of the dawn, Uṣā, who is addressed as the 'gracious goddess, who gives good gifts' and who is implored to 'come speeding nigh to us for our well-being'. Considering that all myths not only reflect real life but are also directly drawn from it, the presence of some benevolent ladies in the Ṛgvedic society may, therefore, be safely presumed. But to become a donor a person needs to not only own property but also exercise complete proprietary right over it. The latter must effectively comprehend the right of alienating by way of gift, sale or mortgage of any item of that property. The socio-economic condition reflected by the *Ṛgveda*, however, would not have permitted much scope for women to have exercised such rights. The chief reason for this was the subsistence level of the Ṛgvedic economy and the predominantly patriarchal-cum-tribal character of its society. In such a social order, minimal quantum of privately owned possessions, mostly of a moveable kind, could possibly have existed, and even over these women *vis-à-vis* their menfolk could not have been expected to exercise any significant hold. Thus, despite women generally enjoying a fair amount of gender parity in the tribal order as existed during the Ṛgvedic period, the maximum that can be assumed about their position as donors is that, as mistress of their household, they might have exhibited some generosity by way of offering food and other sundry items to whoever entreated them.

Sources pertaining to the later Vedic period (*c*. 1000 BC-*c*. 700 BC) do not reveal any significant change in women's position as donors, though considerable changes in material culture are definitely attested. In fact, the beginnings of a surplus economy and a stratified social order if, on the one hand, slightly enlarged the purview of private property, also led to further entrenchment of the patriarchal system, a development which tended to restrict women completely from exercising any form of property right. Yet vestiges of tribal cultural mores which remained visible during this period might have allowed women to continue exercising the limited discretionary right of offering food, etc., to alms-seekers, especially wandering ascetics and renouncers.

It may be noted that during this period women had still not been excluded from participating in sacrificial performances. In fact, in some of the bigger sacrifices such as the *rājasūya* and *aśvamedha*, queens are known to have played an important role in performing various ceremonies.[3] Though no specific references are forthcoming to that effect, it seems very likely that after the performance of sacrificial rites, the king, while distributing gifts among priests and other brāhmaṇas, might have been actively assisted by his royal consorts, the four queens mentioned in the *Śatapatha Brāhmaṇa* (13.5.2.1), namely the *mahiṣī* (chief), *vavātā* (favourite), *parivṛktā* (discarded) and *palagalī* (inferior in social rank). Even in such hypothetical circumstances, women could not have figured as donors in the true sense for they certainly did not exercise any proprietary right over gifted items of wealth.

II

During the subsequent period of the Dharmasūtras (*c*. 600 BC-*c*. 300 BC), which was marked by significant developments in the sphere of surplus economy and entrenchment of the *varṇa*-based patriarchal system, there was a further withdrawal of women belonging to the upper stratum from active economic and social pursuits. They came to be excluded from receiving higher learning as well as from participating in sacrificial performances. The growing marginalization of women in society is reflected by the fact that their role became increasingly restricted to procreation or, at best, to household needs.[4] Consequently, even though there was remarkable growth in the institution of private property with land increasingly gaining in importance, women do not figure as a donor category in contemporary Brāhmaṇical literature. The complete absence of notice to women donors in the latter genre of literature acquires special significance in the light of two other important facts revealed by our sources. First, Brāhmaṇical theorists of this period while denying women's right to inherit their husband's or father's property[5] had, for the first time, conceded to them the right to own moveable property in the form of *strīdhana*. Thus, Baudhāyana (II.2.3.43), Āpastamba (II.6.14.9) and Vasiṣṭha (XVII.46) variously acknowledge the daughter's right to own her mother's ornaments, as well as the wealth given to her by her agnate relations. Second, in contemporary Buddhist literature we come across references to some munificent women donors. In the *Udāna*[6] *Suppavāsā*, the daughter of the Koliyan rājā is said to have 'invited the order of monks headed by the Buddha to seven days food'. The *Therigāthā* (XXXV, Selā) describes how Selā performed a grand feast of offering and worship to the Buddha. From the *Cullavagga* (VI.14.1), we learn that Viśākhā, the mother of Migara, was anxious to have a storeyed building (*prāsāda*) built for the use of the *saṁgha*. We also get references to courtesans such as Āmbapāli making rich benefactions in favour of the Buddhist *saṁgha*.[7]

Considering the fact that women had not only come to exercise some right over moveable items of wealth in the form of *strīdhana* but some amongst them had also begun indulging in munificent gift-making, the absence of references to women donors in Brāhmaṇical literature becomes inexplicable. The phenomenon, instead of appearing as an anomaly, perhaps goes to prove that the Dharmasūtra composers had already begun to draw a fine distinction between the right of absolute ownership and the right of custody and possession, the latter very definitely bound by the rule of non-alienation. Women's ownership over *strīdhana* seemingly meant only having the right of possession and not that of alienation or disposal over it. The distinction between the two levels of ownership is more explicitly expressed, albeit in the context of women inheriting property including land, by such Smṛti writers as Kātyāyana[8] and Nārada (I.28). That the rule of non-alienation applied even in the case of property which the wife had either earned through the pursuit of mechanical arts or obtained as a gift from her agnate and cognate relations is made amply clear by the following injunction of the *Manusmṛti* (VIII.416): 'Whatever is acquired by the wife belongs to the husband.' Even Kauṭilya[9] maintains that under certain circumstances the husband had the right to appropriate his wife's *strīdhana* without having to ever return it. Hence, in the case of both forms of property held by women, inherited as well as independently-owned *strīdhana*, they could exercise only limited ownership. The latter certainly did not include within its purview the right of arbitrary disposal. It is not surprising, therefore, that women, despite owning *strīdhana*, were not able to make gifts; or rather gifts that were big enough to deserve mention in contemporary literature.

As for references in contemporary Pāli texts to munificent benefactions made by women donors in favour of the Buddhist *saṁgha*, it would hardly be correct to assume that the cultural norms set by Brāhmaṇical lawgivers were completely disregarded by the Buddha's followers, their non-conformist attitude notwithstanding. In fact, women living within a common geographical horizon and sharing a common social ethos could hardly be expected to be governed by such widely disparate social norms, unless these formed part of some altogether different and firmly upheld religious code. But the Buddha, unlike his other contemporary, Mahāvīra, paid hardly any attention to formulating a distinct and comprehensive set of social norms and usages for his lay followers. That the latter continued to be governed by Brāhmaṇical customs and traditions is adequately borne out by Buddhist texts such as the *Jātakas*,[10] which very explicitly mention how a wife before giving alms needed to seek her husband's permission. The general dependence of women on their menfolk, especially in matters of gift-making, therefore, can hardly be doubted. Hence, in the light of available data, the only explanation that can be offered is that whereas some women such as Suppavāsā and Selā must have been able to offer food to the *bhikkus* with the due consent and approval of their respective male guardians, others such as Āmbapālī and Sāmā, who were not only engaged in independent callings like that of a courtesan but were also leading unconventional and unregulated family lives thoroughly disapproved of by Brāhmaṇical lawgivers, could not have cared much for the latter's dictates and, hence, were free to use their wealth in whichever way they liked. As Moti Chandra points out, 'It is significant that though the *gaṇikas* were not free persons legally, they had full authority over the assets which consisted of jewellery, income from salary and the gifts received from their lovers.'[11]

III

In the subsequent period of the Dharmaśāstras (*c.* 200 BC-*c.* AD 300), which generally corresponds to the post-Mauryan phase and was marked by remarkable developments in the field of intensive agriculture, trade and commerce, there is a sudden proliferation in the number of women donors. This is effectively attested by votive inscriptions found in large numbers at Mathura, and at other Buddhist and Jaina sites such as Sanchi, Nasik, Kanheri, etc., as well as by contemporary Buddhist texts. Women figure in Pāli literature both as giving daily alms of cooked food to *bhikkhus* as well as making rich donations of precious jewellery and other articles to the Buddhist *saṁgha*. Besides several notices of women offering gifts to *bhikkhus* that occur in the *Dhammapada* (Bk. 26; story 32; Bk. 5, story 15), (I.15) we learn from the *Milindapañho* how an important woman lay follower had supported the venerable Assagutta for thirty years. We even get references to women donors who are said to have built rest-houses for night-shelter.[12]

However, it is from contemporary votive records that we get more definite information about the emergence of women as a distinct donor category during this period. Out of the 133 post-Mauryan votive records found at Mathura and listed by H. Luders,[13] while some do not give information regarding the donor's identity, as many as forty-five votive donations are explicitly recorded in the name of women donors. If the statistical data furnished by them is of any help, then the fact that more than one-third of the donors at Mathura were ladies would positively establish their importance as a donor grouping. The development would appear to be very much in consonance with the continually expanding purview of *strīdhana* revealed by contemporary Smṛti texts. Thus, we find Yājñavalkya (II.143), Kātyāyana[14] and Viṣṇu (XVII.18) adding new categories of wealth over and above the six already listed by Manu (IX.194) that constituted *strīdhana* according to the new Dharmaśāstric ruling. Thus, if Manu (IX.194) recognized what was given before the nuptial fire (*adhyāgni*), what was given on the bridal procession (*adhyavahanika*), what was given in token of love and what was received from the brother, mother or father as the sixfold property of a woman (*strīdhana*), Yājñavalkya (II.143) widened its scope to include what was presented on her husband marrying another wife (*adhivedanika*), the bride's fee which is obtained as the price of household utensils, milch cattle, ornaments and slaves (*śulka*), as well as whatever was obtained after marriage from the family of her husband as also from her cognate relations (*anvadheya*). To this list, Viṣṇu (XVII.18) adds one more, namely those obtained from sons.

Then it is equally significant to note that despite such concessions being made in favour of women, not only had the patrilineal character of society come into sharper focus during this period but there is also a steady decline evident in the general condition and ritual status of women in society.[15] The composers of the Dharmaśāstras, going a step farther than their Dharmasūtra counterparts while allowing women to inherit and own more varied forms of moveable and immoveable property, imposed a serious restriction upon such ownership by withdrawing from them the right of alienation. In this regard, Manu (IX.199) very categorically ordains that a wife ought not to spend anything even from her *strīdhana* property without her husband's sanction. According to Kātyāyana, 'whatever wealth she may gain by arts, as by painting or spinning, or may receive on account of her friendship from any but her kindred, her lord (husband) has dominion over it'. Thus, women, according to a strongly enforced Brāhmaṇical ruling, were not free to dispose of through gift or sale any property they owned without seeking prior approval and sanction from their male guardians, especially their husbands in case they were married.

We are, therefore, confronted with a phenomenon that appears almost dichotomous. Our sources reveal that, on the one hand, women were not only allowed by Brāhmaṇical lawgivers to inherit and own some limited forms of property but they also emerged as an important category of donors. On the other hand, they were becoming completely marginalized and subservient to their menfolk, with their social and economic freedom getting increasingly curtailed. To resolve the apparent dichotomy between women's emergence as an important category of donors and the continual impairment of their position in society, we need to scrutinize the data furnished by both Buddhist literature and votive inscriptions.

A significant finding that emerges from one such analysis is that except courtesans,[16] nuns[17] and two other women donors whose names alone occur,[18] the rest of the women donors are described in the Mathura Jaina votive records as wife, mother, daughter-in-law, daughter and more rarely as sisters. Even in Buddhist texts such as the *Cullavagga* (VI.14.1), a woman donor named Viśākhā is described as the mother of Migara. Thus, a woman's social identity would seem to have been determined chiefly by the nature of the relationship in which she stood to her male guardian on whom she was immediately dependent; he could be husband, father, brother, father-in-law or son. An apparent conclusion that can be drawn from this is that the position of the majority of women as donors was largely due to the consent and active support extended by their respective male relations. This would certainly hold true of women from a more affluent background, such as those belonging to royal families or to flourishing mercantile communities, for their male members are definitely known to have undertaken religious and charitable benefactions on a liberal scale. Incidentally, quite a few women donors of Mathura[19] are stated to have been first wives of their husbands. In a polygamous society, a woman's position as first wife might have considerably enhanced her economic competence and status within the family to enable her to make gifts. In sharp contrast to other women, the position of courtesans as donors is found to be vastly different. The Nādā courtesan, Vasū, for instance, is described merely as the daughter of the Ādā courtesan, Lon Śobhikā.[20] The names of her father or brother are not given. The omission of names of the male members of the family suggests the economic independence of this category of women donors.

Another fact that emerges from a close scrutiny of our data is that the majority of women donors were drawn from an urban background. Our analysis of inscriptional evidence shows that out of the women donors whose names occur in the Sanchi Buddhist Stūpa I inscriptions, twenty-four are from Ujjain, eleven from Nandinagar, five from Kurāragṛha, four each from Puṣkara and Kurār, two from Mahiṣmatī, and one each from Puṇyavardhana and Pemata.[21]

In fact, even the social groupings from which women donors are known to be drawn were generally urban-based. For example, ladies belonging to royal families, which expectedly were stationed mostly in capital cities and towns, figure as donors in early Pāli texts. In the Udāna[22] Suppavāsā, the daughter of the Koliyan rājā is said to have 'invited the order of monks headed by the Buddha to seven days food'. From the Mauryan period, instances of gift-making by queens are recorded in inscriptions too. Thus, in one of his edicts, Aśoka especially wants the donation to be recorded in the name of his second queen.[23] Similarly, which the Mañcapurī cave inscription[24] records the construction of a temple of the *arhats* and a cave for the *śramaṇas* by the chief queen of Khāravela, the Nānāghāṭ cave inscription[25] describes the munificent gifts made by the Sātavāhana queen, Naganikā. Several Buddhist *stūpa* and cave inscriptions at Sanchi, Nasik and Kanheri record gifts made by royal princesses.[26] One of the Nasik cave inscriptions[27] of the time of Nahapāṇa records the gift of a cave by Dakṣamitrā, the wife of Uṣāvadāta, for religious progress.

Another category of urban-based women donors which won considerable recognition from society by its numerous religious benefactions was that of the courtesans (*gaṇikā*). An inscription listed by Luders (no. 102) refers to the setting up of a shrine by the Nādā courtesan, Vasū. In fact, right from the time of the Buddha, courtesans had emerged as an extremely affluent professional grouping. As we learn from the *Kanvera Jātaka* (III, no. 318) the courtesan, Sāmā, undertook the construction of *vihāras* for the *saṁgha*. Similarly, Āmbapāli, the famous courtesan of Vaiśālī, is placed in the same category of Buddha patrons as King Bimbisāra, the royal physician, Jīvaka, and the rich *seṭṭhī*, Anāthapiṇḍika.[28] Nuns belonging to heterodox orders constituted yet another category of women donors with a close urban association, though the exact source of their gift-making cannot be ascertained.[29]

The economic group from which women donors are known to be extensively drawn were the mercantile and artisanal sections of society. In fact, among the women donor category, *sārthavāhinīs* and other female relatives of *seṭṭhīs* and rich merchants are recorded as having made the maximum number of religious donations during the closing and opening centuries of the Christian era.

The fact that the majority of women donors were urban-based acquires special significance when considered in the light of the partisan attitude displayed by Brāhmaṇical theorists towards the fast-disappearing pastoral ethos that had characterized the Vedic period as opposed to the urban ethos and commercial spirit that was gaining ascendance during this period, for which they felt complete disdain and disapproval. This might suggest that the Brāhmaṇical legal strictures were suited more to a rural cultural tradition than the urban. This could also explain why a relatively less stringent social code might have been applicable in societies that were urban-based, as compared to their rural counterparts.

Moreover, the fact that ladies belonging to artisanal and mercantile classes figured more prominently as donors would clearly indicate that they must have enjoyed better economic competence and were, therefore, in a better position to make gifts in favour of religious beneficiaries. It would not be far from the truth to assume that it was the emergent commercial spirit of the age which was, to an extent, responsible for transforming a section of women into an important category of donors; their religious fervour and munificent spirit almost matching that of their male relations.

That *dāna* by women was made mostly out of their personal belongings would seem a safe inference based upon an analysis of the gift-items generally bestowed by them. Our sources reveal that besides giving alms of cooked food to beggars and religious mendicants, women donors also gifted their ornaments. Sumāna is known to have gifted her girdle[30] and Viśākhā is said to have donated her ornaments worth 19,000 crore in order to build a monastery.[31] Women are occasionally known to have even weaved cloth, for the purpose of making gift. Thus, the *Vimānavatthu* (Elephant Mansion, IV.3.41) refers to a 'lay devotee, a woman who lived in Banaras, had a pair of robes woven for the Blessed One'. However, a fairly large number of women donors find mention in the Buddhist and Jaina votive inscriptions recording the installation of images, pillars, gateways, etc. Since young girls are also known to have made gifts, as is very clearly attested by *Itivutthaka* (Splendid Mansion, III.1.79) that contains reference to a 'young girl who was intent on giving alms'), the possibility cannot be ruled out that at least some gift-making by women might have been undertaken out of common family earnings.

Although no positive reference to the gift of land by women occurs in Brāhmaṇical texts, notices of ladies undertaking the construction of monasteries and rest-houses are quite common in the post-Mauryan Buddhist sources.[32] Significantly, the Kuda Buddhist cave inscription records the gift of a *caitya-ghara* by a brāhmaṇa woman.[33] The evi-dence is interesting. Far from underlining any sharp distinctions between the Brāhmaṇical and Buddhist social orders, it seems to accentuate the regional variations in local customs; for instance, notices of the gift of *caitya*-halls are forthcoming mostly from the Maharashtra region. The evidence also affirms the growing import-ance of landed property during the centuries immediately preceding and following the Christian era.

In fact, the rise in the number of gifts made by women during the post-Mauryan period does not necessarily reflect any slackening of male authority in the family. On the contrary, it proves that with the extension of both moveable and immoveable forms of private property, the economic competence of women belonging to a certain social strata had grown considerably by the opening centuries of the Christian era.

IV

The subsequent period, beginning with the rule of the imperial Guptas to almost the end of the first millennium AD, is marked by salient developments in landed economy and feudal formations. Developments related to the fragmentation of power, with ruling dynasties of foreign or indigenous tribal origins making their presence felt in the political arena, combined with the spread of civilizational influences in peripheral zones, impacted contemporary society in a significant manner. The most important outcome as far as Brāhmaṇism was concerned was its complete transformation into a system that comprehended almost all possible existent religious streams, barring only a few that sported a more agnostic aspect such as Jainism and Buddhism. Hinduism, as it has come to be called in recent times, began to exhibit a more popular base and a pan-Indian character. This is especially evident in the case of such religious practices as building temples and monasteries, visiting *tīrthas*, offering ritual *dāna* and observing *vratas*.

A significant outcome of these developments was the growing participation of women in Brāhmaṇical rituals, especially those related to *tīrthas* and *vratas*. Both the practices entailed offering gifts to brāhmaṇas, though the quantum and nature of gift-items offered on such occasions varied drastically from one end of the pole to another; for if, on the one hand, we get notices of royal consorts and princesses building temples, donating land and gifting utensils and other articles of gold and silver, on the other, we hear of tribal belles and ordinary housewives offering earthen jars, bells, lamps, wild fruit, and cooked and uncooked items of food to brāhmaṇas and other religious supplicants. The exceptionally broad social spectrum of women donors and the equally disparate nature and range of their gift-items are two important developments that mark gift-making by women in the early medieval period.

A fact that stands out is that if during the preceding Kuṣāna-Sātavāhana phase it was mostly women belonging to the royal family or drawn from an affluent urban/mercantile background who figured as donors, in the Gupta and post-Gupta phase, though the importance of royal women as donors remained unchanged, those belonging to the mercantile community are rarely heard of. Their place is taken up by a vast conglomerate of housewives drawn from all high and low strata and segments of society. Another significant difference is with regard to notices of women donors that occur in Brāhmaṇical texts belonging to the two consecutive cultural phases. There is no mention in the Dharmasūtra and Smṛti texts, even by way of recommendation, of women undertaking gifts, religious or otherwise (references only pertain to heterodox literature and votive inscriptions). The Purāṇas, however, are full of references to different forms of vows (*vrata*) meant exclusively for women and which had to be necessarily accompanied by gifts made to brāhmaṇas for their fruition.[34] That these were not just theoretical injunctions but were actually practised is attested by both contemporary literature and inscriptions.

An important factor that contributed to the transformation of a vast segment of women from a position of non-donors to that of donors was not so much related to their expanding right to inherit and own property (a development more notional than real but attested by contemporary Brāhmaṇical texts) and their enhanced economic competence, as to their growing right of participation in rituals, especially *vratas* and *tīrthas*, combined with the extremely modest nature of gift-items recommended in the Purāṇas. It was the latter development that enabled even very poor women with meagre or no resources to turn donors by observing vows that simply required some wild fruit like berries or an earthen pot filled with water to be offered to a brāhmaṇa. The flexibility displayed by the authors of the Purāṇas in this regard is quite remarkable and was chiefly responsible for augmenting the popular base and widening the purview of gift-making, especially in the case of women.

While the wealthier category of women donors during the early medieval period was drawn from the royal and feudal backgrounds, as amply attested by inscriptional data, the more common category represented a wider cross-section of society. It comprised women belonging to families ranging from those that were extremely well-off to others less affluent or even downright poor. Besides the lack of a conspicuous rich/poor divide, there was also a complete absence of an urban/rural divide, a feature that had characterized women donors in the preceding cultural phase. The absence of the latter divide could have been, due to some extent, to the onset of forces of de-urbanization during the post-Gupta centuries. In fact, as reflected by our sources, the urban base of women donors during this period is negligible.

One of the factors that could have acted as a leveller was the pan-Indian popularity gained by many regional and tribal *tīrthas*, which had strong local traditions especially as far as the nature of gift-items associated with them was concerned. Consequently, at a *tīrtha* site, the economic background of the donor became less important compared to the ritual efficacy that a traditionally recognized gift-item was supposed to wield, be it an ordinary mask, a water-jar, a piece of cloth or even just a handful of jaggery.

The same holds true of *vrata*-related gifts made by women, though to a more restricted degree. The Purāṇas carry specific injunctions about the kind of gifts to be offered to brāhmaṇas at the successful conclusion of a *vrata*, allowing variations only with regard to their quality and quantum. For instance, a donor with sufficient means could give away a jar made of some metal, even of gold and silver, in place of a plain earthen pitcher originally recommended, though both were supposed to fetch and equal amount of spiritual merit if given with faith (*śraddhā*). Moreover, the compulsions of offering only locally available and traditionally favoured gift articles could not have been as strong or pressing in the case of gifts made at one's residence after the conclusion of a *vrata* as it must have been in the case of regionally located *tīrtha* sites. Nevertheless, the generally modest nature of gift items recommended by the Purāṇa authors and the kind of return expected through them must have contributed greatly towards the numerical growth and expansion of the women donor category.

This is especially true of *vrata*-related gifts that were given for the husband's or son's longevity or for the sake of family prosperity. The predominant patriarchal ethos and feudal values such as obedience, faith and loyalty that were sought to be promoted by contemporary society must have been greatly responsible for encouraging women to observe such fasts in full ritual details, including offering gifts to brāhmaṇas. Consequently, the issues of women's right to property and economic competence could not have come in the way of gift-making. In fact, a husband would have been more than willing to let his wife give gifts to brāhmaṇas out of family earnings, which were meant to ensure his and the family's well-being. The majority of *vratas* recommended for women in the Purāṇas fall into this category. Besides being observed for the husband's long life, there were others meant to beget a male child or to avert some ailment or calamity that assailed the family. The gifts made on such occasions were no longer the concern of just one individual, i.e. the housewife, but of the entire family. A vast majority of women turning donors during this period was, therefore, not an inexplicable phenomenon.

What distinguished women donors of the Gupta/post-Gupta times from their counterparts of the preceding period, however, was the non-arbitrary nature of their gift items. Whereas the former generally conformed to didactic norms laid down in the Śāstras, gifts made by women in the Kuṣāṇa/Sātavāhana period were less tradition-bound and more individualistic, somewhat at par with those of their menfolk. Pāli texts indicate that it was generally the woman who decided when and what gift she wished to give, whether it was an image she wanted installed at a particular religious site or an alms-hall or night-shelter constructed or regular meals organized for monks; though, in most cases, informal consent of the male guardian was invariably sought, especially to determine the logistics of the gift undertaken. It explains the wide range of gift items donated by women during that period, as also the lack of it during the subsequent period. The limited range of gift items is more than evident from the story of Lalitā, the daughter of the Vidarbha king, that occurs in the *Agni Purāṇa* (200.6-18). The princess is said to have given not land or any other opulent variety of gift item made of gold and silver but only a lamp by way of offering.

Some difference in the range and variety of gift items could have been due to the possible scope for women to make gifts in the two cultural phases. While in the earlier phase the desire to make the gift was the only excuse needed for bestowing alms as well as gifts to religious supplicants, in the early medieval period, the occasion for making a gift to the brāhmaṇas was restricted mainly to *tīrthas* and *vratas.* We do not hear of women undertaking *dāna* in a more arbitrary manner, with the possible exception of those drawn from royal families.

The categories of women donors to whom specific references are totally lacking in early medieval literature were courtesans and nuns, as well as those belonging to mercantile and artisanal families or pursuing some independent calling. That at least some of these women categories might have continued making gifts can be assumed in the absence of any direct evidence, especially from the Brāhmaṇical texts which are completely reticent in this regard. However, considering that the Purāṇas prescribe specific *vratas* to be exclusively observed by prostitutes, it may well indicate that the latter were expected to offer gifts to brāhmaṇas, since no fast could be fruitful without it. Moreover, evidence from contemporary works such as the *Kāmasūtra* by Vātsyāyana and the *Mṛcchakaṭikam* by Śūdraka would suggest that some prostitutes led an opulent lifestyle and might have continued to figure amongst donor categories. It is difficult to make a similar assumption in the case of other categories of women, especially those having an independent means of livelihood. In fact, in their case, the information forthcoming from contemporary sources, unlike those of the preceding phase, is minimal.

If the size of women donors expanded unduly during the early medieval phase, there is also evident a dichotomous development. Women began to be increasingly clubbed with property[35] and even relegated to the position of a gift item. This is especially evident from the evidence furnished by the Purāṇas.[36] Thus, according to the *Skanda Purāṇa* (VII.1.28.108), women should be given in the course of a *vrata* observed on the thirteenth day of the fortnight (*striyo deyas trayodaśyām*). The *Brahmavaivartta Purāṇa* (Śrīkṛṣṇakhaṇḍa, 76.54) similarly recommends the gifting of an eight-year old maiden (*kumārim aṣṭavarṣīyam su-viprāya dadāti yāḥ*). The same Purāṇa[37] also mentions how Drumila after begetting a son gave female attendants in gift. Even the gift of prostitutes is recommended in the *Bhaviṣya Purāṇa*[38] (*veśyā-kadambam tu yastu dedyāt suryāya bhaktitaḥ*).

However, our analysis of the Purāṇic references to the clubbing of women with property shows, as we have pointed out elsewhere,[39] that it was chiefly in their role as wives that they were thus equated. Moreover, a scrutiny of the contexts in which these joint references occur makes it amply clear that this was done mainly to emphasize the importance of both (wife and property) as the chief sources of family prestige and, hence, the need to protect and guard them with extra care. Women actually being treated as chattel or alienable items of property or figuring as gift-items as per Purāṇic injunctions are not fully backed by any real evidence. The dichotomy evident in the Purāṇic depiction of women both as donors as well as gift items (*deya*) is, therefore, more fallacious than real.

Our study, thus, reveals that women, in varying degrees, continued to figure as donors throughout the ancient period. This was regardless of their actual economic competence, for gifts undertaken by women were mostly out of common family earnings. Nevertheless, owning some form of property or *strīdhana* (chiefly comprising moveable items), especially in a dominantly commercial/urban material context as during the post-Mauryan phase, considerably augmented their position as donors, bringing it almost at par with that of their male counterparts. However, in keeping with the demands of a predominantly patriarchal society, women's right to make gifts, even to religious supplicants, remained subject to the formal approval and sanction of their male guardians, be it their father, husband, brother or son. Perhaps the only exceptions to this rule were courtesans and prostitutes who stood out not so much for their economic independence but due to leading a totally non-conventional lifestyle and being completely unfettered by any familial constraints.

NOTES

1. *Ṛgveda*, V.56.3.
2. Ibid., V.41.18.
3. Jogiraja Basu, *India of the Age of the Brahmanas*, Calcutta, 1969, p. 97.
4. *Manusmṛti*, II.67; IX.11; Vijay Nath, 'Women as Property and Their Right to Inherit Property up to Gupta Period', *The Indian Historical Review*, vol. XX, nos. i-ii, 1993-4, p. 4.
5. *Baudhāyana Dharmasūtra*, II.2.3.46; Yāska, *Nirukta*, 53: 'Some hold that Daughters do not Inherit.' Nath, op. cit., p. 9.
6. *Udāna*, Mucalinda, II, VIII.17.
7. *Mahā-Ummagga Jātaka*, vol. VI, no. 546; I.B. Horner, *Women Under Primitive Buddhism*, London, 1930, p. 83; D.K. Barua, 'Folk Life of Women as Revealed in the Early Buddhist Texts', *Folklore*, vol. IX, 1986, p. 163.
8. D.N. Mitter, *Position of Women in Hindu Law*, Calcutta, 1913, p. 526.
9. *Arthaśāstra*, III.2.152.
10. *Suvannamiga Jataka*, vol. III, no. 359, 'I wish my lord to give alms to our family priests.'
11. Motichandra, *The World of Courtesan*, Delhi, 1973, p. 48.
12. *Vinaya*, Suttavibhanga (Pacittiya), VI.1.
13. *A List of Brāhmī Inscriptions from the Earliest Times to about AD 400 with the Exception of those of Aśoka*, Appendix to *Epigraphia Indica* and Record of the Archaeological Survey of India, vol. I, X, 1909-19.
14. P.V. Kane, *History of Dharmaśāstras*, vol. III, p. 775.
15. Nath, 'Women as Property and Their Right to Inherit Property', op. cit., pp. 1-15.
16. *Vimānavatthu*, Sirima's Mansion, I.16.
17. *Luder's List*, nos. 327-8, 369, 402, 512.
18. Ibid., nos. 92, 144.
19. Ibid., nos. 27, 48, 50, 122.
20. Ibid., no. 102.
21. Vijay Nath, *Dāna: Gift System in Ancient India*, Delhi, 1987, p. 7.
22. *Udāna*, Mucalinda, II, VIII.17.
23. Allahabad Kosam Queen's Pillar Edict, *Corpus Inscriptionum Indicarum*, I, p. 159.
24. *Epigraphia Indica*, XIII, p. 159.
25. D.C. Sircar, *Select Inscriptions*, book II, no. 60.
26. *Luder's List*, nos. 1186, 1123, 1021, 1132, 1134.
27. *Select Inscriptions*, book II, no. 60.
28. *Mahavagga*, VI.30.5.
29. Nath, *Dāna: Gift System in Ancient India*, op. cit., p. 79.
30. *Therigāthā*, XVI, *Sumanā*; XXIV, Mettika.
31. *Vimānavatthu*, Monastery Mansion, IV.6.44.

32. *Luder's List*, nos. 993, 1965, 1073, 1076, 1127, 1141.
33. Ibid., no. 1050.
34. S.A. Dange, *Encyclopaedia of Purāṇic Beliefs and Practices.*
35. *Garuḍa Purāṇa*, 108.13; 109.48; 114.60; *Harivaṁśa Purāṇa*, II.86.56; III.80.79.
36. *Liṅga Purāṇa*, II.34.4.
37. *Brahmavaivartta Purāṇa*, I.20.51.
38. *Bhaviṣya Purāṇa*, Brahma Khaṇḍa, 93.67.
39. Nath, 'Women as Property and Their Right to Inherit Property', *IHR*, XX, nos. i-ii, p. 8.

5

Brāhmaṇa Recipients of *Dāna*: Changing Parameters

Dāna and brāhmaṇas are synchronous and in a strictly Brāhmaṇical context one without the other is inconceivable. The latter's hegemonic hold on society was both the cause and effect of the continued viability and popularity enjoyed by the institution of *dāna*, though both are known to have undergone variations at different points of history. Brāhmaṇas initially represented a small *varṇa* segment comprising spiritually inclined, learned and morally upright persons, leading an austere life and committed to imparting education and performing priestly duties. *Dāna* and *dakṣiṇā* were the society's mode of showing apreciation and deference for the services thus rendered. Though there has been a lack of consensus amongst scholars about *dakṣiṇā* merely being the fee or remuneration for priestly services, there has been no such misgiving with regard to *dāna*. In fact, the recipients of *dāna*, especially during the later period, were not always engaged in sacerdotal pursuits. Nevertheless, the two (brāhmaṇas as a social category and the institution of *dāna*) not only helped to sustain and augment each other's position but were also instrumental in making it possible for the other to encounter social and economic challenges thrown by commercial enterprise and urbanization.

What accounts for the dialectics of such a brāhmaṇa/*dāna* symbiosis? Why did brāhmaṇas alone emerge as the chief recipients of *dāna*? Since both *dāna* and *dakṣiṇā* came to constitute lucrative sources of income for the brāhmaṇas, we also need to know how far one was distinct from the other? Answers to some of these questions may be sought in the dynamics of the origins and development of *dāna* as a ritual construct and of brāhmaṇa as a *varṇa* stratum, for both show sharp changes throughout the period of their evolution and growth.

I

HOW FAR WAS *DĀNA* DISTINCT FROM *DAKṢIṆĀ*

During the early Vedic period, brāhmaṇas represented just one amongst several categories of ritual specialists involved in the performance of sacrifices (*yajñas*). The two terms *dāna* and *dakṣiṇā* occur commonly in the *Ṛgveda*, though the exact connotation of *dakṣiṇā* remains ambiguous and illusive. The term is found to be so closely akin to *dāna* as to make it difficult to draw a clear-cut line of distinction between the two. The use of the two terms by the composers of the Ṛgvedic hymns would appear to be rather arbitrary. Etymologically, the term *dakṣiṇā* is derived from the etymon *dakṣaya*, which means to impart power or strength. Hence, whatever gifts are made to invigorate and strengthen both the religious rites as well as the sacrificer is called *dakṣiṇā* (*dakṣa kāriṇī hi dakṣiṇā; dakṣaśca balam*).[1] By extension, it came to mean either a gift or a donation made to a priest or the sacrificial fee. The meaning of sacrificial fee may be attributed to *dakṣiṇā* because of a shade of its meaning, namely, 'prolific', a word which aptly describes the cow. K.V.R. Aiyangar[2] and Louis Renou[3] have both accepted the interpretation of *dakṣiṇā* based on this meaning. According to Macdonell and Keith, the authors of the *Vedic Index*, *dakṣiṇā* is the 'gift presented to priests at the sacrifice, apparently because a cow, a prolific one (*dakṣiṇā*) was the usual fee on such an occasion'. The use of the name *dakṣiṇā* for the daughter of Prajāpati and the wife of sacrifice personified would further associate the term with sacrificial rite. Since the term also carries the meaning of completion of any rite, *dakṣiṇā* would appear to be the gift (mostly in the form of a cow) made on the completion of a sacrificial rite to the officiating priest in order to strengthen the sacrifice.

According to Heesterman,[4] *dakṣiṇā* as reflected in the Vedic texts was never a salary or a sacrificial fee, but has to be seen as part of the economic system of Vedic times, that of gift exchange. His chief contention is that *dakṣiṇā* was given to both the *ṛtvij* (officiating priest) and to other brāhmaṇas of the *prasarpaka* category whose role was essentially that of observers. Max Weber[5] also holds that 'the brāhmaṇas accepted only gifts (*dakṣiṇā*) not pay. The giving of gifts for the use of their services was of course a ritualistic duty. Sacrifice without gift brought evil enchantment.' The view that *dakṣiṇā* was not an exclusive payment for priestly service may find support from the fact that it later began to be given along with *dāna*. Thus, in the Purāṇas, it was made mandatory for the donors, while offering *dāna* to brāhmaṇas on occasions ranging from *vratas* and *saṁskāras* to the *śrāddha* rite, to bolster it with *dakṣiṇā*, although the size of the latter could be very small and meant more as a token. In fact, the ritualistic significance of *dakṣiṇā* which bordered almost on the magical, is too far emphasized in literature to be easily overlooked. According to Jaimini's *Mimāṁsā Sūtram*[6] a gift to a *ṛtvik* (priest) is with a view to religious fruit.[7] As J. Gonda[8] points out, *dakṣiṇā* was not given solely in order to pay for services but also to maintain a profitable alliance and to establish a bond between the giver and receiver.

Despite strong objections being raised against regarding *dakṣiṇā* purely as a sacrificial or priestly fee, it needs to be treated at least partly as this. Not only was it paid after the religious ceremony was over but its payment was obligatory, the *yajamāna* having no power to withhold it. The amount to be paid was also largely predetermined if not through actual bargaining (which was discouraged and, hence, may be assumed to be in vogue)[9] then by convention in the form of past precedents. This is apparent from the following verse of the *Āśvalāyana Gṛhyasūtra* (I.23.21) 'He (who is chosen as a *ṛtvij*) should ask: What sacrifice is it? Who are the officiating priests? What is the fee for the sacrifice?' Thus, even though the aspect of *dakṣiṇā* as a religious gift is too marked and cannot be overlooked, view of the available evidence it would be difficult to fully agree with Heesterman's contention that it was never a salary or a sacrificial fee.

In fact, during the post-Vedic times, the distinction drawn between the *iṣṭa* and *pūrtta* forms of ritual gift-making (the former representing offerings made within the sacrificial altar and meant essentially for the gods and the latter denoting other forms of gifts made outside the altar)[10] could not have lessened the ambiguity surrounding *dakṣiṇā* altogether. Yet it helped to somewhat underscore the dividing line between *dāna* and *dakṣiṇā*, for *pūrtta* very definitely fell within the purview of *dāna*. The distinct connotative inflexion of *dakṣiṇā* becomes even more accentuated in the early medieval period when both *dāna* and *dakṣiṇā*, besides being non-interchangeable, had to be offered together to the brāhmaṇa invitees at a religious ceremony. How far *dakṣiṇā* paid along with *dāna* was not wholly meant as remuneration for priests who might have assisted in the performance of the elaborate ritual involved in gift-making is debatable. Nevertheless, by the post-Vedic period, *dakṣiṇā* as a ritual construct had come to be completely distinguished from *dāna*, with both turning into lucrative sources of income for brāhmaṇa recipients.

II

FACTORS CONTRIBUTING TO BRĀHMAṆAS' DOMINANCE AS RECIPIENTS OF *DĀNA*

The appellation brāhmaṇa in the predominantly tribal milieu of the early Vedic period signified essentially just one small and less dominant category of ritual specialists, even though its origins as a priestly class are very definitely affirmed.[11] By the later Vedic times, agricultural expansion eastwards and the growing cultural interaction with the native population led to an exceptional overgrowth in sacrificial ritualism, thereby stepping up the demand for priestly services and inflating the size of the group engaged in the priestly craft. The term brāhmaṇa now came to loosely designate not only the entire sacerdotal class but also teachers, sages and other engaged in activities of a religio-intellectual nature. Although the criterion of birth was becoming increasingly important,[12] it had still not become the sole determinant of brāhmaṇa status. It became possible, therefore, for persons lacking brāhmaṇa parentage but proficient in Vedic learning and engaged wholly in intellectual and ascetic pursuits, as well as exuding an aura of spirituality and moral integrity, to be conferred brāhmaṇahood.[13] It proved to be an important factor in emphasizing and ensuring the innate worthiness of those belonging to the brāhmaṇa stratum.

The brāhmaṇas, moreover, by this time had succeeded in exercising a monopolistic hold over sacrificial ritualism. It is categorically stated in the *Kātyāyana Śrautasūtra* (1.2.8) that only brāhmaṇas are eligible to officiate and eat at sacrifices. Since sacrifices had acquired a more elaborate and complex format, and were believed to be imbued with magical potency, a lot of importance came to be attached to their correct performance. An inadvertent error could adversely affect the outcome of the sacrifice, thus causing much superstitious fear and anxiety in the minds of the performers. The brāhmaṇas officiating at the sacrifices, therefore, had to be extra proficient and dexterous in their task to be able to successfully perform them. The fact that sacrificial ritualism still constituted the chief basis of Brāhmaṇical religiosity must have, therefore, further augmented their dominance in society.

Consequently, their blessings as well as their services in matters both temporal and spiritual came to be much sought after both by kings and members of the other *varṇas*. Gifts to brāhmaṇas began to be recommended and lauded in highly exaggerated terms in Brāhmaṇical texts. According to the *Aitareya Brāhmaṇa* (39.6), the king when anointed should make gifts of gold, fields and cattle. Gifts intended for the brāhmaṇas were declared to be imbued with magical potency. According to one of the *Brāhmaṇa* texts,[14] he who after promising to gift all, does not give all, is reduced to falling into a deep pit or is killed. The *Aitareya Brāhmaṇa* (30.9) enjoins that one should not accept a gift rejected by the priests and, if one accepts it, it should be given over to one's enemy. With *dāna* proving to be the chief source of income for the sacerdotal class, the lawgivers began to device new rituals that could create occasions for making *dāna* to brāhmaṇas. Such gift-making was declared to be absolutely mandatory if the efficacy of a particular ritual was to be maintained.

Another factor that boosted the dominance of the brāhmaṇas was the rise of small kingdoms (*janapadas*) that gradually replaced the tribal chieftaincies of the earlier period. The aspirant ruling chiefs, continually engaged in an ongoing power struggle, were keen to consolidate their nascent power with the help of whatever little surplus they could extract from producers in the form of taxes, for which securing religious validation was an absolute desideratum. To achieve this end, the performance of ostentatious *yajñas* proved to be an important means and their priestly exponents, the brāhmaṇas, became willing collaborators. *Dāna* turned out to be the chief instrument of cementing such a nexus. Vedic sacrifices during this early phase served the politico-religious needs of just two categories of people, the princely sacrificers and their brāhmaṇa officiating priests. Both stood to gain from it, the former by acquiring legal mandate for their kingly power and the latter in the form of munificent gifts liberally bestowed by their patrons. According to a statement contained in the *Mahābhārata* (Sabhā Parva, 12.11), 'One already in possession of a kingdom desireth all the attributes of an emperor by means of that sacrifice which aideth a king in acquiring the attributes of Varuṇa'. In the early Pāli texts, we come across frequent allusions to great sacrifices (*mahāyajñas*), such as the *aśvamedha*, *puruṣamedha* and *vājapeya*, being performed by kings.[15] Even if the latter instances lack adequate historicity, there is definite evidence available to show that even as late as the post-Mauryan period, some of the Śuṅga and Sātavāhana kings performed these great sacrifices to consolidate their political power and to bolster their imperial image, which showed signs of sagging in the face of foreign threats.[16]

Some brāhmaṇas in their position as royal priests succeeded in wielding excessive influence at the court in matters both religious and temporal, a development which must have further added to the power and dominance enjoyed by the brāhmaṇas in general.[17] In the *Baudhāyana Gṛhyasūtra* (1.10.18.7-8), the king is exhorted to appoint a domestic priest who shall be foremost in all transactions. Similarly, according to the *Vasiṣtha Gṛhyasūtra* (XI.313-22), a realm where a brāhmaṇa is appointed as the domestic priest attains prosperity. The influence of the royal priests was as much due to their close personal association with the king as their alleged knowledge of occult sciences and the growing hereditary character of their post. This is borne out by a reference to *purohita-kula* contained in the *Bandhanamokkha Jātaka* (vol. 1, no. 120, p. 264). The fact that the royal priests had also served as the preceptors (*gurus*) of the king must have made the latter all the more dependent on their advice. The king's dependence on the *purohita's* counsel both in matters concerning his own spiritual well-being as well as in state affairs was primarily due to the changed political situation, marked by erosion of the tribal order and the growing need to secure sacerdotal backing, so essential for the consolidation of imperial pretensions. The inordinate influence wielded by the priest is evident from Kauṭilya's[18] enjoinder to the king to follow his *purohita* as a pupil does his teacher, a son his father, or a servant his master. That it was no mere theoretical injunction but was actually being practised by some of the rulers becomes evident from the *Dīgha Nikāya* (XIX, Mahāgovinda Suttanta, II.243) in which King Reṇu addresses his *purohita* Govinda as his father.

Perhaps the chief source of the growing dominance of the brāhmaṇas was the control they were able to establish on the art of writing. By the end of the later Vedic period, works such as the *Nighaṇṭu*, *Niruktam* and *Aṣṭādhyāyī* that dealt with its different aspects, had begun to be composed mostly by brāhmaṇa authors. Consequently, the brāhmaṇas were not only able to completely monopolize the field of education that served as an important means of ideological dissemination but also appropriated the dual role of ritual specialists and lawgivers, with the *Dharma*, *Gṛhya* and *Śrautasūtras* serving as the chief medium of exposition. Thus, if the *Śrautasūtras* expounded the procedural rules of sacrificial ritual, the numerous *Dharma* and *Gṛhyasūtra* texts not only laid down a detailed code of conduct to be followed by member of different *varṇas* but also prescribed the punishments to be meted out in case of transgression of those rules. It is significant that even a distinct code of conduct called *rājadharma* come to be drafted for the members of the ruling class and the latter are known to have readily conformed to it.

In fact, what actually lent efficacy to the *Dharmasūtra* rulings and transformed them into documents of major legislative importance was their adoption by contemporary rulers as the main basis of their governance. Petty rulers desperately seeking to legitimize their power with the support of the priestly class were willing to forfeit their legislative powers in exchange for such validation. Some more powerful kings, however, such as the early Mauryas, with the backing of alternative religious systems, attempted to break free from the legislative constraints imposed by Brāhmaṇical lawgivers, but even they could not completely exorcise the influence exerted by their brāhmaṇa ministers. In fact, we learn from contemporary sources that because of the intellectual sagacity and acumen exhibited by some of its members, the brāhmaṇa *varṇa* became the main recruiting ground for higher bureaucratic posts, especially that of high ministers or *mahāmantrin* who acted as chief counsellors of the king, helping the latter to take crucial decisions on state policies and other important issues. Although brāhmaṇas in their position as *mantrin* could not have performed priestly functions, this did not debar them from receiving *dāna* from their royal patrons. The right to receive ritual gifts had come to be regarded as a duty of all brāhmaṇas, regardless of their vocation.

In their role as lawgivers, brāhmaṇas succeeded in securing for themselves some major social, judicial and fiscal privileges and concessions, which became important factors in their social and economic ascendancy, thereby further boosting their position as recipients of *dāna*. As far as social privileges were concerned, even though the right to receive education was extended to members of all twice-born *varṇas*, in the case of kṣatriyas and vaiśyas it could only be of a limited degree and nature, while the right to impart education was exclusively reserved for the brāhmaṇas.

The same holds true of the right to make and receive gifts. While the right to give *dāna* was allowed to a wide cross-section of society, the right to receive ritual gifts or *pratigraha* was declared to be the exclusive prerogative of the brāhmaṇas, a dictate that prevented members of other *varṇas* from encroaching upon and threatening their position as donees. Other privileges claimed by the brāhmaṇas were exemption from capital punishment and various fiscal impositions. The significance of the latter becomes manifest largely in the context of *brahmadeya* land that began to be granted to brāhmaṇas by royal patrons, a practice that became widely popular during the Gupta/post-Gupta period and was chiefly responsible for giving rise to an affluent landowning community within the brāhmaṇa *varṇa*.

III

FACTORS RESPONSIBLE FOR DECLINE IN BRĀHMAṆA POPULARITY AS RECIPIENTS

By the beginning of the post-Vedic period, although the brāhmaṇas' position as recipients of *dāna* had become well-entrenched, it could not remain unchallenged for very long. There appeared on the scene in very large numbers active members of the newly risen monastic orders (*saṁgha*), who in keeping with the principles of renunciation and non-possession subsisted entirely on alms (*bhikṣā*). A life of total abstinence devoid of hankerings after material wealth not only inspired more respect for them in society but made them worthy recipients of gifts. Since gifts made to both brāhmaṇas and heterodox monks were made more out of religious faith than charity, the retention of the donor's respect by the donee was absolutely necessary. During the centuries following the age of the Buddha, while brāhmaṇas failed to win respect due to lapses in their intellectual and moral bearing, Pāli sources reveal that members of the Buddhist and Jaina orders initially steered clear from such behavioural faults. Monastic rules pertaining to gift articles which could be received and the method of alms-seeking were rigorously framed and enforced to protect and ensure the austere, frugal lifestyle and religious dignity of the monks. Similarly, the *Vinaya* dictates contained in the *Cullavagga* (V.17.45) forbade *bhikkhus* from practising the low arts of divination, spells, omens, astrology, witchcraft and quackery. Brāhmaṇas, by contrast, appear to have erred on the side of lax moral standard, and self-indulgence. According to the *Baveru Jātaka* (III, no. 339), 'When the sweet-voiced Buddha preached the law, from heretics their gifts and praise all men withdrew.'

What served to discredit the brāhmaṇas and make them appear less worthy as recipients of *dāna* was the opulent lifestyle adopted by some of them following the receipt of munificent gifts, especially in the form of land and villages. In the *Dīgha Nikāya* (I.111; I.127), we get a reference to brāhmaṇa Sonadaṇḍa enjoying Champa as his *bahmadeya*, while another mahāśāla brāhmaṇa, Kūṭadanta, is said to have received the village Khanumata in Magadha from King Bimbisāra. The sharp contrast between earlier and later lifestyles sported by brāhmaṇas of the two consecutive periods is effectively brought out in a rhetorical question posed in the *Dīgha Nikāya* (III, Ambattha Sutta, II.9): 'Did those ancient *ṛṣis* whose verses you so chant and repeat, parade about well-groomed, perfumed, trimmed as to their hair and beard, adorned with garlands and gem?' Similarly, the *Aṅguttara Nikāya* (V.20.191) states that 'brāhmaṇas in former times did not hoard treasure, grain, silver or gold; but now they do these things'. This finds reiteration in the *Sutta Nipāta* (II.7) according to which, 'No herds had brāhmaṇas then, no gold or pelf; their love was holy love and holy life.' In the *Maccha Jātaka* (I, no. 34, p. 87), a brāhmaṇa priest is described as coming to the riverside escorted by his attendant slaves. Some brāhmaṇas such as Keniya Jaṭila were so wealthy and resourceful that they could invite and entertain kings on certain occasions.[19]

Moreover, the brāhmaṇas, except for those who had taken the vow of celibacy (*brahmacārin*) and wandering ascetics (*sannyāsin*), generally led a householder's life. They were, therefore, dependent on gifts not only for their own subsistence but also that of their families. This is significant for it partly accounts for the greed and cunning with which brāhmaṇas came to be associated in the Pāli literature, especially in the *Jātaka* stories.[20] According to a story that occurs in the *Dhammapada* (book 26, story II), 'a brāhmaṇa who used to climb a certain *kakudha* tree that grew close to the city-gate at Vaiśālī would grasp a branch and swing downwards, crying out, 'Give me a hundred *kapilas*, give me pennies, give me a slave woman. If you don't give me what I ask for, I will let myself drop from this tree and kill myself making this city as though it had never been a city.' Brāhmaṇas earned further disrepute by their quarrelsome ways as well as by their bargaining over the amount to be paid as sacrificial fee. Lack of respect curtailing the flow of gifts towards them is evident from a statement of the *Dīgha Nikāya* (III, Ambattha Sutta, 1.11): 'The Śākyas neither venerate nor value nor esteem nor give gifts to, nor pay honour to the brāhmaṇas.'

By the beginning of the post-Vedic period, brāhmaṇas had crystallized into a watertight *varṇa* segment, membership becoming strictly restricted by birth. Consequently, true intellectual merit could no longer be ensured in all members of that *varṇa* order. Since the worthiness of a brāhmaṇa depended entirely on his learning and intellectual competence, the absence of these qualities not only undermined the spontaneous respect he inspired earlier but also detracted from his qualifications as a donee. The lack of true learning and wisdom was sought to be made up for by the practice of occult sciences such as necromancy, dream-reading, divining signs and omens. This must have further lowered the popular esteem in which brāhmaṇas as recipients of *dāna* were held. In fact, in the early Pāli texts, it is the *khattiyas* who are declared to be holding the topmost rank in the *varṇa* hierarchy.[21] Laying emphasis on purity of lineage, even an offspring of a *khattiya* father born of a brāhmaṇa mother was not considered to be a true blue *khattiya*.

The brāhmaṇas' position as donee was further compromised by their adoption of economic pursuits that were initially forbidden for them. In view of their ever-multiplying numbers, this was absolutely inevitable. As pointed out by S.C. Bhattacharya,[22] 'It was not possible for a whole *varṇa* to subsist economically on teaching, sacrificing and accepting of gifts. Naturally many brāhmaṇas were forced to take up other professions.' We frequently come across references to brāhmaṇa traders, cultivators, husbandmen, carpenters, etc.[23] Consequently, those brāhmaṇas who did not conform to the prescribed duties of their own *varṇa* must have inevitably fallen short of the high standards which had initially entitled them to the receipt of *dāna*, thus further undermining their position as donee.

Certain other factors also interposed to undermine the brāhmaṇa's position as recipient of *dāna*. The substitution of a semi-pastoral order by a full-fledged agrarian economy, accompanied by the beginning of the processes of urbanization and commercial enterprise undermined the validity and authority of the Vedas and the knowledge contained therein. It also discredited the Vedic sacrificial cult, which had come to constitute the chief basis of the sacerdotal power of the brāhmaṇas at this time. The widening of the cultural horizon due to expanding trade links and growing urbanism engendered a more rational outlook, especially in matters of religious belief. This further detracted from the efficacy of sacrificial ceremonialism, completely eroding its rationale. The spirit of skepticism towards sacrificial ritualism finds expression in the following passage of the *Bhūridatta Jātaka* (VI, no. 543, pp. 109-10), 'If he who kills is counted innocent and if the victim safe to heaven is sent, let brāhmaṇas brāhmaṇa kill, so all were well.' The process of rationalization in matters of religious thought, which had, in fact, been initiated by Upaniṣadic philosophers in the later Vedic period, reached its logical climax in the Mauryan period when Aśoka put a ban on the killing of animals. The latter measure could have been as much inspired by the compassion felt by the monarch for all living creatures as it was by the need to protect cattle wealth in order to promote agricultural production based on plough technology. Whatever the motivation, as B.N. Datta points out, 'the prohibition of animal killing was another dialectical blow to sacerdotal ritualism.'[24] That such a development seriously undermined the scope for brāhmaṇas to receive *dāna* can hardly be doubted.

The rise of territorial kingdoms led to a drastic reduction in the number of tribal chiefs who had constituted the chief clientele of brāhmaṇa priests. The decline in the number of rich patrons, combined with a marked growth in the numerical strength of brāhmaṇas dependent on *dāna* for a living, directly affected the latter's interests as donees. The performance of big *soma* sacrifices, which had earlier been the chief occasion for gift distribution, now became restricted to great rulers whose number was very small. Besides, many of them had started patronizing rival religious sects that advocated *ahiṁsā* as one of their cardinal principles. Nevertheless, we learn from Pāli sources how crafty priests tried to seize every opportunity to fleece their royal patrons by making them perform sacrifices. According to the *Mahāsupīna Jātaka* (I, no. 77, p. 187), some priests, playing on the king's fear arising from a bad dream, coaxed him to offer a sacrifice from which they hoped to reap rich gifts as apparent from their exultant remark: 'Large sums of money, and large supplies of food of every kind will be ours.' According to the *Sutta Nipāta* (II.7.299-309), some brāhmaṇas, seeing the great wealth and splendour of King Okkaka, began to covet it. They persuaded the latter to offer a sacrifice so that they could partake of some of that wealth in the form of gifts. Similarly, in the *Dhammapada* (book 21, story 1), we come across a reference to a king, who on enquiring, 'by what means can the plague with which we are afflicted be abated', is told to offer a sacrifice.

IV

MEASURES TO IMPROVE THE SAGGING IMAGE OF THE BRĀHMAṆAS

The brāhmaṇas consequently lost their pre-eminent position as donee, occasionally even becoming objects of derision and censure, though the heterogeneous character of their *varṇa* saved them from losing their social esteem completely. Thus, during this period, if, on the one hand, we hear of very rich brāhmaṇas such as Canki, Tarukkha, Pokkharasati, Januṣṣoni and Toḍeyya who led an opulent lifestyle, there were also extremely poor brāhmaṇas compulsorily living a frugal life. Similarly, if there were some crafty priests known for their gluttony and crooked disposition, who 'after cramming their bellies to the utmost' are said to take away the remainder,[25] there are also numerous references to brāhmaṇas who, living a truly saintly life, inspired spontaneous faith and respect amongst the people. Brāhmaṇas such as Sunetta[26] and Sela[27] are said to have not only attracted a large student following but to have also enjoyed the respect of the multitude by their vast learning.

Nevertheless, the sharp decline in the popularity enjoyed by the brāhmaṇa donee, especially in the wake of urbanization and, rise of heterodox sects, with the latter actively vying for the patronage of both kings and common householders, forced brāhmaṇa ideologues to rethink and reassess their position, and take corrective measure for regaining it. R.N. Nandi considers 'the developmental character of the *gṛhya* rituals' to represent a 'crisis for the surplus-sharing priestly class, and also attempts to get over it'.[28] Numerous injunctions contained in the *Dharma* and *Gṛhyasūtras* dealing specifically with the conduct of the brāhmaṇas show how great an emphasis began to be laid on a high moral character[29] and Vedic learning to entitle a brāhmaṇa to *dāna*.[30] A person devoid of these virtues was no longer considered fit to be called a brāhmaṇa, for, according to the *Baudhāyana Dharmasūtra* (I.5.10.28), the offence of neglecting a brāhmaṇa cannot be deemed to have been committed against one who is unacquainted with the Veda. *Baudhāyana* (I.1.1.11) at another place contends that as an elephant made of wood, or an antelope made of leather, such is an unlearned brāhmaṇa; those three having nothing but the name (of their kind). According to the *Gautama Dharmasūtra* (V.20), the degree of merit arising from a gift made to brāhmaṇas was bound to vary according to the Vedic learning and moral virtue possessed by the latter.

The Dharmaśāstric rulings, besides emphasizing the changed parameters regarding the qualifications of brāhmaṇa recipients, also drew a clear line between a learned (*śrotriya/vedapāraga*) and a non-learned brāhmaṇa. The worthiness of a donee was now determined not so much by his economic need but by his proficiency in Vedic learning, his high moral bearing and ritual status. In the *Mahābhārata* (Śānti Parva, 37.34), it is stated that 'Just as fire covered with wet wood does not glow so also is a receiver of gifts, devoid of penance, Vedic study and good conduct', and that a non-learned brāhmaṇa deserves to be treated as a mere śūdra. At another place in the same epic,[31] it is mentioned that gifts should not be made to one who is wicked, born to a bad family, nor to one who is not refined by vows. In the *Gautama Dharmasūtra* (V.20), it is specifically stated that 'What we enjoy depends upon our reputation.' That these were not mere theoretical injunctions but that a brāhmaṇa's earnings from gifts actually depended upon his reputation for learning is evident from the Sonadaṇḍa Sutta of the *Dīgha Nikāya*, in which brāhmaṇa Sonadaṇḍa expresses his fear that if he is not able to satisfy by his explanations the questions put by *sāmana* Gautama, his reputation for learning might suffer and, with it, his earnings might also grow less.

Emphasis on Vedic learning as a primary qualification of a brāhmaṇa recipient is reiterated through special privileges allowed to *śrotriya* brāhmaṇas by lawgivers. Thus, according to the *Gautama Dharmasūtra* (X.9), it is the special duty of a king to support and protect, in every way, *śrotriya* brāhmaṇas learned in the Vedas. Manu (VII.134) goes on to declare that the kingdom of that king in whose dominions a *śrotriya* pines with hunger would be afflicted by famine. He even stipulates that, though dying, a king must never levy a tax on *śrotriyas*.[32] In fact, it is significant that the *Mahābhārata* (Śānti Parva, 76.5) goes to the other extreme of suggesting that non-*śrotriyas* should be made to pay taxes and even perform forced labour. In the *Baudhāyana Dharmasūtra* (II.3.5.19), all householders are enjoined to give presents of money according to their means 'to good brāhmaṇas, *śrotriyas* and *vedapāragas*; when they are distressed for a livelihood, or desirous to offer a sacrifice, or engaged in studying or on a journey, or have performed a *viśvajit* sacrifice'. The *Arthaśāstra*,[33] in fact, affirms that the privileges allowed exclusively to *śrotriya* brāhmaṇas had the backing of the state.

In order to further restore the religious dignity and popularity of brāhmaṇas as recipients of *dāna*, the Smṛtikāras emphasized non-accumulation of wealth and non-performance of sacrifice for women and śūdras as some of the other guiding principles to be diligently observed by the *śrotriyas*.[34] Gautama (XX.1) went to the extent of declaring: 'Let him cast off a father who assassinates a king or who sacrifices for śūdras.' Manu (IV.186-7), in fact, did not favour even the acceptance of *dāna* by a learned brāhmaṇa; living by collecting fallen ears of corn was considered by him to be much better for a *śrotriya*. Perhaps for the same reason brāhmaṇas were also forbidden to practice occult sciences for extracting alms. Manu (VI.50) very categorically states that 'neither by explaining prodigies and omens nor by skill in astrology and palmistry nor by giving advice and by exposition of the *śāstras*, let him ever seek to obtain alms'. He (VIII.102) even excluded those brāhmaṇas who followed tainted occupations such as trading, artisanship, domestic service and money-lending from the category of worthy recipients of *dāna*.

Although the Dharmaśāstras clearly aimed at reclaiming the ideal image of the brāhmaṇas, which had suffered greatly in comparison with that of heterodox monks, they were equally concerned about safeguarding the interests of the brāhmaṇa *varṇa* as a whole. Hence, next to Vedic learning and virtuous conduct, it was birth in the highest *varṇa* order and ritual purity which were rated by lawgivers as the chief determinants of the worthiness of a donee. The injunction contained in the *Vasiṣṭha Dharmasūtra* (VI.26) is quite clear in this regard: 'Some become worthy receptacles of gifts through sacred learning and some through practice of austerities. But that brāhmaṇa whose stomach does not contain the food of a śūdra, is even the worthiest receptacle of all'. Thus, according to the guidelines furnished by the lawgivers regarding worthy recipients of *dāna*, although learned and virtuous brāhmaṇas were preferred, all brāhmaṇas by virtue of their birth in that particular *varṇa* stratum naturally became entitled to receive *dāna*.

An attempt was also made to organize the brāhmaṇa priesthood into a well-knit body governed by a certain code of conduct, largely to counteract the stiff competition offered by members of well-organized heterodox sects. Such an impression is confirmed by Dharmaśāstra rulings which specify the exact sacrificial fee to be received by the priest or forbid him to accept a post which has either been rejected or served by another. According to the *Āśvalāyana Gṛhyasūtra* (I.23.20), 'The functions of an officiating priest are not to be exercised if abandoned (by another priest) or at an *ahīna* sacrifice with small sacrificial fee.' The exercise of some kind of control on the priesthood is also indicated by a story about King Lomapāda contained in the *Mahābhārata* (Āraṇyaka Parva, 110.20). According to the story, the king, being guilty of falsehood towards a brāhmaṇa, was shunned so completely by the entire priestly community that he was left without a ministering priest to assist him in his religious rites. Such concerted action on the part of the brāhmaṇas does bespeak some sort of a centralized control exercised by an organized priesthood. In fact, it may bear some comparison with the current practice amongst Gayawāl priests who have been allocated a region or *riyāsata* from where alone they are entitled to receive pilgrims.[35]

V

SACRIFICIAL RITUAL RE-ADAPTED AND PARTIALLY REPLACED BY SACRAMENTAL RITUAL

The remedial measures adopted by lawgivers besides raising the qualification bar for brāhmaṇa recipients, also aimed at redressing certain ideological misgivings that beset the brāhmaṇical belief system in the emergent urban milieu, the most serious being the one related to the ritual killing of animals at sacrifices. In fact, the growing disfavour shown towards the latter, especially in the context of the new cattle-based agricultural technology and fast-paced urban growth, eliminated an important source of gift for the brāhmaṇas. It also provided an edge to the teachings of heterodox leaders, who not only upheld *ahiṁsā* as a cardinal principle of their religious ideology but also favoured the urban ethos. Moreover, as R.N. Nandi[36] points out, 'the older sacrificial cult which gave support to a host of priests for a long period of time was now beyond the competence of householder clients.' There was an urgent need, therefore, to mould and re-adapt sacrificial ritualism to meet the demands of an emergent social order with a prominent urban base.

The newly advanced sacrificial ideology promoted by brāhmaṇical lawgivers lay more in charity and penance than in animal killing. Thus, in the *Vasiṣṭha Dharmasūtra* (XXX.2-5; 7), it is unambiguously declared that 'the offering made through the mouth of a brāhmaṇa which neither spills (blood) nor causes pain (to sentient creatures), nor assails him (who makes it) is far more excellent than an *agnihotra*'. Manu (III.212), adopting an equally unequivocal stance towards sacrificial ritual, proclaims, 'But if no (sacred) fire is available he shall place the offerings into the hands of a brāhmaṇa;

for brāhmaṇas who know the sacred texts declare: 'What fire is, even such is a brāhmaṇa.' A similar injunction is also contained in the *Yājñavalkya Smṛti* (I.315). In fact, as shown by K.V.R. Aiyangar,[37] out of twenty-one periodical sacrifices prescribed in the Dharma-śāstras, it was just one category comprising seven *soma* sacrifices for which an animal victim was required. The rest, namely the seven *havir-yajñas* and the seven *pāk-yajñas*, did not need an animal victim.

That Vedic sacrifice entailing mass cattle decimation was a serious cause of dissent both within and without the Brāhmaṇical system is apparent from the following passage of the *Mahābhārata* (Anuśāsana Parva, 65.38-42): 'Animals have not been ordained to be slaughtered in sacrifices. O Puissant One, these preparations of thine are destructive of merit. This sacrifice is not consistent with righteousness, the destruction of creatures can never be said to be an act of righteousness.' That sacrifice was gradually becoming replaced by *dāna* is more than evident from Manu's (I.86) dictum that 'whereas sacrifice was the chief virtue in the *Dvāpara* age, *dāna* is to be regarded supreme in the *Kali* age'. The gradual rejection of animal sacrifice and its replacement by the principle of *dāna* is attested by the fact that the Sanskrit term *yajña* had, by this time, come to acquire a twofold meaning in Pāli, Brāhmaṇical sacrifice and almsgiving.[38] According to the *Mahāvastu*,[39] 'Following Prince Sudhanu's instructions, the king offered an unobjectionable blameless sacrifice. Several thousand recluses, brāhmaṇas, beggars and wayfarers were given food and drink and clothes.' *Dāna* was now treated at par with sacrifices as far as the resultant religious merit was concerned.

The concept of sacrifice becoming more and more associated with offerings of cooked food instead of animal killing is a development well-attested by contemporary Brāhmaṇical texts, especially the Gṛhyasūtras. Thus, according to the *Sāṅkhyāyana Gṛhyasūtra* (V.3.1.3), 'Having established the sacred fire and having prepared a mass of cooked food, he shall sacrifice with the formula to *Viṣṇu svāha*. In the *Khadira Gṛhyasūtra* (IV.1.10), it is stated that one who desired that his stock of cattle may increase should sacrifice rice and barley. Numerous new occasions and even flimsy reasons came to be suggested when sacrifices involving offerings of cooked and uncooked food had to be performed. According to the *Āśvalāyana Gṛhyasūtra* (III.7.7.10), sacrifice should be performed 'if a dove flies against his house or towards it'. It is stipulated in the *Khadira Gṛhyasūtra* (III.3.13) that when a person's cows are sick, he should sacrifice milk-rice in the cowshed. Similarly, it is stated in the *Khadira Gṛhyasūtra* (II.2.28) that when the child is appearing, a sacrifice for the woman in labour is to be performed. According to the *Sāṅkhyāyana Gṛhyasūtra* (IV.14.2.2: V.2.1; 3.1), sacrifices may be performed when crossing water in order to ensure lucky progress, or on the occasion of the consecration of ponds, wells, tanks and gardens. In the *Gobhila Gṛhyasūtra* (III.3.31), similar sacrificial offerings are recommended even when a span of the roof or the middle post of a house breaks or for a debt which a person is unable to pay. Some of the occasions on which sacrifice came to be recommended would suggest the exploitation of folk-belief and superstitious fears by lawgivers for the purpose of creating more opportunities for brāhmaṇas to extract *dāna*.

Despite some of these drastic modifications affected in sacrificial ritual, the latter was still losing its relevance and validity in the expanding urban milieu. It became imperative for brāhmaṇa theorists, therefore, to replace it by some alternate set of ritual, which could prove conducive to the emergent urban ethos and be a lucrative source of income for the priestly class. Sacramental ritualism fulfilled this requirement to perfection and as many as forty different kinds of *saṁskāras* are enumerated in the Gṛhyasūtras. Our sources are full of references to *dāna* being recommended as well as offered to brāhmaṇas, particularly on such occasions as birth,[40] naming ceremony,[41] *upanayana*,[42] marriage,[43] and funeral rites. In fact, by making the performance of *saṁskāras* by householders mandatory, the lawgivers succeeded in underscoring the line of differentiation between different *varṇas*. Sacramental rites were now considered to be one of the chief determinants of *varṇa* status. According to a well-known Dharmaśāstric dictate, all are born śūdras by birth and it is only through the performance of initiatory rites such as *upanayana* that a person acquires the status of a twice-born. Sacramental rites performed at the time of marriage (*vivāha*) similarly determined a person's status as a householder and defined his duties *vis-à-vis* other members of the family. However, it was in the context of the growing importance of private property, both moveable and immoveable, that sacramental ritual in the form of funeral and ancestral rites (*antyeṣṭi/śrāddha*) became seminal in settling critical issues of inheritance and succession within the family. Most of these sacramental rites, in order to retain their efficacy, had to be accompanied by offerings of food and gifts to brāhmaṇas specially invited for the occasion. In the case of the *śrāddha* rite, brāhmaṇas had to be treated with utmost respect and veneration for they were supposed to act as surrogate ancestors during the ceremony.[44]

Sacramental ritualism, by focusing on and serving certain vital interests of common householders that had a crucial bearing on their financial, social and ritual status, not only made the latter more dependent upon the brāhmaṇas for their priestly services but also helped to develop some sort of *jajamānī* ties between them. Offerings of food and *dāna* to brāhmaṇas during the performance of sacramental rites made up for the declining popularity of sacrifices as a source of gift for the latter. It also vastly broadened the circle of their clientele, the latter no longer drawn merely from royal and rural backgrounds but covering almost the entire spectrum of mainstream society based in prosperous towns and villages. The purview of sacramental ritualism, moreover, no longer directly clashed with that of alms sought by wandering ascetics and monks, for as *rites de passage* (*saṁskāras*) inevitably figured as a perpetual feature of the lives of all householders, regardless of their personal religious predilections. Sacramental ritualism, thus, not only gave brāhmaṇas an easy access into the lives of householders but also gave them an opportunity to extract a portion of the surplus owned by the latter in their capacity as producers.

As pointed out by R.N. Nandi,[45] another significant outcome of the shift from *yajña* religiosity to the one based on *gṛhya* rituals or *saṁskāras* was the integration, however, marginal, of brāhmaṇas to 'the modes and mores of a market-based economy'. The pressures of an urban ethos, moreover, led the lawgivers to adopt a more liberal stance towards the adoption of occupational pursuits by brāhmaṇas that had been originally forbidden for them.[46] According to Nandi, the latter development inevitably 'loosened the brāhmaṇas' habitual adherence to the traditional gift-exchange economy' and also 'sharply divided the *jajamānī* class into practising priests and secular non-priests'.[47] The laxity shown by the lawgivers becomes more apparent from the fact that they allowed brāhmaṇas to accept gifts even from śūdras in times of distress. According to the *Gautama Dharmasūtra* (XVII.5), 'If the means for sustaining life cannot be procured otherwise, they may be accepted from a śūdra'. The *Āpastamba Dharmasūtra* (I.2.7.21) similarly permits money for the teacher to be taken from a śūdra. According to Manu (X.102; X.104), 'A brāhmaṇa who has fallen into distress may accept gifts from anybody, for according to the law it is not possible to assert that anything pure may be sullied.' He (X.107) even cites the example of Bhāradvāja, a performer of great austerities, who accepted many cows from the carpenter Bṛbhu, when he was starving together with his sons in a lonely forest.

In order to further improve the brāhmaṇas' chances of receiving *dāna* by creating more opportunities for its bestowal, lawgivers began to recommend the offering of gifts to them on other occasions as well, such as on a solar or lunar eclipse or on the full moon days of the months of Āṣāḍha, Kārttika, Māgha and Baiśākha, or even at the time of other auspicious planetary conjunctions. Since the institution of *tīrthas* had already taken root by this time, the lawgivers began recommending some prominent pilgrimage sites as appropriate places for the performance of particular *saṁskāras*, the latter having to be inevitably accompanied by the distribution of gifts to brāhmaṇas. According to the *Vasiṣṭha Dharmasūtra* (XI.42), 'The manes consider him to be their (true) descendant who offers to them food at Gayā.' The fact that pilgrimage centres drew their importance from particular sectarian beliefs could hold appeal only for the followers of that religious sect. At a Brāhmaṇical *tīrtha* site, the chances of brāhmaṇas having to share space with the votaries of rival heterodox sects, therefore, did not arise. Consequently, *tīrthas* gained importance as additional and exclusive sources of gifts for the brāhmaṇas.

In order to further boost the brāhmaṇa's scope for gift-sharing, lawgivers also began to utilize and even exploit the ideological concept of sin by attaching undue importance to it, particularly in the context of transgression of *varṇa* laws. They began to prescribe various expiatory measures for sin-atonement or *prāyaścitta*. Though very harsh and severe forms of penance were often recommended, especially in the case of more grievous sins such as the one incurred by the killing of a brāhmaṇa, in the case of milder forms of moral lapses, such as accidentally causing the death of a cat or some other animal, the offering of special kinds of gifts to brāhmaṇas represented the more common mode of atonement. Such expiatory offerings were generally required to be made of precious metals, a ruling which was bound to strain any donor's resources but which must have boosted that of the recipient. All these measures adopted by the lawgivers, particularly the one that converted the *saṁskāra* ritual into a new and exclusive source of *dāna*, besides resuscitating the brāhmaṇas' image as gift-recipients, also reduced the intensity of competitive rivalry for alms-sharing that had existed between them and their chief religious antagonists, the Buddhist and Jaina monks.

VI

BRĀHMAṆA RECIPIENTS ACQUIRING PAN-INDIAN BASE AND CLIENTELE

From the time of the Guptas, a sharp decline in the volume of trade with Central Asia and the Western world arrested commercial growth, a development that had a catalytic effect on the contemporary economy. If, on the one hand, craft production, urbanization, and the money economy suffered retaining only marginal importance, on the other, the thrust on agricultural production increased manifold, turning land into the chief means of production and the most coveted item of wealth. The impact on society and religion was no less, for if the beginnings of a closed economy gave rise to a feudal social order, the centrifugal forces released by such developments spurred both ruling monarchs as well as many aspirant chieftains to focus more attention on the less-developed parts on the periphery of their kingdoms, as well as on the regions that lay beyond and that held greater potential and better scope for agricultural expansion. Lacking the necessary state resources and the infrastructure for undertaking such development, the best way for petty rulers to bring more waste land under active cultivation was by granting it to religious supplicants, chiefly brāhmaṇas and heterodox monastic orders. The beneficiaries of these grants could be instrumental both in economically developing the donated piece of land and making it agriculturally lucrative, as well as in providing the much-needed religious validation for the not very stabilized power of the royal donor, besides being a source of infinite spiritual merit for them.

The growing popularity of the practice of donating *brahmadeya* land greatly affected the brāhmaṇas' position as recipients of *dāna*, for their dependence on the householders for gifts was no longer as consummate. It actually proved to be a timely development because in the wake of urban decline, a large section of the urban population had started moving away from decaying towns towards the agriculturally rich hinterland, thereby cutting asunder the *jajamānī* ties that had developed between them and the brāhmaṇas. Hence, the latter's prospects as gift recipients that had been severely hit by such a movement could be revived and even enhanced by the wide-spread practice of granting land to brāhmaṇas. It is not surprising therefore, that contemporary lawgivers, especially the authors of the Purāṇas, declared the gift of land to be the best of gifts. In ritual efficacy and as a source of spiritual merit it was if not actually superior but definitely at par with the Vedic *soma yajñas*. However, to ensure that only truly deserving brāhmaṇas received such land grants, the stringent rules regarding the latters' qualifications, with *śrotriya*-hood as an essential pre-condition, were formulated.

The practice, besides adding a new dimension to the position of brāhmaṇas as recipients, had several other major repercussions on the structural composition of the brāhmaṇa *varṇa*. It not only gave rise to an affluent landowning segment within it, but also caused it to be further fragmented on account of regional affiliations arising from the large-scale migration of the beneficiaries of land grants to distant parts of the country. The identity of a brāhmaṇa came to be now determined not only by his *gotra*, family lineage and the level of his Vedic learning (proficiency in the number of Vedas) but also by the region from which he originally hailed or where he was eventually settled. However, the most significant impact of the practice of land grants was the unprecedented increase in the geographical reach of the brāhmaṇa recipients. Their activities were now no longer confined merely to the Brāhmaṇical heartland but covered almost the entire subcontinent. Their pan-Indian presence is attested both by the Purāṇas, as well as by contemporary regional literature and epigraphic sources.

An important outcome of migrations by beneficiaries into peripheral regions generally inhabited by indigenous tribes was the close interaction they triggered off between the latter and the brāhmaṇa migrants. Not only was such interaction unavoidable but, to mobilize labour locally for the economic development of the donated land, it even became necessary for the beneficiaries to acculturate the native inhabitants of the area. Such a process of Brāhmaṇization gave fresh scope for the rise of a new and fairly large category of potential clients of the brāhmaṇa priests, a development that was bound to further enhance the latters' prospects as recipients of *dāna*.

Yet what served the interests of the brāhmaṇa recipients was the popularity gained by certain ritual formations, mainly as an after-effect of the ongoing cultural interaction between the tribes undergoing Brāhmaṇization and its chief agents, the beneficiaries of land grants. The interaction, however, could not be completely one-sided for it resulted in certain features that normally characterize pre-literate religions, such as the collective offering of worship to idols crafted of wood or stone, and generally enshrined under trees or within small enclosures, finding its way into the Brāhmaṇical fold largely through Purāṇic adaptations made possible through the extensive use of myths and folklore. The Purāṇas reveal that with *pūjā* (offering worship) fast replacing the Vedic *homa* in popularity, the practice of enshrining Brāhmaṇical deities in temples become more common. That temple-building activities picked up momentum from the Gupta period onwards is attested by archaeological data. Temple worship inevitably created yet another important source of gift for brāhmaṇas, besides giving rise to a special category of ritual specialists in the form of the temple priests (*pūjārī*).

The innumerable temples and shrines that came to be built mostly by royal patrons, and which were generally situated in peripheral zones, soon became the foci of thousands of *tīrtha* complexes that came up throughout the subcontinent and of which copious notices are available in the Purāṇas. Though *tīrthas* as a ritual construct had begun receiving the attention of lawgivers even in the preceding period, it was only from the time of the Purāṇas that the practice gained real popularity and turned into the most lucrative source of gifts for the brāhmaṇas. By professing the special ritual significance of each *tīrtha*, as well as imbuing it with infinite spiritual merit, the Purāṇa composers sought to attract people constituting potential donors from all over the country, though the chief targeted category of pilgrims were those belonging to the fully or even partially Brāhmaṇized tribal groups dwelling in its vicinity and even owing to it a certain religious affinity. What further added to the popularity of the institution was the waiving off of all caste and gender-based restrictions in the context of all *tīrthas*. Consequently, at places of pilgrimage, even those belonging to the substratum of society as well as women now emerged as potential clients and donors *vis-à-vis* the brāhmaṇas. It was a significant development for, despite the modest nature and quantum of their gifts, it still greatly bolstered the overall size of the donor category and was instrumental in augmenting the position of brāhmaṇas as recipients of *dāna*. It, moreover, made the rivalry over gift-sharing with heterodox religious sects inconsequential.

Besides temple worship and *tīrthas*, some other important ritual formations that created more opportunities for brāhmaṇas to receive gifts included new forms of ritual *dāna* that came to be introduced in the Purāṇas. Thus, we hear of the sixteen *mahādānas* that came to be recommended for the first time in the *Matsya Purāṇa*. As attested by epigraphic sources, the performance of *mahādānas* mostly by royal kings and princes seeking religious validation for their newly-founded power became important occasions for the distribution of gifts to brāhmaṇas on a more lavish scale and even ostentatious level.[48] Other forms of *dāna* that came to be prescribed in the Purāṇas for the first time included several kinds of *meru-dāna* and *dhenu-dāna* in which various gift-items such as cereals were piled up either in the form of a hillock or arranged in the shape of a cow to be ritually offered to brāhmaṇas. Considering the great spiritual merit that emanated from them, according to the Purāṇas, such gifts like the *mahādānas* did not require any particular occasion or reason for their performance but could be undertaken at any time.

The Purāṇas, in fact, testify to an unprecedented increase in the occasions for making *dāna*. Thus, it was no longer merely at the time of performing sacramental rites or the *śrāddha* ceremony or even during *soma yajñas* that gifts were distributed to brāhmaṇas. Besides the newly conceptualized *mahādānas* and *merudānas*, as well as thousands of upcoming temples and *tīrthas* which provided new occasions and places for offering gifts to brāhmaṇas, the practice of observing *vratas* also gained wide currency during this period and turned into additional occasions for making *dāna* to brāhmaṇas. The Purāṇas furnish lists of thousands of *vratas* to be observed by men and women alike. In the context of *vratas*, as in that of *tīrthas*, it was the dispensation of gender differentiation which directly contributed to their wider popularity. In fact, a large majority of *vratas* that find mention in the Purāṇas were prescribed mostly for women. Since the observance of these vows for their ritual efficacy had to be necessarily accompanied by gifts to brāhmaṇas, the *vratas* turned into another major source of gifts for the latter.

Significantly, as the occasion, for gift-making multiplied and the geographical horizon of the fast-proliferating brāhmaṇical settlements widened, there was a noticeable erosion of the high standard originally set for brāhmaṇas qualifying as recipients. Spread over almost the entire subcontinent with most settlements far removed from the Brāhmaṇical epicentre, it could scarcely be expected that, despite the passage of so many centuries, all brāhmaṇas living mainly on ritual gifts could continue to uphold the same high standards and impeccable credentials that the original beneficiaries of land grants might have possessed. In fact, there is enough evidence to show that the proximity of immigrant brāhmaṇas to the native population not only considerably diluted the purity of their lineage but also led to their adoption of numerous local cultural traits and traditions that find expression in the Purāṇas.

Consequently, the parameters set for brāhmaṇa recipients, especially as far as their proficiency in Vedic learning and level of erudition was concerned, were inevitably lowered, a development further compounded by a drastic increase both in the overall size of the donor and recipient categories, as well as in the number of occasions for receiving gifts. Thus, despite the continual emphasis being laid by the Purāṇa authors on recipients being morally upright and learned, gifts offered at *tīrthas*, for partaking meals at a *śrāddha* or *saṁskāra* related ceremony, at the conclusion of a *vrata* or even for discharging the duties of a temple-priest did not really require the latter to be exceptionally erudite or even well-versed in the Vedas; possessing bare priestly skills might have proved more than adequate. It is not surprising, therefore, that brāhmaṇa recipients officiating as temple priests or assisting in *tīrtha*-related performances or even partaking of meals at the *yajamāna*'s residence on ritual occasions like *saṁskāra* or *vrata* were accorded very low social status within the brāhmaṇa stratum and an equally low social esteem outside it. In contrast to the latter category of brāhmaṇa recipients, there were others who, as recipients of land grants, had emerged as landed magnates, occasionally sporting a feudal rank and title. The high social status that they enjoyed both within their own *varṇa* as well as outside it had its source as much in their acquired wealth as in their professed learning and purer lineage. Thus, as our sources reveal, there were no fixed parameters regarding qualifications, which could be uniformly applicable to brāhmaṇa recipients of all categories. They invariably varied and corresponded to the special needs and aspects of a particular recipient category.

NOTES

1. *Śatapatha Brāhmaṇa*, II.2.2.
2. *KK*, *DK*, Intro., p. 62.
3. *Vedic India*, p. 100.
4. 'Reflections on the Significance of the *Dakṣiṇā*', *Indo-Iranian Journal*, no. III, pp. 241-55.
5. *The Religion of India*, p. 60.
6. X.222; *SBH*, XXVIII.633.
7. *Aitareya Brāhmaṇa*, VI.30.9.
8. 'Gifts and Giving', p. 140.
9. *Āpastamba Dharmasūtra*, II.5.10.8; 'He shall not choose a priest who is devoid of Vedic learning, nor one who haggles.'
10. *Manusmṛti*, IV.226-7.
11. *Ṛgveda*, II.1.2; 8.91.10.
12. *Aitareya Brāhmaṇa*, VIII.24; *Taittirīya Brāhmaṇa*, I.4.4.
13. *Chāndogya Upaniṣad*, 4.4.1.
14. *Sāṅ.Brāh.*, 25.14, P.V. Kane, *History of Dharmaśāstras*.
15. B.G. Gokhale, 'Brāhmaṇas in Early Buddhist Literature', *JIH*, XLVIII, p. 54.
16. *Mahābhāṣya*, III.2.123; Ayodhya Inscription, *EI*, XX, p. 54; Nanaghat Cave Inscription (of Nāganikā), *SI*, vol. I, book ii, no. 82.
17. *Mahāummaga Jātaka*, VI, no. 546, p. 197.
18. *Arthaśāstra*, I.9.10.
19. *Sutta Nipāta*, III.7.
20. *Bhūridatta Jātaka*, VI, no. 543; *Sigāla Jātaka*, I, no. 113; *Bhikkhā Paramparā Jātaka*, IV, no. 496; *Kuṇāla Jātaka*, V, no. 536.
21. *Cullavagga*, IX.4; *Majjhima Nikāya*, II.128; *Aṅguttara Nikāya*, II.194.

22. *Some Aspects of Indian Society: From c. 2nd Century BC to c. 4th Century AD*, Calcutta, 1978.
23. *Sutta Nipāta*, III.9; *Kāma Jātaka*, IV, no. 467; *Phandana Jātaka*, IV, no. 475; *Daśa Brāhmaṇa Jātaka*, IV, no. 495 contains reference to brāhmaṇas taking to different callings.
24. B.N. Datta, 'Brahmanical Counter-Revolution', *JBORS*, XXVII, 1941, pp. 369-75.
25. *Aṅguttara Nikāya*, book V.20.3; *Dīgha Nikāya*, I, Brahmajāla Sutta, 20, contains a reference to a trickster brāhmaṇa.
26. *Aṅguttara Nikāya*, III.371.
27. *Sutta Nipāta*, III.7.
28. 'Some Social Aspects of the Gṛhyasūtras', *PIHC*, 1977, p. 168.
29. *Āpastamba Dharmasūtra*, I.8.23.5; *Baudhāyana Dharmasūtra*, II.3.5.12; II.10.18.1-2; *Vasiṣtha Dharmasūtra*, VI.30; *Sāṅkhyāyana Gṛhyasūtra*, I.2.2.
30. *Vasiṣtha Dharmasūtra*, III.8, 9, VI.26; *Gautama Dharmasūtra*, VIII.4.5; *Sāṅkhyāyana Gṛhyasūtra*, I.2.6, IV.1.2; *Mahābhārata*, Śānti Parva, 140.35.
31. Śānti Parva, 37.31.
32. *Manusmṛti*, VII.133.
33. Kangle, *The Kauṭilya Arthaśāstra*, pt. III, p. 144.
34. *Manusmṛti*, IV.7.8; *Yājñavalkya Smṛti*, I.128.
35. L.P. Vidyarthi, *The Sacred Complex of Hindu Gaya*, p. 93.
36. 'Some Social Aspects of the Gṛhyasūtras', *PIHC*, p. 168.
37. *Aspects of the Social and Political System of Manusmṛti*, p. 114.
38. P.R. Barua, 'The Brāhmaṇa Doctrine of Sacrifice and Rituals in Pāli Canon', *JASP*, I, p. 94.
39. *Mahāvastu*, tr. J.J. Jones, II, p. 97.
40. *Āpastamba Gṛhyasūtra*, VI.16. 1; *Asatarūpa Jātaka*, I, no. 100, p. 242.
41. *Pañcavudha Jātaka*, I, no. 55, p. 137.
42. *Āpastamba Gṛhyasūtra*, VI.18.4.
43. *Pāraskara Gṛhyasūtra*, I.8.14-18.
44. *Manusmṛti*, II.208-9.
45. *Social Roots of Religion in Ancient India*, Calcutta, 1986, p. 9.
46. *Vasiṣṭha Gṛhyasūtra*, II.24-26; *Āpastamba Gṛhyasūtra*, I.7.20.11-16; *Gautama Gṛhyasūtra*, X.5-6; *Manusmṛti*, X.115.
47. Nandi, *Social Roots*, p. 11.
48. See Chapter on *Mahādāna*.

6

Kanyādāna: Element of Exchange and Gift in Marriage: Genesis and Dimensions

The concept of *kanyādāna* was firmly established by the later half of the first millennium BC, when it had come to figure as an integral part of the marriage ceremony.[1] According to ancient Brāhmaṇical lawgivers, there is no gift better or imbued with more spiritual merit than the gift of a daughter (*kanyādānaparamdānam nabhūtam-nabhaviṣyati; sarveṣudāneṣu kanyādānampraśasyate*).[2] But what was the genesis of this concept? Was it there in the Vedic society right from the inception of the institution of marriage or did it evolve at a later stage of cultural development? To what extent does it reflect the proprietary hold of the father over his daughter? Are its origins traceable to the relegation of the daughter to the position of an item of property?

The earliest reference to the institution of marriage is contained in the tenth book of the *Ṛgveda*. Perhaps the idea of *kanyādāna* also occurs there in the form of the bestowal by the sun-god, Savitar, of his daughter, Sūryā, on her husband.[3] Even the concept of the father's proprietary hold over his daughter would seem to find some vague illusion in the following lines of the same hymn: 'Now from the noose of Varuṇa I free thee, wherewith most blessed Savitar hath bound thee'.[4] That this proprietary right was formally transferred to the bridegroom at the time of the wedding is again evident from the verse: 'Hence and not thence, I send thee free. I make thee softly fettered there.' Interestingly, the ceremony is described as *śikhāmocana* in the *Ṛgveda*.[5] Do we find in these utterances an echo of the *kanyādāna* rite of later times? S. Jayal would dispute such a suggestion.[6] Her chief objection is that Sūryā was wedded not at her father's but at her bridegroom's place, a fact which would exclude the notion of *kanyādāna* from marriage. However, contrary to Jayal's contention, there is enough to indicate that Sūryā's wedding took place at her father's residence, albeit in the absence of the sacred fire. Moreover, the evidence of the verses cited above would very strongly suggest at least the beginnings of the concept of *kanyādāna* in the Ṛgvedic period.

It is remarkable, however, that the rite of *kanyādāna* figures ostensibly as a part of the marriage ritual only from the time of the Dharmasūtras onwards.[7] What makes its omission during the Vedic period[8] more significant is that while in the earlier period consummation of marriage marked the conclusion of the formal rite,[9] it does not figure as such in the Dharmasūtra and Smṛti texts. Although it is relatively easy to account for the latter development in the light of the pre-puberty marriages which began to be recommended in the later period,[10] the omission of the *kanyādāna* rite in Vedic literature is more difficult to explain, especially when we definitely come across the idea of the father giving away his daughter in marriage. What is still more difficult to account for is how the concept came to be emphasized and formally integrated into the marriage ritual from the post-Vedic period onwards. Before taking up these issues connected with the growth of marriage ceremonialism in the Vedic and post-Vedic times, a question which needs some careful probing is what gave the father the right to gift his daughter? Or rather, what is the genesis and the extent of proprietary right exercised by him? The latter question can be answered better if, instead of restricting our field of enquiry to the Vedic society alone, we were to first consider the development of marriage as a social formation in the wider context of early societies.

Sociologists are divided in their views about the beginning of the institution of marriage. J.J. Bachofen,[11] J.F. Mclennan,[12] L.H. Morgan,[13] J. Lubbock[14] and others maintained that the institution of marriage was preceded by a state of promiscuity.[15] The suggestion was later disputed by Darwin and E.A. Westermarck.[16] Regardless of the above controversy,[17] the generally conceded fact is that the origins of the institution lay not so much in the physiological or societal needs as in economic expediency.

The importance of a woman in a primitive group does not rest on her being merely a source of sexual gratification, for which marriage as a binding institution will certainly not be necessary. Her importance is derived entirely from the positive role she plays in economic production. She stands out as a primary producer of food[18] and other essential goods needed by the group. This generalization has a greater bearing for the pre-agricultural societies, which have still not learnt to produce a surplus or utilize slave or hired labour for purposes of production. Even in the relatively more advanced Ṛgvedic society—when, along with pastoral pursuits, incipient agriculture had already made a beginning—we come across frequent references to women being engaged in some of the chief economic pursuits of the time,[19] such as weaving cloth,[20] sewing garments,[21] making bows and arrows,[22] watching the standing crops in the field,[23] milking and tending the cows,[24] and fetching water in jars.[25] Women in the *Ṛgveda* are also known to have taken an active part in tribal wars,[26] which constituted an important economic activity in the tribal milieu.[27] The economic security of man in early societies would, thus, seem to depend very largely upon the cooperation and support he could seek from his womenfolk. Besides contributing to economic production, women in early societies also figure as the producer of producers. The importance of this role may be appreciated better if we bear in mind the continually depleting size of the kinship group, on account of continual inter- and intra-tribal warfare. Under the circumstances, the very physical survival of a group would seem to have depended upon its stock being constantly reinforced through a vigorous process of procreation. It, therefore, became necessary for the group to ensure the optimum utilization of a woman's reproductive powers, even to the extent of permitting a certain amount of license in sexual behaviour. The sanction given to widow remarriage in the early Vedic period,[28] the institution of *samana* which is described in the *Ṛgveda* as 'specially attracting maidens at night',[29] and the laxity evident in the standard of ordinary sexual morality[30] are some of the features of Ṛgvedic life, the significance of which may be understood only in the above context. Similarly, the acquisition of women slaves in very large numbers through wars, and their children being accorded an equal status within the group, was also meant to meet the shortage of females in conquering tribes.[31] The *Ṛgveda* bears reference to women of the *Dāsa* tribes being taken in as *vadhūs* and their children rising to the status of priests and warrior chiefs.[32] Even the fervent prayers contained in the *Ṛgveda* for as many as ten sons,[33] when, in the

Dharmasūtras, the number of sons desired is much less, was not so much directed towards perpetuating the individual patrilineal family as to augment the membership of the tribal group as a whole.

Due to the woman's excessively important role in production and reproduction in early society, it is hardly surprising that she came to be viewed as an 'essential valuable' member of the group. What may have further deepened the impression of her being a scarce commodity was the 'natural' polygamous instinct of man and the fact of more desirable women being always in a minority.[34]

Once women began to be considered an essential valuable to be placed in the same category as food, on which depended the very well-being and survival of the group,[35] their equitable distribution amongst all members became imminent. This could be achieved only through the collective intervention of the group by imposing restrictions on incest, endogamy and exogamy. Through the prohibition of incest,[36] the group clearly sought to ensure that a woman, instead of being completely monopolized by members of her own immediate family, especially her father and brother, would become accessible to other members of the group too. In fact, the roots of incest prohibition lay not so much in nature, as was believed by Westermarck, but in social-cultural needs.[37] As R.S. Sharma[38] points out, the incest prohibition not only forbids but also ordains and is in consonance with the view that marriage is an exchange of women, and that kinship relations are primarily relations between groups rather than relations between individuals.[39] Restrictions on incest were, therefore, tantamount to the enforcement of the rule of exogamy, which necessitates the reciprocal exchange of women. Even endogamy in the form of cross-cousin marriages, for which some amount of evidence is forthcoming from Buddhist literature, is clearly an instance of the 'simplest conceivable system of reciprocity', according to C. Lévi-Strauss.[40] It is significant that in the early Vedic period, in view of the need to expand the circle of marriage alliances within the kinship group so as to ensure its maximum proliferation, the rule of exogamy extended only up to the third or fourth degree on both parents' side.[41] Restrictions upon *gotra* and *sapiṇḍa* marriages are heard of only in a much later period.[42]

Marriage in early society was, thus, essentially an attempt on the part of the group to organize and regulate the distribution of one of its major resources, namely women. Accordingly, when a girl was given in marriage to a member of another family or clan, it automatically established the giver's claim to receive similar gifts of girls in return.[43] Amongst primitive Indian tribes and castes, men even now obtain wives by exchanging sisters or other kinswomen. The custom is called *gurawat* or *adlā-badlā* and is practised by the Barhais, Bhuiyas, Dharkars,[44] etc. The bilateral aspect in such exchanges is specially marked. Since in such marriage exchanges the relationship of reciprocity is not established between man and woman but between the lineage groups by means of women,[45] they become instrumental in not only establishing and strengthening friendly ties between two kinship groups but also in linking them into an ongoing system of exchange. In fact, just as in a tribal milieu, gift-making whether in the form of potlatch or ordinary presentation serves as a means of acquiring power, influence or even sympathy. The gift of a girl in marriage also becomes an instrument for acquiring social prestige and status. Marriage in pre-agricultural societies, therefore, besides serving a major economic purpose, also played a critical role in integrating wider groups and in affecting cultural assimilation. Cultural syncretism through marriage is amply attested by the Vedic texts.[46]

Such gifts of girls in marriage, especially in a tribal social order, emphasize two things, namely the existence of equality and reciprocity between the giver and the receiver, and the fact of kinship relations being, primarily, relations between groups rather than between individuals.[47] Moreover, they also presume the common proprietary hold of the clan or the family over the girl. There are clear indications of this in the *Āpastamba Dharmasūtra* (II.10.27.3), where it is stated that a bride is given to a family of brothers and not to one brother alone. In Vedic literature, the use of the term *deveri*,[48] which literally means second husband, to denote the husband's brother, would also suggest that a bride in the Vedic household was not regarded as exclusively belonging to her husband alone.[49]

It is to be noted, moreover, that in such a social ethos, in which the individual ownership right over daughter or wife is not so clearly recognized, the latter's fidelity towards her husband cannot be expected to be emphasized. In fact, the proprietary right over woman could have meant nothing more than the recognition of the husband's right over her reproductive labour in order to continue the patri-lineage.[50] According to S. Jayaswal, this would explain the sexual freedom and comparatively higher status of women in early Vedic times. Besides evidence cited from the classical literature of different countries by J.J. Bachofen,[51] which attests the prevalence of promiscuity in early societies, its existence in the early Indian society is indicated by several references contained in the *Mahābhārata*.[52] It needs to be pointed out, in this context, that because of their role in economic production, the equitable distribution of women amongst the male members of the lineage group had to be necessarily controlled and regulated through observing certain marriage restrictions, such as those on incest, endogamy and exogamy. Yet it did not actually amount to her being regarded as an item of property. What may tend to create the impression of women being equated with wealth and property is that since they were exchanged between groups of men, they became 'less than persons'[53] and, hence, were treated as objects or as a form of property. But, as pointed out by sociologists, in such marriage exchanges, it was not the woman but only her productive and reproductive labour which was the object of exchange and for which recompense was sought to be offered in the form of bride-price.[54] This may, to some extent, account for the comparative freedom and equal status enjoyed by women in all early societies, including that of the early Vedic period.

Since the element of bilateral exchange in marriage is conspicuous in a tribal order as existed in the early Vedic period, it is not surprising that even though the father is specifically mentioned as giving away his daughter in marriage,[55] yet the term *kanyādāna* is not used in its context, because *dāna* really signifies only unilateral exchange. The element of unilateral exchange in its purest aspect is to be found only in the *daiva* form of marriage, in which the girl is gifted to the officiating priest.[56] *Kanyādāna* as a formal rite, therefore, occurs in Vedic literature only with reference to this particular form of marriage.[57]

In a predominantly tribal set-up, the phenomenon of marriage promoting economic production and reproduction would also seem to be responsible for girls getting married only after they had crossed the age of puberty and were fit to shoulder both these responsibilities. This, in fact, provides the chief rationale for the inclusion of consummation as a formal rite in the marriage ritualism of the early Vedic period.

Besides gift-exchange, the two other chief means of procuring a wife in pre-agricultural societies were through abduction and sale. Whereas the former served as a common mode of procuring wives amongst clans which were mostly warring with each other,[58] the latter emphasizes the need to recompense the girl's family for its loss of a 'valuable resource'.[59] Thus, in the *Ṛgveda* (I.112.9; I.116.1; X.39.7), we come across the story of Vimada who carried off Purumitra's daughter against the latter's wishes. Such a custom is still found in India among aboriginal tribes such as the Gonds and Birhors. As far as marriage by purchase is concerned, Renee Hirschon maintains that 'in regulating the woman's capacities to produce and reproduce, marriage is marked socially by the transfer—the detachment by some and appropriation by others—of valued resources'. Westermarck regards marriage by purchase to be of an universal character in ancient times.[60] Corroborative evidence for this may be found in the common terms for bride-fee, which occur in many Indo-European languages.[61] Significantly, the *Mānava Gṛhyasūtra* (I.7.12) speaks of only two forms of marriage *brāhma* and *śaulka*. The latter must, therefore, have been a popular and prevailing custom in the Vedic age.[62]

The extension of agriculture during the subsequent period of the later Vedas and Dharmasūtras made available slave[63] and hired labour (in the form of śūdras) for economic production. This development severely affected the economic competence of the woman as a primary producer. Unlike the earlier period, references to women taking an active part in economic production are very rare.[64] Consequently, womens' role in society, especially of those belonging to the upper stratum, became confined mainly to procreation and, at best, tending to household needs.[65] Here we may note that the early Brāhmaṇical texts appear to have focused mainly upon the upper stratum to the exclusion of all other sections of society. Rules pertaining to the duties of women expounded in them would, therefore, seem to have a greater bearing for women of that particular social category.

Expanding agriculture also gave rise to the institution of private property and firmly entrenched the patriarchal system of family.[66]

This is borne out by the fact that whereas, in the *Ṛgveda, pitṛs* or manes denote communal ancestors to whom worship is offered collectively, in the *Atharvaveda, pitṛs* denote three ascendants of the male ego.[67] Property inheritance now became patrilineal and the importance of male progeny increased considerably.[68] A major outcome of this development was the overthrow of the 'mother right'. Since, in a patrilineal society, the problem of paternity is vital,[69] in order to ensure the wife's fidelity to her husband, the woman was now required to always remain under the guardianship of some male member of the family, be it the father, brother or son. Thus, according to Friedrich Engels, 'In order to guarantee the fidelity of the wife, that is the paternity of children, the woman is placed in the man's absolute power; if he kills her, he is but exercising his right.'[70] Promiscuity in the case of women, therefore, began to be severely condemned. Monogamy for women began to be enforced;[71] for men could still enjoy a fair amount of sexual permissiveness in the form of polygamy and prostitution.[72] It is stated in the *Gopatha Brāhmaṇa* (III.20), 'One man may have many wives but one wife must not have more than one husband.'

The development thus marked a transition from the concept of collective or group ownership to individual ownership right exercised over the girl, first by the father and then by her husband. In the *Arthaśāstra* (III.2), the term used for it is *svamya*. The development was significant for it would largely account for women being bracketed along with property in contemporary literature.[73] Yāska in the *Nirukta* (3.4), in fact, went to the extent of observing that women could be given away both in gift or sale (*strinām dānavikrayatisarga vidyaṁte*).

Under the circumstances, marriage came to be virtually regarded as the gift of the daughter by the father[74] to the bridegroom. The loss of the economic competence of women led to such gifts bearing a more unilateral character. The use of the term *kaṅyādāna* for marriage becomes appropriate mainly in this context.[75] Significantly, the term 'gift' in the Germanic languages still has two meanings of 'present' and 'betrothal'.[76] Likewise, the term *sadāna* in Arabic means both alms and bride-price.

Along with the change in the concept of individual ownership right, another development there took place, which seems to characterize most patriarchal societies.[77] In order to safeguard and ensure the absolute chastity of the girl, her marriage, soon after she crossed the age of puberty or even earlier, began to be strongly recommended.[78] Consequently, if, on the one hand, it was considered the father's right to gift his daughter in marriage, it now also became obligatory for him to marry her off at the right age. Manu's (IX.93) dictum is quite unequivocal in this regard: 'But he who takes to wife a girl under menses shall not pay anything to her father; for the latter has lost his dominion over her in consequence of his preventing her menses from bearing fruit.' Kauṭilya makes a similar stipulation in the *Arthaśāstra* (III.2).

Compared to the earlier period, the position of the father *vis-à-vis* his daughter, therefore, became more ambiguous, if not wholly reversed. It was no longer a question of right but a matter of duty for him to marry her off before she reached the age of puberty. Instead of asking for the bride-price,[79] as he was prone to do earlier, the father now had to arrange for *vahatu*, i.e. he was required to bedeck the girl with ornaments and fine clothes, and bestow presents on the bridegroom.[80] Just as bride-price compensates the bride's family for the loss of an active productive member, dowry (*vahatu*; the more recent terms used for it being *daj* and *dahej*), in more advanced agricultural societies, compensates the groom's family for the addition of a dependent non-productive member.[81]

A natural outcome of the above development was that marriage through abduction (*rākṣasa*) or purchase (*asura*), which had been greatly favoured in the pastoral stage of culture, began to be condemned in the new social milieu.[82] Manu (III.51; IX.98; XII.6) severely condemns the acceptance of money by the father of the girl from an intended bridegroom. The same postulate was later stretched to the extent that even food offered by the bridegroom or his kinsmen was considered taboo by the members of the girl's family.[83] Even though we may not fully agree with G.M. Tripathi's assertion that the *rākṣasa*, *asura* and *paiśāca* forms of marriage were practised by non-Āryan races of the same name,[84] there can be no doubt that these were more characteristic of the pre-agricultural stage of cultural development.[85] It is significant that except for the *rākṣasa* form of marriage, which continued to be recommended for members of the martial kṣatriya caste[86] (who would not stoop to accept a gift but preferred the forceful abduction of the girl), the other forms became confined mainly to the two lower castes.[87]

Letting a daughter remain unmarried could now bring the greatest dishonour to the father and his entire family. Girls now began to be looked upon more as a burden than an asset from the economic point of view. In the *Atharvaveda* (33.1), the term *kṛpaṇam* has been used for the daughter.[88] The use of such other appellatives as *pitṛsad* and *agru* for the unmarried daughter clearly show the low esteem in which she came to be held in society.[89] Instead of being an object of voluntary gift, she now perforce became a virtual liability to her father. This development was significant for it brought about a vital change in the very concept of marriage. Marriage no longer entailed the transference of proprietary right over the daughter but that of responsibilities of guardianship from the father to the bridegroom.[90] According to the *Vaikhānasa Gṛhyasūtra* (III.2), the father, while bestowing the hand of the girl on the latter, declared in no uncertain terms: 'I will give her for *dharma*, progeny and prosperity'. In reply, the bridegroom had to solemnly vow that he would never fail her in his pursuit of *dharma*, *artha* and *kāma*.[91] Thus, as rightly held by Westermarck, 'the paternal authority of the archaic type . . . formed only a transitional stage in the history of human institutions'.[92]

As the complete relinquishment of property right over the gift-object is deemed central to all forms of gift-making,[93] the gift of a daughter in the changed social ethos could hardly be regarded as a regular gift. It is to be treated as a gift or *dāna* only with due reservations. In fact, it was primarily the economic subservience of the girl to her father which made the bestowal of her hand in marriage bear the aspect of *dāna*. In actual fact, the father does not seem to have wielded any real proprietary hold over the daughter. His control over her did not extend beyond the right of guardianship. Thus, it is clearly recognized in the Dharmaśāstras that if the parents failed to find an eligible husband for her, the latter was free to find one for herself,[94] the clear implication being that the daughter could not be disposed of arbitrarily by the father. She could be given away in marriage only to an eligible suitor.[95] The bridegroom similarly did not acquire through marriage complete proprietary powers over his wife, including those of sale or disposal at will.[96] On the contrary, according to Dharmaśāstric stipulations, he was bound by a definite oath to treat her with due respect.[97]

However, there were certain other factors which tended to emphasize the element of gift in the bestowal of a daughter's hand in marriage. With the break-up of the tribal social order, the element of reciprocity in marriage lessened considerably. Reciprocal exchanges of womenfolk between tribal groups or clans no longer characterized the institution of marriage. Instead, the caste stratification of society led to the tightening of the rules of exogamy. Although, in the *Ṛgveda*, we frequently come across the use of the term *gotra* in the sense of a cowpen or herd or, at best, as explained by Sāyaṇa, in the sense of an assemblage (*samūha*)[98] or group of persons, it is nowhere used in the sense of the descendant of a common patriarchal ancestor, as came to be in the Smṛtis.[99] In fact, even the *Āśvalāyana* and *Pāraskara Gṛhyasūtras* are completely silent about the marriage of persons having the same *gotra* and *pravara*. It is only in the later Sūtra and Dharmaśāstra texts that *sagotra* marriages were totally forbidden.[100] The development, therefore, lent a more unilateral aspect to marriage.[101] A daughter's marriage, accordingly, came to be increasingly imbued with the aspect of *dāna*.

The giving of a daughter's hand in marriage, as in any other form of gift, marked the termination of the latter's association with her natal lineage group and her permanent induction into the lineage or *gotra* of her husband.[102] However, it is significant that even though the girl ceased to belong to her father's *gotra* and could not revert to it even after her husband died, unlike any other pure form of gift, the ties of affection based on blood relationship, were never completely severed between the girl and her parents. As pointed out by M. Strathern 'although disposable they (women) are not alienable in the way that commodities are alienable'.[103] Parents, therefore, continued to exercise claims of affection over her even after she had been formally handed over to the bridegroom.

Another feature which brought into focus the aspect of gift in the marriage of a daughter was the element of self-sacrifice entailed. The daughter was to be given for the happiness and well-being of another family or *kūla*,[104] while the son was to be brought up for selfish motives, i.e. for the continuation and prosperity of one's own family. The sacrifice involved in the gift of a daughter was, therefore, much greater than what was entailed in the gift of the most cherished of material possessions. *Kanyādāna*, hence, came to be regarded as the supreme gift, yielding the highest spiritual merit. Perhaps certain rites connected with ritual *dāna* such as the gift of a daughter made with libations of water and the payment of *dakṣiṇā* at the time of the bestowal of her hand in marriage, may have further heightened its ritual character and given to it a greater semblance to *dāna*. Thus, whereas the element of bilateral exchange in marriage is found to be more prominent in pre-agricultural tribal societies, the element of gift comes to the fore more in the subsequent surplus-producing stratified societies. Here, with the withdrawal of women from public production, marriage tended to bear a more unilateral character. It is not surprising, therefore, that from the time of the composition of the Sūtra texts, the rite of *kanyādāna* began to figure as a prominent, essential part of the marriage ceremony.

NOTES

1. *Baudhāyana Dharmasūtra*, I.2.20.3-5; *Āpastamba Dharmasūtra*, II.5.11. 17-20; *Vasiṣṭha Dharmasūtra*, I.30-32; *Manusmṛti*, III.35.
2. *Mbh.* Anuśāsana Parva, 137, 24-26, tr. K.M. Ganguly, vol. XI, p. 280.
3. *Ṛgveda*, X.85.9.
4. Ibid., X.85.244.
5. Ibid., X.85.24-25.
6. S. Jayal, *The Status of Women in the Epics*, Delhi, 1966, p. 63.
7. *Baudhāyana Dharmasūtra*, I. 2.20.3-5; *Gautama Dharmasūtra*, II.5.17-20; *Vasiṣṭha Dharmasūtra*, I.30-32.
8. S. Dhar and M.K. Dhar, *Evolution of Family Hindu Law*, p. 108.
9. *Ṛgveda*, X.85.
10. *Vasiṣṭha Dharmasūtra*, XVII.70; *Manusmṛti*, IX.88.
11. J.J. Bachofen, Mutterrecht, Stuttgart, 1861.
12. J.F. McLennan, *Studies in Ancient History*, comprising a reprint of *Primitive Marriage*, London, 1886.
13. L.H. Morgan, *Ancient Society*, London, 1877.
14. J. Lubbock, *The Origin of Civilization and the Primitive Condition of Man*, London, 1870.
15. F. Engels, *The Origin of the Family, Private Property and the State*, Calcutta, 1943, p. 4.
16. E.A. Westermarck, *History of Marriage*, London, 1891, pp. 116-71.
17. C. Staniland Wake, *The Development of Marriage and Kinship*, Chicago, rpt., 1967, pp. 14-53.
18. V. Gordon Childe, *Man Makes Himself*, p.123.
19. V. Nath, 'Women as Property and Women's Right to Property', *IHR*; A.S. Altekar, *The Position of Women in Hindu Civilization*, p. 179.

20. *Ṛgveda*, II.3.6 (*tantum*).
21. Ibid., II.32.4 (*śivyatvapaḥ*); X.71.9.
22. Altekar, op. cit., p. 179.
23. *Ṛgveda*, VIII.80; VIII.91.5-6.
24. Ibid., IV.12.3.
25. Ibid., I.191.14 (*udakam kumbhiniriva*).
26. Ibid., V.30.9; I.112.10.
27. R.S. Sharma, 'Conflict, Distribution and Differentiation in Ṛgvedic Society', *PIHC*, 1977, p. 179.
28. *Rgveda*, X.18.7-8; *Atharvaveda*, X.3.1-12.
29. Ibid., I.48.6; I.123; II.124.8; IV.58; VIII.2.5; X.86.10; B.S. Upadhyaya, *Women in Ṛgveda*, New Delhi, 1974, pp. 40-5.
30. Macdonell and Keith, *Vedic Index*, p. 480; G.S. Ghurye, *Vedic India*, p. 229.
31. S. Jayaswal, 'Women in Early India, Problems and Perspectives', *PIHC*, 1981, p. 55.
32. *Ṛgveda*, VIII.19.36; VIII.46.33; Braj Deo Prasad Roy, *The Later Vedic Economy*, p. 60.
33. *Ṛgveda*, X.85.45.
34. Maurice Godelier, *Perspectives in Marxist Anthropology*, Cambridge, 1977, pp. 37-8.
35. P.S. Schebesta, *Among Congo Pygmies*, 1933, p. 128; 'The more women available, the more food'.
36. Sufficient evidence contained in the *Ṛgveda* (X.10) proves its observance in the early Vedic period. Lewis H. Morgan, *Systems of Consanguinity and Affinity of the Human Family*, Washington, 1871.
37. E. Adamson, Hoebel and Everett L. Frost, *Cultural and Social Anthropology*, pp. 174-6.
38. R.S. Sharma, *Perspectives in Social and Economic History of Early India*, New Delhi, 1983, p. 35.
39. Godelier, op. cit., p. 48.
40. Ibid.
41. *Śatapatha Brāhmaṇa*, I.8.3.6.
42. *Manusmṛti*, III.5.
43. Lucy Mair, *An Introduction to Social Anthropology*, p. 197.
44. E.A.H. Blunt, *The Caste System of Northern India*, p. 69.
45. Lévi-Strauss, op. cit., p. 116.
46. *Vājasaneyī Saṁhitā*, XXIII.30-1; *Taittirīya Saṁhitā*, VII.4.19.2-3.
47. Robin Fox, *Kinship and Marriage*, p. 117; Maurice Godelier, *Perspectives in Marxist Anthropology*, Cambridge, 1977, p. 104.
48. *Ṛgveda*, X.18.7-8; *Atharvaveda*, X.31.12.
49. A.N. Saha, 'Evolution of Family and Matrimonial Law', *Folklore*, XXII, i, pp. 3-4.
50. Jayaswal, op. cit., p. 57.

51. J.J. Bachofen, *Das Mutterect*, Stuttgart, 1861; F. Engels, *The Origin of the Family, Private Property and the State*, p. 10.
52. P.V. Kane, *History of Dharmaśāstra*, vol. II, pt. i, p. 438; R.S. Sharma, *Perspectives in Social and Economic History*, pp. 35-8.
53. M. Strathern, 'Subject or Object', in *Women and Property: Women as Property*, pp. 163-4.
54. Max Gluckman, *Politics, Law and Ritual in Tribal Society*, Oxford, 1977, p. 47.
55. *Ṛgveda*, X.85.
56. *Āśvalāyana Gṛhyasūtra*, VII.6.2.
57. Dhar and Dhar, op. cit., p. 113.
58. Haripada Chakraborty, *Socio-economic Life of India in the Vedic Age*, p. 87; S. Rao Shastri, *Women in the Vedic Age*, p. 31.
59. Renee Hirschon, ed., *Women and Property: Women as Property*, p. 10.
60. Westermarck, op. cit., pp. 116-71.
61. Schrader, *Prehistoric Antiquities of the Aryan People*.
62. *Ṛgveda*, X.27.12; Haripada Chakraborty, op. cit., p. 86.
63. R.S. Sharma, *Śūdras in Ancient India*, p. 51, 'Slaves working on land are first heard of in the Śrautasūtras'.
64. Altekar, op. cit., p. 179.
65. *Manusmṛti*, IX.11.
66. Engels, op. cit., p. 79.
67. Jayaswal, op. cit., p. 56.
68. R. Thapar, *Ancient Indian Social History*, p. 32.
69. Robin Fox, op. cit., p. 115.
70. Engels, op. cit., p. 58.
71. *Mahābhārata*, Sabhā Parva, 61.35.
72. *Aitareya Brāhmaṇa*, III.12.12.
73. Sharma, *Perspectives in Social and Economic History*, pp. 39-43.
74. *Pāraskara Gṛhyasūtra*, I.4.15.
75. *Śatapatha Brāhmaṇa*, IV.1.5.6-7.
76. Levi-Strauss, op. cit., p. 63.
77. Mair, op. cit., p. 91.
78. Kane, op. cit., p. 445; Altekar, op. cit., p. 54.
79. *Mahābhārata*, Anuśāsana Parva, 45.19-20.
80. *Manusmṛti*, III.27-28.
81. Ursula Sharma, 'Dowry in North India: Its Consequences for Women', in *Women and Property: Women as Property*, op. cit., p. 67.
82. *Mahābhārata*, Ādi Parva, 67.12; Anuśāsana Parva, 45.19-20; XIII.44.8; *Āpastamba Dharmasūtra*, II.6.13.10; *Baudhāyana Dharmasūtra*, I.2.20-1.
83. Jonathan Parry, 'The Gift, the Indian Gift and the "Indian Gift"', *Man*, XXI, 1986, p. 461.
84. G.M. Tripathi, *Marriage Forms under Ancient Hindu Laws*, pp. 7-11.

85. R.M. Das, *Women in Manu and His Seven Commentators*, p. 130.
86. *Mahābhārata*, Ādi Parva, 219-22.
87. Sharma, op. cit., p. 50.
88. *Aitareya Brāhmaṇa*, VIII.31.3.
89. Shivraj Shastri, *Ṛgvedic Kāl Mein Pārivārika Sambandha*, Meerut, 1962, p. 233.
90. Mair, op. cit., p. 91; Altekar, op. cit., p. 47.
91. Ram Gopal, *India of the Vedic Kalpasūtras*, pp. 225-6.
92. Westermarck, op. cit., p. 235.
93. *Pūrva Mīmāṁsā*, VI.7.1.7; *Manusmṛti*, VIII.199.
94. *Baudhāyana Dharmasūtra*, IV.1.14; *Vasiṣṭha Dharmasūtra*, XVIII.59; *Manusmṛti*, IX.90; *Mahābhārata*, Anuśāsana Parva, 44.15.
95. *Manusmṛti*, IX.88.
96. *Mahābhārata*, Anuśāsana Parva, 44.45.
97. *Vaikhānasa Gṛhyasūtra*, III.2; *Mahābhārata*, Ādi Parva, 68.40.
98. *Ṛgveda*, II.23.18; VI.65.5.
99. Haripada Chakraborty, op. cit., pp. 77-8; Macdonell and Keith, op. cit., p. 475.
100. *Gobhila Gṛhyasūtra*, III.4.5; *Āpastamba Dharmasūtra*, II.5.15.
101. *Mahābhārata*, Anuśāsana Parva, 44; Parry, op. cit., p. 462.
102. Kane, op. cit., p. 481.
103. Strathern, op. cit., p. 165; C.A. Gregory, 'Gifts to Men and Gifts to God', *Man*, vol. XV, no. iv, 1980, p. 641.
104. Mair, op. cit., p. 92.

7

Mahādāna: Dynamics of Gift-Economy

Dāna or ritual gift-making has been integral to the Brāhmaṇical belief-system right from the age of the *Ṛgveda*.[1] In fact, the ritual symbolism of *dāna* as inferred through semantic and contextual analysis proves it to be a major and constant source of gaining prestige, and an important means of imparting ritual purity and status in widely different social and religious contexts.[2] The concept of the sixteen *mahādānas* or great gifts is not met with earlier than the time of the epics and the Purāṇas, when it came to be imbued with a definite ritual connotation. This sudden development, therefore, raises certain key questions: How do we account for such a ritual formation? What special circumstances led to its conceptualization? What is perhaps most important is the precise time of its origin. Even though the institution of *dāna* had been in existence since the inception of the Brāhmaṇic religious system, it was only after a lapse of almost fifteen centuries that the concept of *mahādāna* could be formulated and provided with a ritual format by the composers of the Purāṇas.

Terms such as *mahādāna*,[3] *mahādānika*[4] (officer-in-charge of donation), *mahādānapati*[5] (munificent donor) and even *mahādānapatnī*[6] (liberal female donor) occur in post-Mauryan inscriptions. These terms do not always figure in Brāhmaṇical religious contexts and the epigraphic records in which they appear are forthcoming from outlying regions such as Taxila in Peshawar and Nāgārjunakoṇḍa in Āndhra. The term *mahādāna* as used in these inscriptions and in early Buddhist texts, instead of bearing any special ritual connotation, simply denotes munificent gift-making. It also does not have any association with the number sixteen. In fact, even in the *Mahābhārata* (Āśrama-Vāsika Parva 5.15; 19.15; 23.17), although *mahādāna* is used in a more specialized sense, any detailed procedure connected with it is conspicuously lacking.

The earliest theoretical exposition of the concept of sixteen *mahādānas* is found in a section of the *Matsya Purāṇa* (Chapters 271-89), which is believed to have been composed as late as *c.* AD 550-650[7] in the western Deccan[8] region, where the practice of land grants is also known to have initially taken roots.[9] It is interesting, therefore, to find out if there existed some kind of linkage between these two forms of ritual gift-making, both of which originated in the same region of the Indian subcontinent and gained currency almost at the same time.

The composer of the *Matsya Purāṇa* was apparently aware of the innovative nature of the *mahādāna* rite. In a verse (274.18), he declares: 'Sixteen great ordinances that have not been mentioned elsewhere until now, I shall now explain before you.' The relevant section of the *Matsya Purāṇa*, besides enumerating the sixteen great gifts (viz., *hiraṇyagarbha*, *brahmāṇḍa*, *viśvacakra*, *saptasāgara*, *kāmadhenu*, *kalpapādapa*, *kalpalatā*, *aśvaratha*, *hiraṇyāśva*, *hemahastiratha*, *ratnadhenu*, *mahābhūtaghaṭa*, *tulāpuruṣa*, *gosahasra*, *dharādāna*, *pañcalāṅgalaka*), furnishes the guidelines and procedural format pertaining to each *mahādāna*. It also mentions the purpose and degree of spiritual merit obtained through the great gifts.

An identical list of sixteen *mahādānas* with minimal procedural details is also contained in the *Agni Purāṇa* (Chapter 210.1-4), dated roughly between AD 800 to 1500[10] though it is difficult to determine the place of its first compilation.[11] In this text, there is evidence of a slight change in focus. Its composer, instead of devoting more space to the *mahādāna*, has dealt with other innovative forms of *dānas* such as the ten different kinds of *merudānas* (gifts of hills formed of various precious substances) and an equal number of *dhenudānas* (gift of different articles arranged in the shape of a cow). It is to be determined, therefore, as to how far the composer was seeking to widen their popular base and context by suggesting such variables and diluting the opulent nature of the *mahādānas*.

In the *Liṅga Purāṇa* (II.28-43), which is dated around *c.* AD 1000,[12] the sixteen *mahādānas* receive a more elaborate treatment, though their names and visages are found to have undergone considerable change. Perhaps the only features which are common to both sets of *mahādānas* are the number sixteen and the element of symbolism so strongly manifest in their names and ritual details.

Out of the sixteen *mahādānas* listed in the *Liṅga Purāṇa*, four appear in their original forms, namely *hiraṇyagarbha*, *hiraṇyāśva*, *gosahasra* and *kalpapādapa*. The popularity of these four great gifts is attested by contemporary epigraphic records.[13] This may also account for their remaining relatively untampered. Of the remaining twelve *mahādānas*, *tulāpuruṣa*, though at par with *hiraṇyagarbha* in popularity, is renamed *tulādhirohana*; *dharādāna* appears as *suvarṇamedinī*; *viśvacakra* becomes *viśveśvara* and *hemahastiratha* has been recast as *hiraṇyagajadāna*. Another variant of *hiraṇyagajadāna*, which figures for the first time, is a *mahādāna* called *hiraṇyavṛṣa*. It seems to have replaced the *pañcalāṅgalaka mahādāna*. The author of the *Liṅga Purāṇa*, by substituting the *hiraṇyavṛṣa* for the *mahālāṅgalaka*, was perhaps trying to retain the agrarian cast and spirit of this particular *mahādāna*. The concept of some *mahādānas,* such as *hemadhenu*, *tiladhenu*, *tilaparvata* and *sūkṣmaparvata* would seem to be based upon the various forms of *merudānas* and *dhenudānas* listed in the *Agni Purāṇa*. Amongst the more innovative forms of *mahādānas* introduced by the author of the *Liṅga Purāṇa* are *lakṣmīdhara*, *lokapāla* and *kanyādāna*.

Before trying to account for the changing Purāṇic tradition related to the *mahādānas*, a scrutiny of the context in which the sixteen great gifts are discussed in the *Matsya Purāṇa*, as well as an analysis of the procedural details furnished therein, may help determine the precise nature and historical dialectics of such a ritual formation.

An analysis of the contents of those chapters of the *Matsya Purāṇa* which immediately precede the section devoted to the sixteen great gifts is quite revealing. The sequential order of thematic discussion shows that whereas the *mahādāna* ceremonial is dealt with at great length from Chapter 274 onwards, the three chapters immediately preceding it mention, in the Purāṇic prophetic style, the names of numerous supra-regional, regional and sub-regional political powers which shall rule over the earth during the Kali age, characterized by innumerable ills (273.24-34).

The mention of the Śrīparvatīya Āndhras (273.17), Ābhiras, Gardabhilas (273.18), Kilakilas (273.24), etc., in the list of local dynasties and along with such foreign powers as the Śakas (273.18), Tuṣāras, Yavanas and Hūṇas (273.19) is significant, as it tends to underline the role of these ruling dynasties in causing political ferment during the period when the Purāṇas as a separate genre of literature began to be written. The phenomenon is found to be particularly prominent in the western Deccan, where the *Matsya Purāṇa* is believed to have been composed. That many of these local dynasties were either of tribal or doubtful origin is clearly indicated by their names such as the Gardabhilas or the Kilakilas. This is especially evident in the case of the Guruṇḍas as they are clubbed with the śūdras and attributed a *mleccha* origin (273.22).

As for the exposition of the Kali age paradigm, despite an ongoing debate[14] on its nature and adequacy in making a convincing case in favour of a feudal formation in early medieval India, the data contained in the *Matsya Purāṇa* does indicate some kind of social turmoil and cultural ferment. This is especially so when viewed from the Brāhmaṇical perspective, which may have been as much the result of the disaffection felt by the śūdra peasantry labouring under serious social and economic constraints as the outcome of resistance by preliterate groups undergoing acculturation. Significantly, the latter had come to be referred to by the generic term *mlecchas* in contemporary Brāhmaṇical literature.[15] Thus, of the many evils which are said to have assailed the Kali age, the worst, according to the author of the *Matsya Purāṇa*, was the intermixing of the members of twice-born classes with the *mlecchas* (273.25), as well as the flouting of *varṇa* and *āśrama* rules by them. It is significant to note here that the description of how people during the Kali age shall become unrighteous and subsist on 'fruits, roots and leaves of trees', 'clad in tattered garments, barks and skins' and 'wander over the earth in search of livelihood', appears to be less apt for the people belonging to the mainstream social order and more applicable to the mountain and forest-dwelling ethnic groups. These were already affected by agricultural expansion in peripheral areas during the centuries following the Christian era, and were under increasing pressure from acculturating agencies, and finding it hard to adjust to an alien mode of production and social ethos. The fact that a very large number of such nomadic groups and tribes have been identified and listed by the composers of the Purāṇas[16] shows their deep concern for the impact that such a social upheaval was likely to have on Brāhmaṇical society and the urgent need to diffuse the crisis in the best manner possible.

The treatment of political and social upheaval being immediately followed, in the *Matsya Purāṇa*, by an exposition of a wholly innovative form of gift-making, therefore, can make sense only if there existed some sort of causal connection between the two developments—a connection which also provided the rationale for such a sequential thematic ordering by the author. If we correlate the *mahādāna* ceremonialism with the phenomenon of the rise of local dynasties and the problems created by the processes of acculturation projected through the Kali age paradigm, it becomes obvious that the practice of making great gifts was meant largely to offset the gravity of the political situation and diffuse the crisis that threatened the traditional social order. The formulation of *mahādāna* ritual in a Purāṇic text composed in the western Deccan region around the middle of the first millennium AD is of great significance, since the earliest epigraphic record attesting the practice of land grants is also forthcoming from the same area. It even roughly corresponds to the same period because the broad time-frame allotted to the *Matsya Purāṇa* cannot be assumed to be exact. In fact, we have to make due allowance for a gestation period when the idea of *mahādāna* must have germinated and developed. We need, therefore, to look for the origins of the two ritual formations in the process of social-economic change triggered off during post-Mauryan times and accentuated in western parts of peninsular India, which occupied a geographically and commercially advantageous position. Determining the extent to which these forms of ritual *dāna* served as substitutes for each other and fulfilled a similar purpose, and identifying the specific donor-categories targeted through them, is possible only by referring to the socio-economic developments during the early centuries of the Christian era, when the Kali age crisis is believed to have deepened.

During the post-Mauryan phase, the western Deccan experienced maximum economic growth, especially in the field of trade and commerce, accounting for the prosperity of the region in general and of the mercantile community in particular.[17] However, to meet the growing demand for Indian goods in foreign markets, there was a need to promote agricultural production and boost cash-crops, besides stepping up commodity production. Thus, the reclamation of waste-land became necessary. In contemporary records of land grants, we come across recommendations for planting specific kinds of trees of commercial value.[18] Any agricultural expansion in the forested areas was bound to be resented by the indigenous groups dwelling there. It goes to the credit of the leaders of non-conformist religious systems and the brāhmaṇas, who were quick to realize the need to win over such tribal segments by at least partially integrating them into the mainstream social order.

It was, therefore, as much the need to promote agricultural expansion in peripheral areas as to acculturate the pre-literate groups which stood in its way, that land grants began to be issued by ruling chiefs and rulers in favour of religious institutions and brāhmaṇas.[19] The latter, in their role of religious ideologues and as repositories of religious authority, were best equipped to perform the task of disseminating traditional cultural values amongst ethnic groups rooted in strong tribal traditions.

Besides being instrumental in the reclamation of wasteland, land grants to religious beneficiaries proved to be an important means of gaining spiritual merit and social prestige for the royal donors. It easily accounts for the popularity of the institution of land grants with royal donors in general, but more specially with those ruling chiefs who lacked an illustrious ancestry and were still trying to gain religious validation for their newly-won political power. Our sources, especially Purāṇic and epigraphic records, testify to the rise of numerous political powers from relative obscurity to political eminence in the western Deccan. Amongst the more well-known powers which dominated the political scene in the region around this time, the names of the Ābhiras,[20] Ikṣvākus,[21] Cuṭus, Ānandas,[22] and Nāgās, are especially noteworthy. Significantly, most of them betray strong tribal antecedents and influence.

Although the practice of making land grants was confined mostly to rulers and their kinsmen in the beginning, gradually even the landowning commercial magnates began to utilize this new form of ritual gift-making to earn spiritual merit and prestige.[23] However, the beneficiaries of their munificence were mostly monastic institutions, belonging to non-conformist sects such as Buddhism and Jainism. The prosperous mercantile community evidently found these religious systems more amenable to their needs and interests than the traditional Brāhmaṇical system.[24]

Such a development was bound to create stiff competition for patronage and gift-sharing between the active members of dissenting religious sects and the brāhmaṇas. It became, therefore, necessary for Brāhmaṇical ideologues to woo the affluent merchant community more actively. This is amply manifest from the Purāṇas who began lauding the acquisition of wealth in no uncertain terms. According to the *Matsya Purāṇa*, 'One should acquire, increase and protect wealth' (274.1). The author of the same Purāṇa also commends the acquisition of wealth by a virtuous person (274.2). The *Liṅga Purāṇa* (II.28-56), similarly stipulates that on the occasion of *tulādhirohaṇadāna*, *homa* had to be performed to the accompaniment of the *mantra*, '. . . may we be the lords of wealth'. In fact, one of the sixteen gifts listed in the *Liṅga Purāṇa* (II.36) is *Lakṣmīdharadāna*, which was meant to increase the prosperity of the performer (*mahādaiśvaryavardhanam*).

It was in keeping with this more accommodative Brāhmaṇical stance towards material prosperity in general, and towards that of traders and merchants in particular, that new and more innovative forms of rituals began to be formulated, which could hold greater appeal for the latter segment of society. Several *mahādānas*, especially the *saptasāgara mahādāna*,[25] appeared to have been conceived mainly to fulfil this need.

If some *mahādānas* were meant for the rich merchants wanting to celebrate their newly-acquired wealth, there were other forms of great gifts such as the *tulāpuruṣa mahādāna* or the *hiraṇyagarbha mahādāna*, which appear to have been more specifically designed to confer ritual status and validate the newly-established royal power of the performer. They were ideally suited for those tribal chiefs who were trying to participate in the mainstream power struggle. In this respect, the great gifts are found to discharge almost the same function which was served by land grants, except that in the case of the *mahādānas*, the ritual symbolism associated with them made them a more potent means of elevating ritual status. It explains the greater appeal of the great gifts for the members of the newly-established dynasties of the western Deccan.[26]

MAHĀDĀNAS: THEIR RITUAL SYMBOLISM

The *mahādāna* ceremonial procedures as delineated in the *Matsya Purāṇa* focus mainly upon the occasions on which they were supposed to be performed, the articles to be gifted, the qualifications of officiating priests, the criteria for selecting gift recipients, the special *mantras* to be used and the particular deities to be invoked on the occasion. The relevant section of the *Matsya Purāṇa* also specified numerous other ingredients needed for the *mahādāna* rite, as well as the size and the structural layout of the place of its performance.

MAHĀDĀNA: A MECHANISM OF VALIDATION AT PAR WITH VEDIC SACRIFICE

Our study shows that the composer of the *Matsya Purāṇa* was attempting to model the *mahādānas* on the lines of Vedic sacrifices. This is evident from the invocatory verses, which had to be recited at the commencement of the *mahādāna* ceremony. The deity had to be invoked with the words: 'Be pleased to guard this sacrifice' (274.47). The procedural stipulations, moreover, required the construction of sacrificial altars (*vedī*) and sacrificial cavities (*kuṇḍa*) at the ritual site. Such structural components being generally associated with Vedic *yajñas* further emphasized the sacrificial aspect of the *mahādānas*. The qualifications prescribed for the officiating priests also made it incumbent for them to be well-versed in the Vedas (*veda-vida*, 274.37) and specially proficient in Vedic ritual-lore (*veda-vidhānadakṣa*).

As in the case of Vedic sacrifices, the generally opulent character of the *mahādānas* must have similarly restricted the purview of the donor categories. Only members of a very small elite group, comprising ruling chiefs and commercial magnates who had the necessary wherewithal, could afford to undertake them. Moreover, the pastoral base of some of the gift-items, which were required to be distributed at the *mahādāna* rite, made the entire ceremonial reminiscent of the great *soma-yajñas* of Vedic times. For example, at the *gosahasra mahādāna*, each *ṛtvija* or priest had to be presented with a minimum of 10 cows, for, according to a covering injunction, the gift of one cow is downright sinful (278.20). In fact, the conceptualization of this particular *mahādāna* would seem to have been largely inspired by the current practice of giving, at the time of any *yajña* performance, 1,000 cows as the sacrificial fee (*dakṣiṇā gavām sahasram*). The latter finds frequent mention in inscriptions belonging to the early centuries of the Christian era.[27] The degree of spiritual merit derived from a *mahādāna* is also stated to be at least at par with the Vedic sacrifice. For instance, the performance of the *kalpa-pādapa mahādāna* is said to yield as much merit as an *aśvamedha* sacrifice (277.18).

Such an explicit attempt to cast the *mahādānas* in the Vedic sacrificial mould suggests a certain identity of purpose which they were expected to serve, as well as some common politico-economic expediencies which occasioned them. Most anthropologists agree that any grandiose ceremonial which involves an ostentatious display of wealth, either through wasteful destruction of valuable resources or through gift distribution or both, is meant to gain prestige and status within the group.[28]

In a traditional social order based on prestige economy, a ritual of this nature also performs an important legitimizing role. It becomes instrumental in sacralizing political power.[29] Religious support and the sanction of political authority becomes especially necessary when the contest for power gains urgency and momentum on account of the socio-economic forces of change and transition operative at the time. Transition from one mode of production to another is amply attested by our sources both in Vedic/post-Vedic as well as Gupta/post-Gupta times.

Whereas in the earlier period the pastoral-tribal order was fast giving way to a territorial state-system marked by attendant developments in the field of technology and surplus-production, in the later phase, the unicentric imperial structure, backed by a flourishing market-economy, was gradually eroded and replaced by a polycentric state system with a prominent feudal and regional base.

Consequently, despite vastly different material conditions prevailing during these two phases of early Indian history, the similarity in the nature of contest for political power provided common grounds for the growth of rituals, manifesting a remarkably similar cosmo-regal aspect. Both Vedic *yajñas* and Purāṇic *mahādānas* expectedly lent validation to the freshly acquired power of political contenders, particularly those belonging to obscure marginal groups who were finding it difficult to gain wider recognition for their regal status and authority. This is especially true of the later phase when strongly activated forces of agricultural expansion brought a large peripheral tribal segment within the vortex of mainstream culture and polity.

In Gupta/post-Gupta times, the demands of a rapidly advancing agrarian economy, the compulsions of commercial developments of a somewhat residual nature, and the constraints imposed by competing dissenting sects had come to negate the pastoral base of *yajña* ritualism and undermined its scope and viability.[30] In fact, as pointed out by V.S. Pathak, sacrifices such as *aśvamedha* and *rājasūya* were little heard of during the early medieval period in northern India.[31] The *Brahmā Purāṇa*, as quoted by Aparārka, describes the abandonment of sacrificial rituals in the Kali age.[32] Even epigraphs from the sixth century AD onwards occasionally mention the decline of Vedic activities in the Kali age.[33] The composer of the *Matsya Purāṇa*, therefore, displayed remarkable ingenuity in substituting *dāna* for sacrificial ritualism and adapting it to the specific requirements of the emergent social order, marked by agricultural expansion, regional state formation and a strongly manifest feudal ethos. The feudal aspect is reflected by the very prefix *mahā* used to emphasize the grandiose scale of the new form of gift-making.

The agrarian base of *mahādāna* is revealed by the inclusion of the gift of land or *dharādāna* (Chapter 284) in the list of sixteen great gifts. It was apparently done not so much to upgrade and glorify an already popular and widely practised form of gift-making as to emphasize its functional utility in and relevance to a predominantly agricultural milieu. However, in conformity with the general opulent nature of *mahādānas*, the performer of the *dharādāna* was required to gift a golden replica of the earth, shaped like Jambūdvīpa with mountains, rivers and oceans depicted on it. This aspect of the *mahādāna* is more clearly brought out in the *Liṅga Purāṇa*, in which it has been renamed *suvarṇamedinī mahādāna*.

Another form of great gift which fitted perfectly into the agrarian mould was the *pañcalāṅgalaka mahādāna* (Chapter 283). It entailed the gift of five ploughs made of wood of the finest quality, along with a plot of land and five pair of oxen with their horns covered with gold. However, as in the case of *dharādāna*, the rite connected with the *pañcalāṅgalaka mahādāna* also required the donor to gift five ploughs made of 5 to a 1,000 *palas* of gold.

Besides the agrarian base and feudal tenor of the *mahādānas*, their cosmo-regal aspect is strongly manifest through the procedural norms related to some of them. For example, the performer of *tulāpuruṣa mahādāna* was required to put on regal attire, including a coat-of-mail, sword, shield and ornaments (274.65). The Purāṇic injunction further stipulates that 'the king (*nareśvaraḥ*) eager for his prosperity should place more gold than that of his weight on the floor'. In the case of *gosahasra mahādāna*, its performer is stated to reign as a king for 100 *kalpas* (278.25). The exposition of the *mahādāna* ritual in the *Liṅga Purāṇa* (XXVIII.14) commences with an explicit reference to the sixteen types of charitable gifts which kings were supposed to undertake. In the context of *kalpapādapa mahādāna*, it is specially stated that by performing it a king will become an emperor (*rājā sārvabhaumo-bhaviṣyati*, *Liṅga Purāṇa*, I.32.9).

That the *mahādānas* had come to replace Vedic *yajñas*, especially after the seventh century AD, is affirmed by epigraphic data. Some of the kings who claim to have performed the *hiraṇyagarbha mahādāna* include Attivarman and Dāmodaravarman of the Ānanda dynasty,[34] Mādhavavarman of the Viṣṇukuṇḍin dynasty,[35] and Dantidurga of the Rāṣṭrakūṭa dynasty.[36] The *tulāpuruṣa mahādāna*[37] is known to have been performed by Yaśaḥkarṇa of the Kalacuri dynasty,[38] Jayapāla of Kāmarūpa,[39] the Candella ruler Dhaṅga,[40] the Kacchapaghāta ruler Mahipāla,[41] the Rāṣṭrakūṭa kings Dantidurga,[42] Indra III[43] and Govinda IV,[44] as well as the Gāhaḍavāla ruler Jayacandra.[45] King Lakṣmaṇasena of Bengal granted a village as *dakṣiṇā* when he performed the *hemāśvaratha mahādāna*.[46] The Gāhaḍavāla ruler, Govindacandra, is known to have performed the *pañcalāṅgalaka mahādāna* in Vikram Saṁvat 1181.[47] Similarly, the Candravatī grant belonging to Vikram Saṁvat 1156 mentions the performance of *gosahasra mahādāna* by another Gāhaḍavala king, Candradeva.[48]

Here, an analysis of the regional distribution and family background of the above-mentioned rulers may provide an insight into the developments related to *mahādāna* ritualism. Our study shows that all of them were trying to establish their royal credentials and stake their claim to political power in widely dispersed areas such as Assam (Jayapāladeva of Kāmarūpa), Bengal (Lakṣmaṇasena), different parts of the Deccan (the Rāṣṭrakūṭas of Mālkheḍ, the Viṣṇukuṇḍins and the Ānanda-gotras), and central India (kings belonging to the Candella, Kalacuri and Kacchapaghāta dynasties). In fact, excluding the Gāhaḍavāla rulers who were able to establish their rule over Kanauj after a close contest for power, the rest of the kings were engaged in a political struggle in regions other than the

Sanskritic core cultural zone. This would point to the popularity of *mahādāna* ritualism more in the peripheral zones, where forces of acculturation were visibly active, than in the upper and mid-Gaṅgā Valley regions.

The dynastic antecedents of a majority of the rulers mentioned above is less definitely known. Whatever we do know about them generally pertains to the domain of the mythical. Thus, no definite account of the ancestral background of Jayapāladeva of Kāmarūpa is forthcoming, though H.C. Ray considers him to be a scion of the dynastic line founded by Brahmapāla.[49] The latter claims descent from Naraka's race, which clearly represented a non-Āryan stock.[50]

The origins of the Senas of Bengal is equally shrouded in obscurity. According to Ray, they had come from Karnataka and settled in Rāḍha in West Bengal.[51] Similarly, the Rāṣṭrakūṭa kings like Dantidurga were still in the process of establishing their political hold over acquired territory and must have needed some kind of ritual validation for their newly-won power. As far as the Viṣṇukuṇḍins are concerned, although one of their kings claims the title of *Āndhrapati*, nothing positive is known about their dynastic antecendents.[52]

The origins of the Ānanda-gotras as well as that of some of the other powers which arose in the western Deccan was undisputedly tribal.[53] The same appears to be true of the Candellas of Jejākabhukti, the Kalacuris of Dahala and the Kacchapaghātas of Gwalior. In the case of the Candellas, both epigraphic evidence and traditions trace their genealogy to the Moon. In the Augasi grant, however, they are described as belonging to the line founded by sage Candrātreya (Candrātreya *vaṁśa*).[54]

Epigraphic records furnish an equally mythical lineage for the Kalacuris, connecting them with the Haihayas.[55] The latter, according to epic and Purāṇic tradition, were the descendants of Sahasrajīt, a son of Yadu.[56] In the case of the Kacchapaghātas, on the other hand, nothing is known about their ancestry.[57] Significantly, the nature of relationship of Mahipāla, the Kacchapaghāta king who claims making the great gift, with his immediate predecessor is also somewhat obscure.[58] This might have lent further urgency to the need for him to perform the *mahādāna* rite.

The wide popularity gained by the *mahādānas* mainly with the founders and scions of newly established dynasties would seem to underline its validatory role. In fact, in the new material context, the *mahādānas* appear to have served more or less the same function as was discharged by the *vrātyaṣṭoma* ritual in the earlier phase. The Vedic rite was specifically meant to be performed by *vrātya*, or fallen kṣatriyas, to overcome their social discredibility.[59]

REGENERATIVE ASPECT OF *MAHĀDĀNAS*

The sacramental aspect, particularly of the *hiraṇyagarbha mahādāna*, is highly accentuated. Whereas in most rites of passage, initiation by symbolically cutting asunder a person's bonds to his previous status in life is subtly achieved through a series of encoded ritual acts,[60] in the case of the *hiraṇyagarbha* rite, its very nomenclature and the main ceremonial performance is found to centre upon the theme of ritual rebirth. As pointed out by V.S. Agarwala, the word *hiraṇya* denotes the fecundating principle which is the Vedic symbol of *prāṇa* or life.[61] Since the other word *garbha* stands for the womb, the two terms put together would signify the life-giving process or the act of regeneration.

The ritual procedure enjoined in the *Matsya Purāṇa* (275.4-6) further required the performer of the *hiraṇyagarbha mahādāna* to get a jar made of gold shaped like a lotus with a golden string around it. It had to be filled with clarified butter and milk. Ten weapons, jewels, a sickle, gold, etc., had also to be placed inside this jar. On its two sides were placed a golden begging bowl, along with sesamum and other gems. The performer, while holding an image of the creator, Brahmā, in his hand, was required to sit with his head bent between his ankles, impersonating a foetus in the womb. The officiating priest then performed pre-natal rites such as *garbhādhāna* (performed at the time of conception), *puṁsavana* and *sīmantonnayana* (275.15-17). These were followed by post-natal ceremonies beginning with *jātakarma* which is normally performed immediately after the birth of a child. According to a stipulation contained in the *Liṅga Purāṇa* (II.29.12), at the *hiraṇyagarbha* ceremony, the rites beginning with *garbhādāna* should end with the rite of *viśvajīt*, which was meant to be performed only by kings. That the whole ceremony was a re-enactment of the birth of the person is clear from the words, which according to the *Matsya Purāṇa*, the performer of the *hiraṇyagarbha* had to address to the presiding deities: 'O Best of the *devas*, as I was born of thee in the mortal world, so let me be born again of divine form.' The rite later concluded with the distribution of all used articles and other valuable gift-items amongst brāhmaṇas, priests and the preceptor.

We come across a similar procedural format and ritual symbolism suggestive of the spiritual rebirth of the donor in the *brahmāṇḍa mahādāna.* According to the injunctions contained in the *Matsya Purāṇa* (Chapter 276), the *brahmāṇḍa*, or the cosmic egg symbolizing primeval creation, had to be made with 20 to 1,000 *palas* of gold, depending upon the means of the performer.

In this context, it is remarkable that amongst all the precious metals, gold, variously referred to as *hema*, *hiraṇya* and *suvarṇa*, is especially known in the Brāhmaṇical belief system for its purificatory quality. Since purification is an essential part of the sacralizing process, by combining an auspicious symbol such as *kumbha* with a purifying agent like gold, the Purāṇic composers sought to transform the *mahādāna* rites into a doubly potent legitimizing instrument. Since *hiraṇya* also symbolizes *jyotiḥ* or the light of Brahmā which manifests itself as *prāṇa* or the life-infusing principle, the cosmic egg in the *brahmāṇḍa mahādāna* being fashioned of gold made it into a powerful symbol of both ritual purification and rebirth.

Ritual rebirth in the *mahābhūtaghaṭa mahādāna* (Chapter 289) was similarly symbolized through the imagery of a golden jar (*ghaṭa* or *kumbha*) representing the womb. The analogy of the womb with the pitcher or jar is as common in tribal mythical lore as it was integral to the Vedic tradition. The fusion of two different strains of symbolism pertaining to rebirth and purification thus made the *mahādāna* an effective means of status elevation and change. Gold was, in fact, the predominant metal required to be used in the fashioning of most ingredients and gift-items related to all the 16 forms of *mahādānas.* Even the images of various deities, to whom worship was to be offered as part of the ritual performance, had to be made exclusively of gold. Beside highlighting the sacralizing role of the *mahādāna* ritual, such exaggerated importance being attached to gold was bound to also accentuate its opulent character.

MAHĀDĀNAS: THEIR OPULENT AND COSMO-REGAL ASPECT

The element of opulence is best projected in the *tulāpuruṣa mahādāna*, which held great appeal for both aspirant rulers and rich merchants.

According to the rules of this *mahādāna*, the donor was weighed against gold, which was later distributed among brāhmaṇas and ministrant priests. By incorporating a commonly held belief imbued with a strong magical overtone, namely, that a person could dispel evil influences by merely gifting some valuable substance which was equivalent to his own in weight, the author of the *Matsya Purāṇa* managed to impart to the *mahādāna* rite greater ritual efficacy and popular appeal. Moreover, his insistence upon gold being used as the chief precious metal at the *tulāpuruṣa mahādāna* transformed an ordinary folk practice into an impressive courtly ceremonial with all the attendant regalia. According to the *Liṅga Purāṇa* (II.28.77-8), the *mahādāna* rite was to be accompanied by vocal and instrumental music as well as dancing, which were supposed to add 'beauty and splendour to the ceremony'.

A large number of early medieval epigraphs testify to the *tulāpuruṣa mahādāna* being performed by rulers such as Mahipāla of the Kacchapaghāta dynasty,[62] Candrādityadeva of the Gāhaḍavālà dynasty,[63] Dhaṅga of the Candella dynasty,[64] Yaśaḥkarṇadeva[65] of the Kalacuri dynasty, and Indra III[66] and Govinda IV[67] of the Rāṣṭrakūṭa dynasty. That the *tulāpuruṣa mahādāna* was equally instrumental in sanctifying and validating political power is evident from the Rāṣṭrakūṭa inscription. The latter specifically mentions how the *tulāpuruṣa mahādāna* was performed by the Rāṣṭrakūṭa kings on the occasion of their *paṭṭa-bandha* ceremony, which was apparently a part of the coronation rite.[68] Thus, by highlighting the cosmo-regal aspect of *dāna* through the use of cosmic and other popular symbols, as is especially evident in the case of the *brahmāṇḍa* and *viśvacakra* forms of *mahādānas*, the author of the *Matsya Purāṇa* was able to both retain the centrality of the institution of ritual gift-making as well as to make it a more direct instrument for providing religious sanction to the political power of the performer.

In this context, we also need to take note of the fact that much before their being formally incorporated into the list of 16 great gifts, some forms of ritual gifts were already current and even widely popular. For instance, besides frequent epigraphic notices of the gift of land (*dharā* or *bhūmi*), we also come across a reference to the gift of the desire fulfilling *kalpa*-tree in the Hāthīgumphā inscription, which cannot be dated later than the second century BC.[69] Similarly,

Sanskrit and Pāli literature belonging to the pre-Christian era is replete with references to such gift-items as cows (*go*), horses (*aśva*), elephant (*hasti*), chariots (*ratha*), precious stones (*ratna*), etc. The composer of the *Matsya Purāṇa*, therefore, has to be credited with remarkable ingenuity and the power of discernment in selecting only those gift-items which could augment the cosmo-regal aspect of *mahādānas*.

MAHĀDĀNA: THEIR POPULAR BASE AND APPEAL

To extend the purview of this innovative form of ritual gift-making, the purposive scope of *mahādāna* was enlarged beyond the legitimizing and status-conferring powers to comprehend the general fulfilment of all desires. This was done through the adoption of some common symbols representing divine boon-conferring powers. Thus, besides using such explicit motifs as *kalpavṛkṣa*, *kalpalatā* and *kāmadhenu* after which some of the *mahādānas* were named, certain other auspicious signs (*maṅgala cihna*) such as jewels (*maṇi* or *ratna*), the heavenly elephant Airāvata, and the heavenly horse Ucchaiśravas, which are widely mentioned in literature and are found depicted in contemporary art, were also incorporated to lend a popular contour to the *mahādāna* ritual as well as to emphasize its wider context.

In the case of the *kalpalatā mahādāna* (Chapter 286.3-5), it is ordained that the desire-fulfilling creeper should be made of gold and adorned with various fruits, flowers and birds, which must also be made of gold. A couple of *vidyādharas* and *siddhas* should also be shown plucking flowers and fruits. A similar stipulation is made regarding the *kalapapādapa mahādāna* (Chapter 277.3-4). The procedural rule pertaining to it enjoins that besides the boon bestowing tree being shown laden with fruits and flowers, four other trees such as the *pārijāta* and *mandāra*, should also be made of gold and decorated with birds and fruits.

Yet another popular motif steeped in Vedic and Purāṇic mythical lore and effectively employed by the author of the *Matsya Purāṇa* was that of the ocean. In popular imagination, the unfathomable sea has always stood as a storehouse of rich treasures, guarded by the creatures of the subterranean region. This common folk-motif received further embellishment in the Purāṇas, in which the ocean is depicted as a repository of gems of all kinds and forms (*nānā-ratnasamanvitā*, *Matsya Purāṇa*, II.34), ranging from precious stones of heavenly hues to divine damsels such as Rambhā and animals such as the elephant Airāvata, the horse Ucchaiśravasa and cow Kāmadhenu. Fourteen of these heavenly beings and objects emerged from the ocean when it was churned by the gods (*devas*) and the demons (*asuras*). Besides the famous wish-fulfilling tree, creeper and cow, some of the other auspicious things which came out of the sea included the lustrous *bhadramaṇi*, *pāñcajanya śaṅkha* (conch-shell), *amṛta* (elixir), and the goddess of fortune and wealth, Lakṣmī.

Significantly, most of these objects stood as symbols of prosperity, immortality, wish-fulfilment and royal splendour. They also served as common symbolic referents to the *cakravartin* ideal. The *Matsya Purāṇa* (142.63) lists the *aśva* (horse), *hasti* (elephant), *ratha* (chariot) *cakra* (universal wheel), *maṇi* (jewel), *nidhi* (treature), etc., as insignias of a universal monarch. The names of at least four *mahādānas*, *hiraṇyāśva*, *aśvaratha*, *hemahastiratha* and *ratnadhenu*, were definitely based upon the *cakravartin* symbolism and project a highly accentuated cosmo-regal aspect.

Besides symbolizing material well-being and wealth, the sea was also viewed as a powerful cosmic symbol in both Vedic and Purāṇic mythology.[70] The concept, based on an analogy with the liquid content of an egg, regarded the great mass of water enveloping the earth as representing the fluid within the cosmic egg or *brahmāṇḍa*. The liquid, in the form of the primeval and infinite ocean called *Ekārṇava*, was believed to have existed as an undifferentiated mass till it fissioned into seven separate seas or *saptasāgara*, symbolizing the seven causal principles of creation. In ritual performances, these seven seas were represented as seven different kinds of fluids such as *kṣīra*, *ghṛta*, *dadhi*, *udaka*, *surā*, *lavaṇa* and *ikṣu*.

Basing the *saptasāgara mahādāna* upon the same cosmo-regal symbolism related to the ocean, the procedural rules pertaining to it (*Matsya Purāṇa*, Chapter 287) required the performer to get seven sacrificial pits or *kuṇḍas* made of gold which, after being filled with the seven above-mentioned ingredients, had to be gifted to brāhmaṇas. As suggested by Agarwala,[71] the *saptasāgara mahādāna* ritual was perhaps required to be performed near the *samudrakūpas* which excavations have revealed at some prominent *tīrtha* sites such as

Mathura, Prayaga and Ujjain. Moreover, the *saptasāgara mahādāna* may have been targeted at a particular donor category, namely, the rich merchants whose leanings towards dissenting sects like Buddhism and Jainism were becoming a matter of grave concern for the Brāhmaṇical ideologues who knew that for traders, especially those undertaking hazardous maritime ventures,[72] a safe homecoming could have been nothing less than a new birth. When, in the traditional social order, such risks were further compounded by social disapprobation, it was natural for them to turn more towards those religious systems which displayed a less rigid stance. Under the circumstances, the *saptasāgara mahādāna* seems to have been conceived for the specific purpose of helping to safeguard and reaffirm the ritual status of seafaring merchants and, at the same time, enabling them to celebrate their newly acquired fortune.

The popular appeal of the *mahādānas* was sought to be increased in many other ways as well. One was by diluting the opulent quality of some of the great gifts by introducing a certain amount of flexibility in the use of precious metals and other valuable substances, as well as scaling down the volume of the gift articles. It was also done by reducing the number of priests to be engaged for the performance of a *mahādāna* rite. For instance, in the case of the *kalpapādapa mahādāna* (277.17), it is stated that if the performer cannot afford much money, he should only worship the preceptor. It was an important concession, for it meant an exemption from the payment of exhorbitant fees and gifts to a large number of ministrant priests whose services had to be normally requisitioned. A similar stipulation is also made in the case of *hiraṇyāśva mahādāna* (280.3). With regard to the *viśvacakra mahādāna* (285.3), it is stated that a person with limited means could get the image of *viśvacakra* made of only 20 *palas* of gold, which was, however, the lowest limit to which relaxation was permissible.

By recommending the performance of *mahādānas* on wide-ranging occasions, the author of the *Matsya Purāṇa* sought to further ensure their broader context and purview. For instance, the *tulāpuruṣa mahādāna* (274.19-23) could be made if a person acquired wealth, visited some *tīrtha* or temple, dreamt a good or bad dream, performed a sacrifice or *śrāddha* rite, or even at the time of his marriage or some other festivities. That the *mahādānas* had come to be performed on widely different occasions is clearly borne out by contemporary inscriptions.

To maximize the popular appeal of the *mahādānas*, their purposive scope was made very comprehensive. The *tulāpuruṣa mahādāna*, besides dispelling all ills, was considered to be the bestower of virtue and longevity. The *hiraṇyāśva mahādāna* was supposed to confer numberless benefits upon the performer (*anantam phalamasnute*, 280.1-2). The *ratnadhenu mahādāna* is similarly described as the giver of high benefits (288.1). By leaving the nature or resultant benefits unspecified and vague, the composer of the Purāṇa was apparently trying to give a wide berth to officiating priests and brāhmaṇas in interpreting them to the best of their clients' interests. The *kāmadhenu mahādāna*, likewise, is said to fulfil all desires of a temporal and spiritual nature (279.1-2). In fact, the *mahādānas* are stated to be the dispellers of all ills, including the effects of bad dreams (*duḥsvapnanāśam*, 275.4). In the case of the *mahābhūtaghaṭa mahādāna*, it is stated that its performance led to the attainment of inexhaustible wealth. The *kalpapādapa mahādāna* (277.19) and the *gosahasra mahādāna* (278.1), on the other hand, were believed to be efficacious in liberating the manes, as also the members of present and future generations. The latter *mahādāna* is especially distinguished by its power to liberate 'grandmothers' (*mātāmahānāms*, 278.24). Such pointed gender categorization as done in the *gosahasra mahādāna* appears as a new feature and helps us to identify the section of society sought to be wooed through this innovative form of gift-making. This *mahādāna* may have been intended to attract mainly tribal ruling chieftains seeking entry into the mainstream culture and politics whose own social ethos was marked by gender parity, so conspicuously lacking in the Brāhmaṇical system.

An analysis of the explicitly mentioned purposes of the various *mahādānas* shows that out of the sixteen forms of great gifts, no less than ten were specifically meant to dispel sins of varying nature and degree, advertently or inadvertently committed by the donor. Such an excessive preoccupation of the author of the *Matsya Purāṇa* with the concept of sin expiation would appear to have significant contextual implications. In fact, if we relate it to the other common motif permeating Purāṇic mythology, then we find that the two put together served as an excellent means of rationalizing and justifying the obscure antecedents of many of the ruling chiefs aspiring for a better political and ritual status. Whereas the motifs of sin and curse helped to explain their present low status, the *mahādāna* form of gift-making was meant to ward off the effect of any sins which they might have committed in present or past births, or of some curse from which they might suffer, and thus to help them regain their original and true ritual status. This is particularly manifest in the case of those *mahādānas* in which the symbolism of rebirth has been overtly adopted.

ABSORPTION OF POPULAR CULTIC BELIEFS IN *MAHĀDĀNA* CEREMONIALISM

The popular contour of the *mahādānas* was also emphasized by incorporating divinities of a more local and non-Brāhmaṇical origin into the list of deities to be invoked at the time of ritual performance. Besides worship being offered to the Brāhmaṇical triad of Brahmā, Viṣṇu and Śiva (274.6: 53), and to their respective consorts, Sāvitrī, Lakṣmī and Pārvatī, as well as some of the Vedic gods such as Indra, Agni, Sūrya and Soma, certain other deities of a more titular character who had to be invoked to ensure the success of the ceremonial included the *lokapālas* or the divine guardians of the four quarters, the *grahadevatās* or the ruling deities of the planets (274.29), and the *devamātaras* or mother goddesses. Another deity whose worship was enjoined was Ananta, the presiding deity of the netherworld (*pātāla*). The fact that the deity is said to be eulogized and worshipped by Nāga women and the *kinnaras* (274.50) clearly points to its tribal affiliations.

An invocation to Lokeśa or the *lokapālas* is found to be an integral feature of most *mahādāna* rites. In fact, in the *Liṅga Purāṇa*, its author has gone to the extent of replacing one of the original great gifts mentioned in the *Matsya* and *Agni Purāṇas* by a *mahādāna* which is specifically called *lokapāla*. Such importance being attached to the worship of the guardian spirits of different quarters of the earth acquires special significance when viewed in the light of Rupert Sheldrake's observation on the seminal character of guardian spirits of nature in the religious beliefs of all early societies when man had still not distanced himself from nature.[73] Instead, man tried to nurture and reinforce the consonant quality of his proximity and links with nature through animistic beliefs. By incorporating these ideas in the *mahādāna* ceremonial, the composers of the Purāṇas were no doubt seeking to win over a segment of society which continued to cherish such beliefs.

The invocation at the time of the *mahādāna* rite of semi-divine and semi-mythical beings such as the *dānavas*, *yakṣas*, *rāksaṣas*, *piśācas*, *gandharvas* and *nāgas* (274.53), who in Purāṇic mythology represented mainly the malevolent forces of nature, seems somewhat strange, especially when they are known to manifest close cultural affinity with primitive tribal groups and were openly hostile towards Brāhmaṇical rites and beliefs. Hence, besides the need to appease and propitiate them in order to stop them from causing harm to the performance, the only other reason why it was thought necessary to invoke them along with the other gods, could have been the newly arisen expediency to invest the *mahādāna* rite with a more popular colouring so as to attract the common people. Such mythical and semi-mythical categories could scarcely be expected to appeal to more refined minds.

The popular aspects of the *mahādāna* ceremonial becomes still more evident from the way in which the author of the *Matsya Purāṇa* has tried to overcome the Brāhmaṇical and non-Brāhmaṇical sectarian divide by enjoining, in the case of the *aśvaratha mahādāna* (281.7), that the performer must 'consecrate the deity to whom he is devoted'. By making such a stipulation, the author very pointedly tried to lift the *mahādāna* ceremonial above narrow sectarian constraints and give it a wider base and appeal.

In the subsequent period when the *Liṅga Purāṇa* was composed, the tilt towards more popular cultic beliefs was almost complete so that they, particularly Tāntric ones, had come to virtually replace the Smārtta element in the *mahādāna* ceremonial. The deities who were now required to be invoked at the *tulādhirohaṇa mahādāna* were no longer Brahmā, Viṣṇu or other Vedic gods but mainly Śiva and Devī in her multiple aspects of Vistarā, Subhāgā, Vardhanī, Pradakṣiṇā, Appāyaṇī, Vimalā, Sārā, Arahdyā, Sukhā, etc. (11.28.67-9).

The *Matsya Purāṇa* contains a list of goddesses whose images had to be worshipped at the time of the *mahākalpalatā mahādāna*. It includes, besides Brahmā and Anantaśakti (286.6), the names of other female divinities such as Gādinī, Nairṭyā, Patākinī (286.9) and Śaṁkhinī (286.10). Whereas Gādinī and Patākinī had to be shown riding their respective mounts of buffalo and deer, Nairṭya had to be shown holding a sword. The Purāṇa, moreover, stipulates that the images of these deities should be made in their girlish forms with a coronet on their heads and with their hands in the posture of offering some boon (286.11). The names and mounts, as well as the manner in which these goddesses were required to be portrayed, are all suggestive of their tribal bearing. By emphasizing their boon-giving powers, their popular aspects were clearly highlighted.

ROLE OF THE PRECEPTOR IN *MAHĀDĀNA* RITUAL

Another significant feature of *mahādāna* ceremonialism was the importance attached to the *guru* or spiritual teacher. The preceptor was not only required to participate in and even officiate at the rite (*Matsya Purāṇa*, 275.17-18), but was also to be the chief recipient of gift offerings (284.17). The *Matsya Purāṇa* (274.37-8) even outlines the qualities which must characterize a *guru*. Besides being proficient in Vedānta and possessing a cheerful disposition, he also had to be born in an Āryan family. The latter stipulation was perhaps meant to ensure that the performer of the *mahādāna* rite did not engage the services of a teacher with doubtful antecedents and qualifications.

As far as the bestowal of gifts upon the *guru* at the *mahādāna* rite is concerned, the *Matsya Purāṇa* (274.56) categorically enjoins that he must be given double the share of what is given to the *ṛtvijas* (*dviguṇam gurave dadyāt*). In the *tulāpuruṣa mahādāna*, the performer, after alighting from the scale, had to first give half of the whole offering to the preceptor (*tato avatīryya gurave pūrvamardham nivedayet*: *Matsya Purāṇa*, 274.71) and the rest was to be made over to the priests. Moreover, all the ritual articles used in the course of the worship had to be offered to the guru (*tatropakārṇam sarvam gurave vinidayet*, 275.24). It was further laid down that in case of limited resources, the performer could make do with the services of the *guru* alone (*svalpe tvaika agnivat kuryyāt gurave cābhipūjanam*: *Matsya Purāṇa*, 277.17). Thus, in the context of the *brahmāṇḍa mahādāna*, it is clearly stated in an ordinance that when only a small amount is spent by the devotee, the preceptor alone should offer libations into the sacrificial fire as in the *agnihotra*. He alone should be given all the clothes and ornaments, etc. (276.16).

Such excessive importance being accorded to the *guru* in *mahādāna* ceremonialism is in consonance with the general tenor of the Purāṇas[74] in which the preceptor figures prominently in all sorts of contexts, ranging from the educational to the edificatory and ritualistic. But whether the *guru* as represented in the Purāṇas, was merely the archetypal teacher of the Smārtta tradition or was, in fact, the Purāṇic counterpart of the tribal *bhopa* or shaman requires probing. The position of the *guru* in the Smārtta tradition is found to be essentially endemic to the Brāhmaṇical educational system. His role in other religious activities of a ritualistic or priestly nature appears to have been almost minimal and more through default. It certainly did not go beyond the performance of initiatory rites, especially those which marked the beginning of the educational career. In the Dharmaśāstra[75] texts, three different categories of teachers have been distinguished, namely, the *upādhyāya*, the *ācārya* and the *guru*. While the *upādhyāya* was considered qualified to teach only a portion of a Veda, and the *ācārya* regarded intellectually equipped to initiate the pupil and teach him the Veda together with the *kalpa* and *rahasya*,[76] it was only the *guru* who could perform all the rites for the individual beginning with the *garbhādhāna*, as well as deliver instructions, in the Vedas.[77] This injunction, besides emphasizing the relatively wider scope of a *guru's* duties, also accentuates the closer and more lasting nature of ties which bound him to his pupil.

It would appear, therefore, that although sacramental rites had come to figure prominently in Brāhmaṇical ritualism from as early as the time of the Dharmaśāstras, and the *guru's* role in them was conceded by lawgivers, it remained confined to this. General sacerdotal functions could never be comprehended within the purview of a preceptor's common set of duties. In the Purāṇas, on the other hand, although the *guru* is clearly distinguished from the *ṛtvija*, he is known to officiate in religious performances other than the purely initiatory, as is evident from the level of his participation in the *mahādāna* ritual.

Field studies show that in most pre-literate societies admission to adulthood is possible only by going through painful initiatory rites[78] performed by tribal elders under the guidance of the *guru*, variously called *bhopa*, *bhagat* or *mahārāja*, who invariably combines the function of a ritual practitioner with those of an exorcist, medical healer and even a moral preacher and guide. This counsel is much sought after and valued in all matters pertaining to the individual and group well-being.[79] His role is less than that of a teacher who provides spiritual guidance and imparts higher learning of a generalized nature[80] and more akin to that of a *guru* of the Tāntric[81] and *bhakti*[82] traditions, who initiates the disciple into the mysteries and secrets of a particular kind of religious knowledge, shared only by a limited group. For instance, the most significant life cycle rite of the Vīraśaivas for attaining adult religious status is the *ayyacar* (initiation) ceremony, at which it is the *guru* who officiates.[83] In tribal, Tāntric and *bhakti*-based religious systems, the *guru*, therefore, served as a strong legitimizing agent. The importance which began to be attached to the *guru* in the *mahādāna* ceremonial reveals an overt attempt on the part of the Purāṇa composers to draw upon both tribal and Tāntric traditions. Perhaps it was also meant to emphasize the validatory role of the sixteen great gifts.

Significantly, the depiction of the Purāṇic *guru* in the role of a ritual officiant becomes more prominent in the later Purāṇas, which reveal a stronger Tāntric orientation. In the *Liṅga Purāṇa*, the *guru* has been specially glorified. In one of its verses, it states that though the preceptor is one, he represents the glorious Brahmā, Viṣṇu and Maheśvara (II.44.9). How far a similar trend, perceptible in the earlier Purāṇas, was the outcome of the tribalization of the *guru* of the Smārtta tradition is a possibility worth considering. The plausibility of such an explanation would reinforce our view that the new genre of Purāṇic literature was targeted mainly at those sections of society which stood on the periphery of the mainstream social order and were still under the strong influence of tribal traditions.[84]

TĀNTRIC ELEMENT IN THE *MAHĀDĀNA* CEREMONIAL

Yet another important feature of *mahādāna* ritualism as developed in the Purāṇas is its constantly varying form. Compared to how it is projected in the *Matsya Purāṇa*, the *Liṅga Purāṇa* indicates considerable changes both in the ritual format and the general tenor of this new form of gift-making. For one, the prefix *mahā*, which gave it a distinct feudal colouring, is dispensed with. In fact, it is more on the basis of the sixteen different kinds of gifts listed rather than the occurrences of the term *mahādāna* that we are able to identify the gifts mentioned in the *Liṅga Purāṇa* with the original set of sixteen.

Moreover, in the *Liṅga Purāṇa*, the Tāntric orientation of most ritual stipulations pertaining to the sixteen gifts is clearly manifest. For instance, with regard to the *tulādhirohaṇadāna* (II.28.47-52), it is stated that a mystic diagram (*maṇḍala*) should be drawn in the middle of the altar. Other Tāntric symbols such as the thunderbolt (*vajra*), lotus (*padma*), discus (*cakra*), noose, sword, iron club, trident, etc., had also to be drawn on different sides of the altar. Similarly, the Tāntric character of the *mantras*, which had to be used in the ritual performance of the gifts, is equally conspicuous. Thus, in the *hiraṇyagarbha* ceremony, the rites had to be performed by repeating the *śaktibīja-mantra* (II.29.13). Similarly, on the occasion of *sūkṣmaparvatadāna*, the *nyāsa* rite was recommended (II.31.5). The *hiraṇyagarbhadāna* is stated to be the bestower of all *siddhis* (II.29), a purpose never admitted in the *Matsya Purāṇa*.

Significantly, the roots of Tantrism, according to D.P. Chattopadhyaya,[85] lie in the pre-literate magical beliefs and rituals related to agricultural operations. If we recognize such a causal connection between the rise of Tantrism and primitive agricultural rites and cultic beliefs, then the growing assimilation of Tāntric rites and practices in the later Purāṇas in general and in the *mahādāna* ceremonial in particular, will have to be attributed largely to the accelerated pace of interaction between the established religious systems and pre-literate traditions due to the penetration of mainstream cultural forces into the remote tribal areas.

The shifting focus of *mahādāna* ceremonialism is also perceptible in the changing character of recipient categories, as well as in the degree of emphasis laid on the qualifications of the officiating priests. Our analysis of the relevant section of the *Liṅga Purāṇa* dealing with the sixteen gifts shows that besides employing such descriptive terms for the *ṛtvija* as 'an excellent brāhmaṇa' (II.29.8; II.39.4), the author of the text did not deem it necessary to specify other professional requirements as done by the composer of the *Matsya Purāṇa* (274.36-7). Instead of furnishing such qualificatory details as high birth or good looks and cheerful disposition, the *Liṅga Purāṇa* attaches greater importance to his sectarian bias (II.43.7). In fact, its Śaiva leanings are reflected both in the criteria laid down for the selection of officiating priests as well as of gift recipients. For the first time in the *Liṅga Purāṇa* (II.28.71-2) we come across references to *yogins*, who had to be honoured and fed at the *mahādāna* rite. They are described as the sole masters of Śaiva philosophy. At another place in the *Liṅga Purāṇa* (II.28.80-1), it is specifically laid down that all used articles had to be given to one 'who regularly performs the Pāśupata rite and who smears holy ashes (*bhasman*) all over his limbs'. In fact, most injunctions pertaining to the sixteen gifts insist on preference being shown to the devotees of Śiva as donees (II.28-95).

Amongst the recipient categories, the brāhmaṇas now figureless prominently than before. There are also references to some additional groups who were required to be fed and given *dakṣiṇā* at the time of gift-making. Thus, the author of the *Liṅga Purāṇa* (II.28.95-6) enjoins that on the occasion of *tulādhirohaṇadāna*, poor, blind, wretched, old, lean and sick people as well as children should be duly fed and given *dakṣiṇā*. The same is recommended in the case of *hiraṇyāśvadāna* (II.39). The stipulation pertaining to *viśveśvaradāna* (II.34.5), on the other hand, required a virgin girl to be worshipped and offered gifts. Even in the case of brāhmaṇa recipients, those who were poor had to be preferred (II.30-1). The projection of the poor and infirm as a more deserving recipient category was perhaps meant to make royal donors more conscious of their duty towards the marginalized sections of society. However, it seems also to betray a definite attitudinal change on the part of later Purāṇic composers. More than that, it suggests the sharpening of class disparities by the opening centuries of the second millennium AD.

Such an inference is further substantiated by the growing importance of monetary gifts at the *mahādāna* ceremony. The *Liṅga Purāṇa* recommends the use of *niṣkas* or gold coins not only for the purpose of gift-distribution but even for the making of the images of deities and other articles to be used for gift-making. Thus, at the *hiraṇyagarbhadāna*, a splendid image of a girl had to be made with 30 gold coins (*trisanniṣkena*, II.29.11). Similarly, while in the case of the *suvarṇamedinīdāna* a replica of earth had to be made with 1,000 gold coins (II.32), on the occasion of *kalpapādapa-dāna* the *kalpa*-tree had to be crafted with 100 gold coins. At the *viśveśvaradāna*, the idol of Viśveśvara was to be made with 10 gold coins. Other ritual and gift objects like *hemadhenu, hiraṇyāśva, hiraṇyagaja, hiraṇyavṛṣa* were also required to be made of a specified number of gold coins.

The substitution of metallic currency for precious metals as a gift-item is a significant change which affected the format and tenor of the *mahādāna* ritual. It is symptomatic of some major socio-economic developments taking place around this time, especially the revival of the monetary economy in a rather big way.[86] Yet even the less opulent quality of gift-items recommended in the *Liṅga Purāṇa* would seem to suggest a declining feudal ethos, and an attempt on the part of the Purāṇa composer to recast *mahādāna* ceremonialism to suit the needs of a changing social order.

The variations in the ritual format and tenor of the sixteen great gifts, as projected in the *Matsya* and *Liṅga Purāṇas*, besides emphasizing the elements of change and continuity, highlight their purposive role and character. This clearly reaffirms our basic proposition regarding the twofold objectives served by the *mahādānas*. The first important purpose was to provide ritual validation for the power and social status of political aspirants of tribal and obscure origins. This is evident from the fact that most of the great gifts noted above are known to have been performed not by rulers whose power was already firmly established but by those political adventurers and founders of new dynasties who, besides having prominent tribal antecedents, were still seeking to augment their newly-won political power. Some of the great gifts appear to have been specifically formulated for the purpose of putting the stamp of ritual and social approbation on the wealth amassed by rich merchants and commercial magnates.

Another equally important purpose served by the *mahādāna,* especially from the point of view of the Brāhmaṇical sacerdotal class, was to win over a vast clientele from amongst those sections of society who had either tended to lean more heavily towards such religious systems as Buddhism and Jainism, or else were still undergoing acculturation and continued to have strong tribal affiliations. In the case of the latter, the *mahādānas* apparently served to facilitate their entry into the mainstream social order.

Our study, thus, not only throws light on the functional base of *mahādāna* ritualism but also underscores the symbolic nature of its relationship with the processes of acculturation intensified by agrarian expansion in virgin tracts during the post-Gupta centuries.

NOTES

1. V. Nath, *Dāna: Gift System in Ancient India: A Socio-Economic Perspective,* Delhi, 1987, pp. 13-14.
2. V. Nath, 'Ritual Symbolism and Status Conferring Role of Dāna', Proceedings of the Indian History Congress, Golden Jubilee Session, Gorakhpur, 1989-90, pp. 80-95.
3. *EI*, VIII, no. 8, verse, 23; XVI, no. 23, pp. 299-301.
4. Ibid., VII, no. 9, lines 34, 91, cf. p. 87.
5. Taxila Copper Plates, *CII*, II, pt. 1, p. 28.
6. *EI*, XX, no. 1, line 9, p. 16.
7. R.C. Hazra, *Studies in the Purāṇic Records on Hindu Rites and Customs,* Delhi, 1975, pp. 44-5.
8. Ibid., p. 52.
9. Himanshu Prabha Ray, *Monastery and Guild: Commerce under the Sātavāhanas*, Delhi, 1985, pp. 110-11.
10. Hazra, op. cit., pp. 138, 185.
11. Ibid., p. 139.
12. Ibid., p. 95.
13. *IA*, IX, 102; *EI*, II no. 1, verse 21, line 18, p. 4; IX, no. 4, line 54, p. 37; XIII, no. 26, verse 19, line 21, p. 292; XIV, no. 15, line 1, p. 197; XVIII, no. 25, line 1, p. 197.
14. B.D. Chattopadhyaya, 'Political Process and Structure of the Polity in Early Medieval India: Problems of Perspective', Presidential Address, Section I, Proceedings of the Indian History Congress, 44th Session, Burdwan, 1983, p. 25; B.N.S. Yadava, 'The Accounts of the Kali Age and the Social Transition from the Antiquity to the Middle Ages', *IHR*, V, nos. 1-2, 31-64; R.S. Sharma, 'The Kali Age: A Period of Crisis', in S.N. Mukherjee, ed., *History and Thought: Essays in Honour of A.L. Basham*, Calcutta, 1982, pp. 186-203.
15. Aloka Parasher, *Mlecchas in Early India*, Delhi, 1991, p. 179.
16. D.C. Sircar, 'Purāṇic Lists of People', in *Geography of Ancient and Medieval India*, Delhi, 1960, pp. 21-37; N.Y. Desai, *Ancient Indian Society, Religion and Mythology as Depicted in the Mārkaṇḍeya Purāṇa*, Baroda, 1968, pp. 222 ff.
17. Ray, op. cit., pp. 90 ff.
18. Ibid., p. 102.
19. Swati Dutta, *Migrant Brāhmaṇas in Northern India*, Delhi, 1989, pp. 7-25.

20. Buddha Prakash, 'The Abhiras: Their Antiquity, History and Culture', *JBRS*, XL, pt. 3, 249 ff.; Mamta Choudhary, *Tribes of Ancient India*, Calcutta, 1977, p. 14.
21. K. Raghunath, 'Religion of the Ikshvaku Times', *JIH*, LVI, 1978, 429-35.
22. V. Sundara Rama Sastry, 'The Anandagotras of Andhradesa: A Study of the Social Mechanics of their Origin', Proceedings of the Andhra Pradesh History Congress, Warangal, 1990, pp. 42-3; M. Rama Rao, *Journal of Andhra History and Culture*, I, 11; idem, *Studies in Early History of Andhradesa*, Madras, 1974, p. 90; A.M. Shastri, *Early History of the Deccan: Problems and Perspectives*, Delhi, 1987.
23. H. Luders, *A List of Brahmi Inscriptions from the Earliest Time to about* AD *400 with the Exception of those of Aśoka*, Varanasi, 1973, nos. 1000, 1024, 1073.
24. K. Raghunath, 'Religion of the Ikshvaku Times', op. cit., p. 432; B.S.L. Hanumantha Rao, 'Religion, Politics and Society in Early Deccan', Presidential Address, Ancient Indian Section, PIHC, 53rd Session, Mysore, 1993, pp. 46-7.
25. Agarwala, 'Saptasāgara Mahādāna', *Purāṇa*, I, pp. 2, 206-12.
26. Gorantala Plates of Athivarman, *IA*, IX, 102.
27. *EI*, XXIII, no. 7 (A, B, C), p. 52; XXIV, no. 10, line 32, p. 56.
28. M. Herskovits, *Cultural Anthropology*, rpt., Delhi, 1969, p. 164.
29. Murray Milner, Jr., *Status and Sacredness: A General Theory of Status Relations and an Analysis of Indian Culture*, New York, 1994, p. 84.
30. Two inscriptions found in Jodhpur (*EI*, XI, no. 12, p. 45) issued by the Cāhamāna rulers but made public by Jaina monks strongly deprecate the killing of animals and recommend *abhayadāna* instead. *ABORI*, XL, 1959, 226.
31. V.S. Pathak, 'Vedic Rituals in Early Medieval Period: An Epigraphic Study', ibid., p. 222.
32. Ibid., also note 1.
33. *EI*, I, no. 8, pp. 229, 307.
34. Gorantla Plates, *IA*, IX, 102 ff.; Mattepad Plates, *EI*, XVII, no. 18, pp. 327 ff.
35. P. Arundhati, *Brahmanism, Jainism and Buddhism in Andhradesh*, Delhi, 1990, p. 61.
36. *EI*, XVIII, no. 26, verse 9.
37. V.B. Mishra, *Religious Beliefs and Practices of North India during the Early Medieval Period*, Leiden, 1973, p. 70.
38. *CII*, VI, i, no. 56, line 18, p. 294; no. 57, line 18, p. 304.
39. Ibid., XVIII, no. 26, verse 22, p. 292.
40. Ibid., I, no. 19 (iv), verse 52, p. 146.
41. *IA*, XV, 36.
42. Ibid., XI, 112.
43. *EI*, IX, no. 4, line 55.

44. Ibid., VII, no. 6, line 46.
45. Ibid., VI, no. 11 (5), line 22, p. 126.
46. Ibid., XII, no. 3, lines 43-8.
47. *JASB*, LVI, pt. 1, 108.
48. *EI*, XIV, no. 15, p. 197.
49. H.C. Ray, *The Dynastic History of Northern India*, Calcutta, 1936, p. 255.
50. Ibid., p. 249.
51. Ibid., p. 355.
52. S. Sankaranarayan, *The Viṣṇukuṇḍins and their Times*, Delhi, 1977, pp. 18-30.
53. Sastry, op. cit., pp. 42-8.
54. *IA*, XVI (1887), 202, 207-10; cf. Ray, op. cit., p. 706.
55. Ray, ibid., p. 752.
56. Ibid., p. 738.
57. Ibid., p. 821.
58. Ibid., p. 827.
59. *Atharvaveda*, XV; A.C. Banerjea, *Studies in the Brāhmaṇas*, Delhi, 1963, pp. 81-172.
60. Monika Vizedom, *Rites and Relationships: Rites of Passage and Contemporary Anthropology*, London, 1976, p. 25.
61. V.S. Agarwala, 'Hiraṇyagarbha', *Purāṇa*, II (1960), 292.
62. *IA*, XV (1886), 36.
63. Chandravati Plate of vs 1156, *EI*, XIV, no. 15, p. 197, lines 1-2.
64. Ibid., I, no. 19 (iv), verse 52.
65. *CII*, VI, pt. 1, no. 56, verse 21.
66. *EI*, IX, no. 4, lines 54-5.
67. Ibid., VII, no. 6, line 46.
68. Ibid., VII, no. 6, line 46; IX, no. 4, lines 54-5.
69. Ibid., XX, no. 7, line 9.
70. V.S. Agarwala, 'Hiraṇyagarbha', *Purāṇa*, II, 1960, 285-306.
71. V.S. Agarwala, 'Saptasāgara Mahādāna', *Purāṇa*, I, pt. 2, II, 206-12.
72. Shyamsunder Nigam, *Economic Organization in Ancient India (200 BC-200 AD)*, Delhi, 1975, pp. 167-8.
73. Rupert Sheldrake, *The Rebirth of Nature*, London, 1990, p. 138.
74. Hazra, op. cit., p. 262.
75. *Manu*, II.141.
76. Ibid., II.140.
77. Ibid., II.142.
78. H. Webster, *Primitive Secret Societies*, New York, 1932, p. 38; B. Spencer and F. Gillen, *Native Tribes of Central Australia*, London, 1899, p. 401; A.W. Hewitt, *Native Tribes of South-East Australia*, London, 1904, p. 530.
79. R.B. Lal, 'Social-Religious Movements among the Tribals of South Gujarat', in K.S. Singh, ed., *Tribal Movements in India*, New Delhi, 1983, pp. 285-308.

80. F. Barth, 'The Guru and the Conjurer', *Man* (NS), XXV, 640-53.
81. Sanjukta Gupta, 'The Mandalas as an Image of Man', in Richard Gombrich, ed., *Indian Ritual and its Exegesis*, Oxford University Papers on India, II, i, pt. 33, N.N. Bhattacharyya, *History of Tantric Religion*, New Delhi, 1982, p. 145.
82. Murray Milner, *Status and Sacredness*, op. cit., p. 197.
83. William McCormack, 'The Forms of Communication in Virasaiva Religion', *Journal of American Folklore*, LXXI, 1958, 326.
84. Vijay Shankar Upadhyay, 'A Note on the Tribes mentioned in the Medieval Records', *JBRS*, XLVII, 1961, 405-7.
85. D.P. Chattopadhyaya, *Lokayata: A Study in Ancient Indian Materialism,* Delhi, 1978, p. 286.
86. K.M. Shrimali, 'Cash Nexus on Western Coast, *c.* AD 850-1250: A Study of the Silaharas', in A.K. Jha, ed., *Coinage: Trade and Economy*, Anjaneri, 1991, pp. 178-93.

8

Almsgiving: How Far is it a Distension of *Dāna*

The unique contours of ritual *dāna* as it evolved and developed in ancient India have thrown into focus one chief category of recipients, namely the brāhmaṇas, who from Vedic times stood out as its main beneficiary. The qualifications of recipients as laid down in Brāhmaṇical law books could vary enormously from one period to another, from one socio-economic order, pastoral/rural or predominantly urban, to another. The only factor that remained constant was their brāhmaṇa identity. Even though erudite (*vedapāraga/śrotriya*) brāhmaṇas were always to be preferred over those who were less learned or lacked *bona fide* credentials, in the absence of the former, the latter were declared to be the most deserving recipients of ritual *dāna*. Thus, in the strictly Brāhmaṇical context, the practice of *dāna* and the importance enjoyed by brāhmaṇa donees represented synchronic phenomena, symbiotically linked, and constituting part of a single cultural syndrome.

In contrast to the Brāhmaṇical stereotype that we come across in Buddhist and Jaina literature, there are copious notices of numerous other categories of recipients, the more prominent being monks and indigent beggars. The continually swelling number of the former and their complete dependence on alms (*bhikṣā*) is attested not only by Indian texts but also by foreign accounts. Contemporary literature also throws light on the nature of gift-items offered to them, as well as the organized manner in which such alms were generally distributed. The present study, through an analysis of certain characteristic features, of the two systems of gift-making (Brāhmaṇical and heterodox) both common as well as others that set them apart, seeks to highlight their basic similitude, and establish that one was essentially an extension of the other. Though in the case of heterodox almsgiving, the recipient categories and the ritual entailed in making the gift varied considerably, the same underlying principles governed both forms of gift-making.

The emergence of these new categories of alms-seekers: monks, wayfarers and beggars, was a purely surplus-based urban phenomenon that, unlike the Brāhmaṇical gift system, cut across the wide social spectrum of castes and tribes (*varṇas/jātis*). Nevertheless, all the requisite elements of *dāna*: donor (*dātā*), donee (*pratigrahīta*), gift-item (*deya*), time (*kāla*), place (*sthāna*) and faith (*śraddhā*), deemed absolutely necessary for its efficacy by brāhmaṇa theorists, are found to be present also in alms given to monks; though the measure and form in which they occur could somewhat vary.

One area in which the maximum difference in the two systems of religious gift-making can be found is in the procedure or mode of offering gift-items, for alms offered to monks were not completely devoid of ritual. In fact, it is significant that heterodox sects, despite vehemently disparaging Vedic ritual, still adopted many of its usages, mostly in deference to popular feeling. For instance, in the Brāhmaṇical practice of *dāna*, we find that the pouring of water by the donor constitutes the most significant part of the gift-making rite, without which no gift was considered complete (*sarvānyudakapūrvāni dānāni*).[1] It not only marked the formal annulment of the donor's right of possession over the gift-object but also of the mystical bond between the two. The gift-item, thus absolved of its power of transmitting the sins of the previous owner, was rendered safe for the donee to receive. Contemporary Buddhist texts reveal a similar practice of besprinkling water being adopted at the time of making gifts. In the *Dhammapada* (III.16.9), we get a reference to the water of donation being poured into the right hand of Tathāgata. From the Mathura Lion Capital inscription,[2] we learn how Kṣatrapa Soḍāsa gifted a piece of land with libations of water to the teacher, Buddhadeva.

The practice in both systems of gift-making would suggest a common underlying belief in the strong mystical bond which seemingly exists between the donor and the gift-object. According to van der Leeuw, 'To give is to convey something of oneself to a strange being, so that a firm bond may be forged.'[3] The universal nature of such a belief is indicated by an ancient Chinese custom, which recognizes the indissoluble bond of a thing with its original owner. Even today, the man who sells property retains the right during the rest of his life to weep over it.[4] The gift-item, therefore, became a potential carrier of the donor's sins and even disease to the recipient.[5] Once gifts came to be regarded as a means of transmitting the donor's sins, they automatically became imbued with danger for the donee. It was for this reason that the Dharmaśāstra composers not only recommended discriminate *pratigraha*, i.e. acceptance of gifts from only worthy and virtuous donors,[6] but also prescribed the chanting of special *mantras* and the rite of besprinkling water to sever the mystical bond between the donor and gift-item. The belief must have been so widely current that even leaders of non-conformist sys-tems such as Buddhism had to take cognizance of it, and allow their followers to observe some of these rites to safeguard the interests of both the donor and recipient. Heterodox leaders, making concession for popular beliefs and sentiments, are known to often make procedural amendments; this is quite evident from the Buddha's remark in the *Cullavagga* (V.33.3): 'Laymen are given to lucky phrases (*gihi bhikava maṅgalika*). I allow you, O *bhikkhus*, to reply, "May you live long", to laymen who say to you, "Long life to your reverence." ' Respect shown for popular sentiments by the Buddha becomes even more manifest from another concession recorded in the same text.[7] According to it, when, despite a woman's insistence that the *bhikkhus* step over the cloth spread in their honour for good luck's sake and they would not do so for fear of offence, they were told by the Buddha: 'I allow you, O *bhikkhus*, when asked to do so for the sake of good luck to laymen to step over the cloth laid down for ceremonial purposes.'

In other respects, too, almsgiving by members of alternate systems is known to be attended by many of the norms laid down by Brāhmaṇical lawgivers. The emphasis laid on maintaining an attitude of faith or *śraddhā* is as strong in the case of heterodox sects as in the case of the Brāhmaṇical concept of *dāna*. In the *Baudhāyana Dharmasūtra* (I.5.10.6; II.8.15.6), it is unequivocally stipulated that, 'want of faith is the greatest sin'. If gifts are given or received without touching them with the thumb, the performer of the act is not benefited. In Buddhist texts, too, we come across numerous references to lay donors who, while offering alms to monks, manifested a similar attitude of devotion and faith. In the *Majjhima Nikāya* (CX, Cula Punnama Sutta, III.22), a donor who does not distribute alms properly, is 'casual in his giving' or 'gives neither with his own hand nor with consideration' is severely denounced. The five right ways of giving, according to the *Aṅguttara Nikāya* (III.172), are to give in faith, to give carefully, to give quickly, to give firmly, and to give so as not to injure oneself or the donee. That this was no mere theoretical injunction but was actually put into practice by donors who showed the utmost respect and veneration for the recipient monks is sufficiently borne out by our sources. The *Pīṭha Jātaka*[8] describes how a lay donor, saluting a monk, took his alms-bowl and led him to his house where he offered him a seat. The *Cullavagga* (IV.4-6) refers to a certain householder who, along with his wife and children, used to stand at the place of alms and serve. Similarly, according to the *Majjhima Nikāya* (XXXV, Cula Saccaka Sutta, I.286), Saccaka served the confraternity of monks headed by the Buddha with his own hands and 'without stint till all had eaten their fill'. The importance of personally serving food to the donee is best illustrated by the *Keśava Jātaka* (vol. III, no. 346, p. 94), which refers to the distribution of the choicest food in the king's palace, 'but there are none to give it with their own hands, with marks of affection and love, but the king's ministers dispense the food and the Brethren do not care to sit down and eat it'.

It was mainly to ensure that respect was shown to recipients that Brāhmaṇical lawgivers stipulated that the gift of food was to be made only to a small group of people at a time. According to the *Baudhāyana Dharmasūtra* (II.8.15.10), even a very wealthy man should not be anxious to entertain a large company, for it 'destroys the respectful treatment of the invited guests'. That the members of heterodox sects attached as much importance to this adage is evident from the *Mahāvagga* (VI.25.1). It refers to a certain minister who, having invited 1,250 *bhikkhus*, got ready as many different dishes so that each *bhikkhu* could be served a special dish.

Moreover, the concept of retribution following the callous bestowal of *dāna*/alms occurs as much in Brāhmaṇical law books as in Buddhist texts. The *Dīgha Nikāya* (XXIII, Payasi Suttanta, II.354) alludes to the retribution which overtook Prince Payasi for not bestowing his gifts 'with his own hand', 'with thoroughness' or even 'with due thought'. In the case of recipients of a religious order such as brāhmaṇas and monks, the concept of retribution was directly linked with a belief in their spiritual prowess, as well as their inherent potential for causing harm to the donor in case they felt offended by the callous mode of gift-making. According to the *Bṛhaspati Smṛti* (49), a brāhmaṇa's anger is fiercer than a discus: 'One should not make a brāhmaṇa irate, for there is no re-growth for him who has been destroyed by a brāhmaṇa's ire.' The Jaina text *Uttarādhyayana Sutta* (Lec. XX.45) contains a similar injunction for lay donors: 'Prostrate yourself before him (monk) for protection if you want to save your life and your property, for in his wrath he might reduce the world to ashes.'

Perhaps it was the same portentous fear of the donee causing harm to the donor which led both Brāhmaṇical and heterodox leaders alike to stipulate that *dāna* should be given only to persons who were really meritorious; brāhmaṇas of cat-like conduct (*bidālavrati*) or who were hypocrites (*bakavrati*) were to be excluded from the category of deserving recipients of *dāna*.[9] The *Saṁyutta Nikāya* (III.3.4) similarly enjoins that a gift bears fruit only when given to a person 'no matter what his social class, who has left the world and has abolished five qualities and is possessed of five qualities'. Perhaps the practice of making the donee recite the benediction 'may welfare attend thee',[10] was meant chiefly to offset the danger of the donor even unwittingly falling prey to the former's wrath. The Buddha went a step further and enjoined his disciples that, in return for the alms they received, they should help the *upāsakas* achieve spiritual progress through religious and moral sermons.[11] The practice inevitably invested *dāna* with a bilateral aspect. The idea finds further exposition in the *Dhammapada* (354) in which the Buddha speaks of two kinds of *dāna*: the material gift or alms which the monk receives from lay folks and the spiritual gift or *dhamma dāna* which he himself confers in return. The practice became so firmly established that, in due course of time, lay disciples more or less came to expect religious sermons from the *bhikkhus* as a matter of right in return for the alms.

The concept of spiritual merit or *puṇya* accruing to the donor in return for the material gift he bestowed was another feature central to ritual gift-making.[12] However, it tended to undermine the unilateral basis of such gifts. Once *dāna* to brāhmaṇas and other religious mendicants came to be viewed as a reciprocal exchange in which the gift of material goods was requited in the form of spiritual merit, it automatically acquired a bilateral character. The concept of *puṇya* being integral to ritual gift is found to be as much entrenched in alternate religious systems as it was in the Dharmaśāstras. The Buddha gave it a more tangible expression when he exhorted monks to reciprocate alms by giving sermons for the moral edification and spiritual advancement of donors. The practice became so widespread that, according to the *Uddālaka Jātaka* (vol. IV, no. 487, p. 189), some monks reportedly complained that though people were willing to give them alms, 'they make us show gratitude by declaring the law'. Hence, *dāna*, although apparently unilateral, had come to be tacitly regarded in both systems as an equitable exchange, with the balance tipped in favour of the religious beneficiaries. This inevitably created a unique situation in which the donee, instead of labouring under an obligation, was regarded as doing a favour to the donor. This is evident from the Buddha's injunction to the *bhikkhus* to turn their bowls down, i.e. withhold the right to bestow alms to the donor in case he was guilty of some grave moral misdemeanour.

With religious recipients having an edge over donors in both Brāhmaṇical and alternate systems, the best form of *dāna* was considered to be one in which the donor, displaying respect for the donee, supplicated the latter to receive gifts. Consequently, gifts made at the donee's residence were regarded as ideal.[13] References contained in the epics to kings personally visiting sages in their hermitages and showering munificent gifts upon them indicate that it was a common practice for the donor to voluntarily seek out the recipient and beseech him to receive gifts. That such gifts continued to be regarded very highly even up to the time of the Purāṇas is apparent from the following statement contained in the *Agni Purāṇa* (209.55): 'It was the custom in the golden age (*Kṛta-yuga*) to make a gift to a person by calling at his house. In the *Tretā* age a brāhmaṇa used to be invited to the house of the giver and sent honoured with a gift. In the *Dvāpara-yuga* it was the custom to make a gift to a person who had asked for it, while in the present *Kali-yuga* gifts are made to persons who actually run after the giver.' Buddhist literature, likewise, abounds with references to lay folks carrying gifts for teachers as well as to monasteries for the resident monks. Thus, the *Ṭiṭṭira Jātaka* (vol. III, no. 438, p. 320) recounts how the natives of a country, saying 'a famous professor is living in the forest and giving lessons in science' brought presents of rice for him. According to the *Viśvanta Jātaka* (vol. I, no. 69, p. 167), 'folks came to the monastery with a quantity of such cakes for the Brotherhood'. Similarly, while in the *Cullavagga* (V.181), we get references to people who 'came to the *ārāma* bringing perfumes and garlands', from the *Mahāvagga* (VIII.5.1), we learn how people went to the *ārāma* with robes to be presented to the *bhikkhus*.

However, in both Brāhmaṇical and heterodox literature, references to donors respectfully inviting donees to partake of meals and gifts at the formers' residence are plentiful. Thus, if Dharmaśāstra composers such as Manu (III.187), Yājñavalkya (X.10.225) and Viṣṇu give formal approval to the practice of brāhmaṇas being invited and honoured by the donor at his own residence, from the Buddhist texts we learn how, once the proffered invitation had been duly accepted, the donors went about making elaborate arrangements to accord all possible honour to the august invitees. We learn from the *Cullavagga* (VI.41) that having gained the Buddha's consent to dine at his residence, the *seṭṭhī* of Rājagṛha bade his slaves and servants to rise early the next morning and cook various delicacies. The same text also refers to Anāthapiṇḍika making elaborate preparations for receiving the confraternity of monks invited by him.[14]

Gifts made on an inordinately large scale, however, must have made it necessary for wealthy donors, especially kings, in both the systems to engage the services of a large number of officers and servants. If, from the *Keśava Jātaka* (vol. III, no. 346, p. 94), we learn about a king's ministers dispensing food to monks, the *Dhammapada* (book 11, story 9) describes how food was presented to a recluse at the door of a rest-house by novices and probationers. Even epigraphic notices are forthcoming to prove that bureaucratic machinery was employed for organizing gift-making activities. In Mauryan and post-Mauryan inscriptions, we come across references to officers exclusively deputed with the task of administering royal donations. From the Delhi Topra Pillar Edict VII,[15] we learn how 'both these and many other chief (officers)' were occupied with the delivery of gifts made by the emperor as well as by the queens.

According to one Nasik Cave inscription[16] during the time of the Sātavāhana king, Kṛṣṇa, the cave was caused to be made by the officer-in-charge of the śramaṇas at Nasik. The Manikiala Stone Inscription[17] refers to the donation master of the Kṣatrapa Vespasi.

This development was by no means confined to heterodox systems alone. In fact, in the case of the Brāhmaṇical system, the large-scale distribution of gifts by kings was generally undertaken by their minions. According to a description of gift distribution contained in the *Mahābhārata* (Aśvamedhika Parva, 87.61), 'a large number of men taking innumerable vessels in their hands distributed the food unto the regenerate classes by hundreds and thousands. The attendants of the Pāṇḍavas gave away unto the brāhmaṇas diverse kind of food and drink.' At another place in the same text,[18] we are told how 'tellers and scribes under the orders of Yudhiṣṭhira ceaselessly asked the old king, 'Do thou command, O Monarch, what gifts should be made to these', and as soon as the king spoke, they gave away what he directed.' In the *Rāmāyaṇa* (Bāla Kāṇḍa, XIV), too, we come across a reference to the assisting priest placing all the king's gifts before the holy sages, Vasiṣṭha and Ṛṣyaśṛṅga and begging them to distribute them.

If we can discern a certain similarity between the two procedural modes of offering gift, the dissimilarities between them are equally striking. In fact, in consonance with the predominantly urban ethos in which the heterodox sects evolved and developed, the gift-making practised by them manifests an exceptionally remarkable organizational spirit, which is lacking in the Brāhmaṇical system. Our sources reveal wide-ranging procedural formations that seem to be directly inspired by such an organizational spirit. It is found to be especially manifest in the case of gift-distribution lasting for several days, which, from Buddhist texts, appears to be a common practice. The *Vimānavatthu* (First Chair Mansion, 1.1) mentions how King Pasenadi of Kosala had inaugurated for seven days an unparalleled almsgiving for the order of monks. In the *Therigāthā* (LXIV), we learn how Uppalavanna gave great gifts for seven days to the Buddha and the order. A similar reference to almsgiving lasting for seven days also occurs in the *Dhammapada* (vol. III, 17.3, p. 103).

In fact, it was mainly the economic expediency arising out of urbanized living and the growth of trade and a money economy which occasioned variations in the gift-making procedure. These were bound to occur in the case of gifts distributed through the institution of alms-halls, through the ticket system or when gifts to the *saṁgha* were deposited personally by the donor. Distribution of gifts through the ticket system appears to be a completely novel and purely urban phenomenon. The numerous notices that are forthcoming vouch for its popularity. The *Mahā-Sutasoma Jātaka* (vol. V, no. 537, p. 259) refers to the distribution of milk by tickets. The *Vimānavatthu* (Sirima's Mansion, 1.17) mentions alms being given daily to eight members of the order chosen by lot. The *Dhammapada* (Bk. 11, story 1) describes how a lady 'gave regularly the eight ticket food and from that time on, eight monks came regularly to her house'.

Improvements are known to have been effected in the mode of alms-distribution to suit the donor's convenience, as is evident from a passage of the *Dhammapada* (book 2, story 1). It describes how a daughter, disturbed by the noise caused by alms-seekers at her father's refectory, suggested that in order to make the people receive their alms peaceably and quietly, the refectory should be provided with a fence with just two gates, through which people could enter and exit one at a time: 'From that time on there was no more tumult in the refectory.' The growing popularity of the practice of building alms-houses[19] could have been partly due to the increased commercial and religious traffic on the highways. We learn how *dānaśālās* or *sattraśālās* were constructed at the city gates or at other vantage points in the city, where alms entailing a fixed expenditure could be distributed in an organized manner. Thus, if the *Kurudhamma Jātaka* (vol. II, no. 276, p. 253) refers to an alms-hall situated on the eastern gate of the city, the *Vessantara Jātaka* (vol. VI, no. 547, p. 250) describes how 600,000 pieces were distributed daily at an alms-hall.

Characteristic of the organized nature of the newly emergent urban life was the manner in which perpetual meals for the *saṁgha* were instituted by lay devotees, or the way in which the residents of a whole street or city used to club together to make gifts of cooked food or other articles to the *bhikkhus*. Thus, we learn from the *Kundakapava Jātaka* (vol. I, no. 109, p. 252) how at Sāvatthi, 'the Brotherhood with the Buddha at their head used to be entertained by a body of people or a whole street would club together or sometimes the whole city entertained'. The *Keśava Jātaka* (vol. II, no. 221,

p. 138) similarly informs: 'At that time the citizens of Rajagaha used to club together for the proposed almsgiving.' Notice of such a practice is also contained in the *Duddada Jātaka* (vol. II, no. 180, p. 59): 'The people were all glad to give him alms. They clubbed together and made a collection and provided plenty for the band of anchorites.' According to the *Mahāvagga* (I.30), 'At that time an arrangement had been made at Rajagaha that the *bhikkhus* were to receive excellent meals successively (in the houses of different rich *upāsakas*).'

Instituting perpetual meals for the members of the *saṁgha* was another practice for which we get copious notices. The *Cullavagga* (IV.4.6) refers to a certain householder possessed of good food, who 'used to give perpetual alms to the *saṁgha*, a meal for four *bhikkhus*'. Similarly, according to the *Vimānavatthu* (Slave Woman's Mansion, I.18), a devotee is said to have informed the superintendent of meals about appointing four perpetual meals for the order: 'From tomorrow on let the worthy gentlemen come to my house'. Such practices clearly reveal the extent to which organized efforts were made to meet the changed economic conditions.

The growing commercial preoccupation of the contemporary society, moreover, was solely responsible for giving rise to yet another procedural variation of making *dāna*. It involved the deposition of a fixed capital with a guild, with instructions to use the interest accruing from it for the construction and maintenance of a religious or charitable building or for institutions such as monasteries and alms-halls. This form of religious endowment must have especially suited the newly-arisen category of donors, namely the rich merchants and big business magnates.

Some procedural variations, especially those related to alms-begging rules, would appear to have their source not so much in economic contingency as in the strong competitive spirit arising out of sharing space with rival religious sectaries. Candidly acknowledging their dependence on alms, the monks tried to win the acclaim of their patrons by leading a life of continence and moral uprightness, as well as by their general pleasant demeanour and correct mode of conducting themselves at the time of receiving alms. We learn from the *Khantivadi Jātaka* (vol. III, no. 313, p. 26) how a householder, becoming pleased with an ascetic 'for the propriety of his deportment, brought him into the house and fed him with the food prepared for him'. The *Siri Jātaka* (vol. II, no. 284, p. 280) contains another such reference. According to it, an elephant trainer, once taking a fancy to the ways and manners of a recluse 'fed him and gave him lodging in his own grounds, waiting upon him continuously'. Buddhist monks are specially enjoined in the *Cullavagga* (VIII.4.5) to eat the alms they received with 'mind alert, paying attention to the bowl' and not putting the whole hand in the mouth. According to an injunction contained in the *Aṅguttara Nikāya* (IV.3.28), a monk must be content with any sort of food he receives and should always speak in its praise. Even while going around for alms, monks were strictly bidden by the Buddha to keep their lips sealed and proffer no request (*Sutta Nipāta*, III.11.32-3). According to the *Mahāvastu*,[20] the Buddha also advised his disciples to stand in silence and merely point to their alms-bowl while seeking alms. In fact, as can be inferred from the following passage of the *Cullavagga* (VIII.5.2), the Buddha wanted monks to be extra careful and not show any over-anxiety to receive alms: 'The monk should take notice whether the lady of the house seems willing or not to give away. If she wipes a spoon and puts aside a dish, he should stand still, perceiving that she seems willing to give. After the food has been given, he should cover up the bowl with his robe and turn back slowly and carefully.' As pointed out by R. Spence Hardy,[21] a similar code of seeking alms for monks is also prescribed in the *Milindapañho*: 'It is forbidden to the priest to proclaim his purity or attainments to the householders in order that they may gain honour or gifts. When persons come to the temple, he may not go up to them or address them, nor is he allowed to be continuously pressing them and urging them to give.' Heterodox alms-seeking rules were, thus, governed largely by pragmatic considerations as well as a strong competitive spirit amongst different sectarian groups and categories of alms-seekers. Brāhmaṇa recipients, on the contrary, being mostly householders, were not solely dependent on alms for their daily subsistence and, therefore, could not be expected to be bound by a similar strict code. Despite such procedural dissimilarities occasioned by the change of material context or the level of dependence on *dāna*, there was a lot in common between the two systems, the Brāhmaṇical and heterodox mode of offering gifts.

In fact, in matters of gift-items, the two systems, when placed in common material contexts, do not show any marked difference. In the predominantly pastoral/rural Vedic phase, cattle and slaves figure as the most popular gift-items. In the urban milieu of post-Vedic times, the list of most coveted gift-items comprised mainly food, both cooked and uncooked, and a wide range of finished goods, including both items of daily use as well as luxury articles.[22] Significantly, the list of popular gift-items during the urban phase is found to be more or less common to both the Brāhmaṇical and heterodox systems of gift-making.

From the Sātavāhana times onwards, even villages and land for residential purposes began to figure prominently in both Brāhmaṇical and heterodox lists of gift-items. Thus, if the gift of villages and land to brāhmaṇas is widely recommended in the *Baudhāyana Dharmasūtra* (IV.79), *Āpastamba Dharmasūtra* (II.10.26.1), *Vasiṣṭha Dharmasūtra* (XII.3), *Manu Smṛti* (IV.233) and *Viṣṇu Smṛti* (3.77-81), Buddhist texts, too, abound with notices of the gift of land and villages to religious beneficiaries. The *Dīgha Nikāya* (IV, Sonadaṇḍa Sutta, 1) and the *Majjhima Nikāya* (II.164) refer to land gifted by Bimbisāra of Magadha and Pasenadi of Kosala. The former text[23] also mentions the gift of the village of Ukkatha by Pasenadi. A reference to the gift of as many as sixteen villages occurs in the *Mahāummaga Jātaka* (vol. VI, no. 546).

Our sources furnish enough evidence to show that gift-making, as it was practised by heterodox sects, was largely an extension of ritual *dāna* that had been conceptualized and moulded by Brāhmaṇical ideologues. The two are found to share not only a basic common format and a somewhat common range of popular gift-items but also numerous procedural norms and beliefs underlying those practices. This was quite natural considering the common geographical space and time they shared. Whatever disparity existed was largely in response to the needs arising out of certain economic conditions or to the particular demands of different segments of society involved in this gift exchange.

Alms given to the non-religious category of recipients constitutes another form of gift-making that may be classified as *dāna* but in a more restricted sense. Our sources abound with references to alms-seekers such as wayfarers, tramps, indigent beggars and those who, like performing acrobats (*sailūṣa*), pursued occupations which made them constantly move from one town or village to another but provided an inadequate means of living. In the *Saṁyutta Nikāya* (I.2.3.3), we get a reference to paupers, cripples, wayfarers and beggars as seekers of alms. The *Mahāvastu*[24] refers to alms being distributed to the blind, helpless, poor and destitute. That beggars soliciting alms was a common sight in contemporary society is evident from a passage of the *Mahābhārata* (Anuśāsana Parva, 133.2), which refers to the destitute, blind and distressed *(dināndhkṛpānadisu)*. The *Mahāsupīna Jātaka* (I, no. 77, p. 191) similarly refers to beggars and religious mendicants seated on the highway, at the street-corners and at the doors of the king's palace. Two of Aśoka's edicts[25] refer to the measures adopted by the emperor to provide relief to the old, orphaned, poor and miserable. From the Mathura stone inscription of Huviṣka,[26] we learn that provision was made for alms-distribution amongst the destitute, hungry and thirsty.

The need for alms in the case of these varied categories of seekers, however, could not have been the same. For example, in the case of wayfaring travellers, such a need could be only temporary and of a limited nature. Drawn mainly from a shifting population that moved to and fro between market towns and cities, merchants, religious mendicants and pilgrims, and even royal agents and wayfarers unable to carry enough provisions to last the entire journey,[27] must have needed a temporary shelter and a meal to take care of their journey as well as their stay in strange towns. In the *Milindapañho* (I.32), Nāgasena, voicing his apprehension in undertaking a long journey, (Great, Sir, is the distance. It will be difficult to get food on the way. How shall I get there?) is reassured that, if he keeps going straight, he will get food on the way. Wayfarers were essentially a product of the economic situation created by the emergence of urban centres and the growth of trade during the Kuṣāṇa-Sātavāhana period.[28] The unprecedented increase in traffic on the highways that resulted from such developments is indicated by the fact that people with means had come to realize the need for constructing alms-halls and resting places for wayfaring travellers. Our sources testify to a large number of almshouses and rest-houses built by the rich, both within and outside the city gate.[29] According to certain Jātaka stories,[30] it had become almost customary for the city's rich to build five to six alms-halls at different points. From the *Milindapañho* (I.2), we learn how the city of Sagala was adorned with hundreds of alms-halls of various kinds. The Garha (Jasdan) stone inscription of Rudrasena I[31] refers to a *sattra* erected by the brothers of Khara(r)patha. According to the *Kurudhamma Jātaka* (II, no. 276, p. 253), eight brāhmaṇas, taking money for their journey, donning their travelling garb and without resting more than one night in a place, travelled quickly until, after a few days, they took their meal at the alms-hall at the city gate. A passage of the *Vinaya* (Pacittiya, XXI.1) mentions how alms-food came to be prepared in a public rest-house by some guild not far from Sāvatthi.

That rest-houses were meant to chiefly benefit weary travellers is indicated by a statement of the *Dīgha Nikāya* (III, Ambattha Sutta, II.4). According to it, hospices were invariably constructed at the meeting point of important highways so that whoever passed by could be supplied with alms. The *Kulavaka Jātaka* (I, no. 31, p. 79) also creates a similar impression. According to the *Mahā-Umagga Jātaka* (VI, no. 546, p. 158), the donor had so arranged the hall that there was, in one part, a place for destitute women to lie, in another, a lodging for brāhmaṇas and śramaṇas, in another, a lodging for other sorts of men, and in yet another, 'a place where foreign merchants could stow their goods, and all these apartments had doors opening'. That alms, besides being dispensed in alms-halls, were otherwise also offered to wayfarers is affirmed by the *Itivutthaka* (I, Splendid Mansion, I.1.2), which mentions how common people gave alms according to their means to wayfarers and tramps. The *Dīgha Nikāya* (V, Kutadanta Sutta, XIII) similarly mentions how a noble donor kept an open house 'a welling spring whence śramaṇas and brāhmaṇas, the poor and the wayfarers, beggars and petitioners might draw'.

Belonging to the same category as wayfarers were professional dancers, acrobats and other kinds of entertainers, the demands of whose profession made them tramp from one place to another in search of a livelihood and who, in the absence of regular or adequate earnings, often had to subsist on alms. Thus, the *Mahāvastu*[32] describes how some young actors who had come from Takṣaśilā to Benares went to a merchant's house to beg for alms. According to the *Ucchiṭṭha Bhaṭṭa Jātaka* (II, no. 212, p. 117), the Bodhisattva was once born in a family of poor acrobats that lived by begging. The *Mahābhārata* (Śānti Parva, 37.29) also refers to performing artistes and members of other professional groups, leading a gypsy life and occasionally subsisting on alms. However, in the *Mahābhārata* as well as in the *Viṣṇu Smṛti* (III.54), such performing artistes are declared to be unworthy of receiving alms. According to a verse of the *Mahābhārata*, 'A pious man should not make a gift to those who are given to dance and song.' Yet the bias shown by earlier Brāhmaṇical texts against such professional groupings is not fully endorsed by some of the later Purāṇas, which considered some skill to be necessary for begging.[33] According to the *Śiva Purāṇa* (II, Pārvatī Khaṇḍa, 30.26), even Śiva had to take the form of a dancer-actor, with a small drum (*ḍamaru*) in his right hand and a horn in his left, for the purpose of begging alms. In the *Kūrma Purāṇa* (25.12), however, begging is said to be generally bad, for whatever is gained without asking is nectar and alms received after begging is akin to death (*ayacitaṁsyadamṛtam mṛtāmbhaikṣyamtu yacitam*). Nevertheless, in the *Skanda Purāṇa* (IV.35.206), certain categories of alms-seekers such as a wanderer (*adhvagaḥ*, i.e. one who goes along a path), one who has meagre maintenance (*kṣīṇavṛtti*), a student (*vidyārthī*), those who want to sustain their preceptor (*gurupoṣaka*), one who has renounced the world (*yati*), and a *brahmacārin* are declared to be *dharma-bhikṣukas*. Alms to them, therefore, would be considered meritorious. Moreover, the fact that alms to wayfarers and tramps are invariably clubbed, in heterodox literature, along with those offered to brāhmaṇas and monks, might suggest that the popular mind had come to accept and even concede a certain degree of parity between gifts offered to the two different categories of recipients, religious and others beyond such parameters. For example, according to the *Peṭavatthu* (II.2), a wealthy brāhmaṇa of Benares was 'a well unto recluses and brāhmaṇas, indigents, tramps, wayfarers and beggars'. It may not be, therefore, incorrect to treat such alms as a distended form of *dāna*.

The same logic may also apply to alms given to beggars; though compared to wayfarers and tramps, their dependence on alms was far more complete and of a lasting nature. This is manifest from the rhetorical question posed in the *Pañcatantra*:[34] 'What beggar has come to exalted station?' The *Losaka Jātaka* (vol. I, no. 41, p. 109) refers to a beggar family which became even more impoverished after the birth of a child. The presence of wayfarers and tramps in a society emphasizes its expanding commercial horizon, its proliferating cities and townships, and a fading parochial mindset. The prevalence of beggary is symptomatic of economic disparities and the growing hiatus between the rich and poor. It also suggests greater competition and insecurities besetting economic life. Pāli literature pertaining to the NBPW cultural phase affirms the presence of the very rich *seṭṭhīs* and *gahapatis* owning 80 *koṭis* of wealth,[35] as well as the extremely poor (*daliddas*) who lived on the leavings of other people's food.[36] Some economic disparity could have resulted from sharp fluctuations in the fortunes of individuals, be it due to losses suffered in trade, in the wake of some natural or other calamity, as an aftermath of frequently raging inter-state wars, or even on account of social ostracization. The *Asampadāna Jātaka* (vol. I, no. 131, p. 286) refers to Piliya of Benares who, having got into difficulties and losing all his property, was reduced to beggary. Similar references are also forthcoming from some of the other *Jātakas*.[37]

The pitiable condition of beggars as they went about soliciting alms is thus described in the *Pañcatantra*:[38] 'Stammering in the throat, sweat on the countenance, pallor and trembling, the same signs that mark a dying man mark also a beggar.' In the *Sama Jātaka* (vol. VI, no. 540, p. 38), beggars are described as being 'clothed in rags and carrying potsherds in their hands'. According to the *Indriya Jātaka* (vol. III, no. 423, p. 276), beggars often received nothing better than 'gruel made of broken lumps of rice, solid food stale or decaying, or sprouts dried and burnt'.

Though feelings of pity and compassion were behind alms given to beggars, beggary as an institution was generally disliked and was very often a source of annoyance to the people. This is apparent from the *Peṭavatthu* (II.7.6) which describes the deep aversion that the wealthy Dhanapāla felt for beggars, so that, while taking meals, he would lock his doors to prevent them from seeing him. This is also corroborated by the *Maṇikaṇṭha Jātaka* (vol. II, no. 253, p. 197). Besides their unkempt and unpleasant looks, especially in the case of lepers and the maimed, it was their large numbers which the householders found disconcerting. The *Visayha Jātaka* (vol. III, no. 340, p. 85) refers to six hundred thousand beggars all repeatedly crying out, 'Give to us also.' The fraudulent ways and duplicity employed by some of them to evoke pity may have also fostered feelings of distrust and apathy towards them. For instance, according to the *Culla-Paduma Jātaka* (vol. II, no. 193, p. 83), a wicked wife once took her paramour upon her shoulders and went begging among the people. The *Jātakas* are, in fact, full of references to false ascetics and monks, who, according to the *Dhajavihetha Jātaka* (vol. III, no. 391, p. 189), would go about in ascetic garb during the day and indulge in sinful acts at night. More than anything else, it was their greed and indolence which earned the scorn and contempt of the people. The *Aditta Jātaka* (vol. III, no. 424, p. 280) mentions a householder who, on seeing 'alms being devoured by worthless greedy people' in his alms-hall, was exceedingly annoyed. Yet the householder's response to beggars was not necessarily always unfavourable or antagonistic. In fact, to a large extent, it also depended on the prevailing economic conditions, which could range from prosperity to drought and famine. The *Mahāvagga* (VI.32.1) mentions how, at one time, the city of Vaiśālī was 'well provided with food, the harvest was good, alms were easy to obtain'. We even chance upon statements such as the one that occurs in the *Mahāvastu*: 'Time and again when he saw a beggar the sight gladdened his heart.'[39] That many rich people distributed alms at their own doorstep is affirmed by the story of Aṅkura that occurs in the *Peṭavatthu* (I.9.40). According to it, 60,000 cartloads of food were distributed daily at his house.

To what extent can alms to beggars be regarded as *dāna* is, however, a question that cannot be answered in categorical terms. Even though some of the essential elements of *dāna* such as a proper time, place and reverence (*śraddhā*) displayed in the act of giving may be lacking in the case of the bestowal of alms to beggars, their unilateral character and the belief and hope of earning spiritual merit (*puṇya*) through them are two prominent features that draw them close to the concept of religious *dāna*, bringing out their commonality of form and purpose. Viewed from such a perspective, alms to beggars may also be treated as yet another distended form of *dāna*. Such a conclusion may also find support from the *Chāndogya Upaniṣad* (IV.1-2)[40] in which Janaśruti Pautrāyaṇa is highly lauded for erecting shelters everywhere in order to feed all people at all time coming from different quarters. Though the reference pertains to a period when social stratification and economic disparities had still not become deep-rooted, the idea of offering food to the needy being considered as a spiritually elevating and meritorious act is quite apparent from it. Our study, therefore, indicates that almsgiving to different categories of recipients, be they monks, wayfarers, tramps or beggars, represented the diversification of ritual *dāna* in all its mutations.

NOTES

1. *Āpastamba Dharmasūtra*, II.4.9.8, *Gautama Dharmasūtra*, V.19.
2. *Corpus Inscriptionum Indicarum*, vol. II, pt. I, pp. 48-9.
3. *Religions*, p. 351; J. Gonda, 'Gifts and Giving', *Selected Studies*, vol. IV, *History of Ancient Indian Religion*, Leiden, 1975, p. 129.
4. M. Mauss, *The Gift*, London, 1954, p. 62.
5. S.C. Mitra, 'On Some Indian Ceremonies for Disease Transference', *JASB*, NS, XIII, 1917, p. 13.
6. *Manusmṛti*, IV.191.
7. *Cullavagga*, V.21.4.
8. *Pīṭha Jātaka*, vol. III, no. 337, p. 79; *Jātakas*, ed. V. Fausboll, 6 vols., London, 1877-98; tr. E.B. Cowell, Cambridge, 1895-1913.
9. *Manu Smṛti*, IV.192; *Viṣṇu Smṛti*, XCIII.7.
10. *Bṛhaspati Smṛti*, 49.
11. S. Tachibana, *The Ethics of Buddhism*, rpt., London, 1975, p. 228.
12. *Viṣṇu Smṛti*, 93.1-4.
13. *Manu Smṛti*, IV.250.
14. *Cullavagga*, V.4.8.
15. *Corpus Inscriptionum Indicarum*, vol. I, p. 136.
16. D.C. Sircar, *Select Inscriptions*, vol. I, bk. ii, no. 75, p. 189.
17. *Corpus Inscriptionum Indicarum*, vol. I, p. 150.
18. *Mahābhārata*, Āśramavāsika Parva, 20.7-8.
19. *Dīgha Nikāya*, III, Ambattha Sutta, II.4.
20. *Mahāvastu*, tr. J.J. Jones, Sacred Books of the Buddhists, vol. XVI, London, p. 419.
21. *Eastern Monachism*, London, 1850, p. 70.
22. Vijay Nath, *Dāna: Gift System in Ancient India*, pp. 148-51.
23. *Dīgha Nikāya*, III.2.6.
24. *Mahāvastu*, tr. J.J. Jones, vol. I, pp. 76-7.
25. Kalsi rock edict V, *CII*, p. 33; Delhi-Topra Pillar Edict VII, *CII*, p. 136.
26. *Select Inscriptions*, vol. I, bk. II, no. 49.
27. *Mahāvagga*, VIII.1.8; VI.34.21.
28. Kameshwar Prasad, 'The Kuṣāṇa Towns in India: Problems and Methods', Proceedings of the Indian History Congress, 34th Session, Chandigarh, 1973, pp. 36-9; V.K. Thakur, *Urbanization in Ancient India*, pp. 80-3; 99;

B. Gafurov, 'Kusana Civilization and World Culture', *Kusana Studies in USSR*, p. 9.
29. *Vessantara Jātaka*, VI, no. 547; *Bilarikosiya Jātaka*, IV, no. 450; *Sivi Jātaka*, IV, no. 499; *Nimi Jātaka*, VI, no. 541; *Kurudhamma Jātaka*, II, no. 276; *Janasandha Jātaka*, IV, no. 468; *Mahābhārata*, Anuśāsana Parva, 133.3.
30. *Khadiraṅga Jātaka*, vol. I, no. 40; *Visayha Jātaka*, vol. III, no. 340; *Śaṅkha Jātaka*, vol. IV, no. 442, p. 9.
31. *Epigraphia Indica*, XVI, no. 17, p. 239.
32. *Mahāvastu*, tr. J.J. Jones, op. cit., p. 169.
33. S.A. Dange, *Encyclopaedia of Purāṇic Beliefs and Practices*, sv alms.
34. *Pañcatantra*, tr. Franklin Edgerton, London, 1965, p. 52.
35. *Mahāvagga*, V.1.29.
36. *Dhammapāda*, bk. 2, story 9.
37. *Mahāsutsoma*, vol. V, no. 537, p. 253; *Sama Jātaka*, vol. VI, no. 540, p. 38.
38. *Pañcatantra*, tr. Edgerton, op. cit., p. 9.
39. *Mahāvastu*, vol. I, tr. J.J. Jones, op. cit., p. 4.
40. P.V. Kane, *History of Dharmaśāstra*, II, pt. ii, p. 838.

9

Peasantry and the Dynamics of the Ritual Gift System

Sources pertaining to the early period of Indian history indicate an extremely marginal role played by peasants in ritual gift-making. They do not figure as a prominent category of donors, especially during the period *c*. 600 BC to *c*. AD 300.[1] Votive inscriptions belonging to the centuries immediately following the Christian era contain a few references to husbandmen tillers (*halakiyas*) as donors,[2] although *gahapatis* with a prominent agricultural base stand out as a donor category.[3] The absence of references to peasant donors can be explained in more than one way. It could have been due to their low economic competence to make gifts, combined with the fact that the actual tillers of soil had come to be differentiated from the rich landed proprietors.[4] Yet the essentially rural background of the peasantry as a social segment, as well as the rather modest nature of their gift-items, which necessarily must have excluded cattle, gold or land, could have also been responsible for the gifts made by them not being recorded in contemporary sources.

Right from the later Vedic times, the peasants constituted the main bulk of the population. The gift-economy had all along figured as a major factor in both social and economic life.[5] Hence, some kind of dialectical relationship between the two seems inevitable and, therefore, requires careful probing. In this context, the role of peasants as producers of food is especially significant,[6] for food has always figured as a major item of gift. The sharing of food is a symbolic mode of recognizing parity in ritual status in most traditional societies.[7]

I

Before attempting to assess the nature and degree of impact exercised by such a dialectical interaction, we would need to take cognizance of certain important developments characterizing the general format and purposive character of *dāna* ritualism, as well as some major structural changes besetting the composition of the peasantry, especially during the Gupta period and the centuries immediately thereafter. Regarding changes in the gift-system, the Smṛti and Purāṇic literature reveal an unprecedented extension of *dāna* ritualism. Besides elaborate rituals centering round the sixteen *mahādānas*, ritual *dāna* became the focal point of all sacramental, expiatory and fertility-related agricultural rites which gained popularity during this period. *Dāna* also came to be closely associated with temple and *tīrtha*-based ritualism.[8] In fact, *dāna* ritualism even acquired a Tāntric hue. The *Matsya Purāṇa* reveals Tāntric influence in the prescription of *maṇḍalas* in the *śrāddha* ritual.[9]

Perhaps the most crucial development related to the ritual gift-system was the growing popularity of land as an object of *dāna*. Although references to the gifts of villages and, occasionally, even of land occur in pre-Mauryan and Mauryan literature, actual instances of the gift of land, especially for agricultural purposes, are recorded mainly from the Sātavāhana times onwards. The growing incidence of the practice of land grants during the centuries following the Christian era marks an important stage in the development of the agrarian economy and is generally acknowledged to have had a significant impact on the condition of agricultural producers, as well as on the changing mode and relations of production.[10] Another major development pertaining to ritual gift-items was the concept of *utsarga* which gained popularity during this period through its wide endorsement in contemporary legal texts. The dedication of tanks, gardens, wells,[11] etc., as a form of ritual gift-making is commonly reported from the Kuṣāṇa-Sātavāhana times and would seem to be directly linked with developments in the field of agricultural production.

Another gift-item which gained popularity from the post-Vedic period but more so during the Gupta/post-Gupta centuries was food, particularly grain. In the *Matsya Purāṇa*, there is not a single ritual in which food does not figure in the list of gift-items. The composer of the text, introducing some innovative forms of ritual gifts, lists ten *parvata dānas* and another ten *dhenu dānas*, which entailed the gift of various cereals arranged in the shape of a hillock or cow. The changing pattern of gift-items, besides reflecting the growing importance of the agrarian economy, would also bespeak cognizance on the part of Brāhmaṇical lawgivers of the need to extract agricultural surplus from potential donors, be they householders or producers of food themselves, namely the peasants, even though the latter have never been categorically distinguished in the role of donors in the Dharmaśāstras.

Change is also evident in the purposive role played by *dāna* in the early period of Indian history. In the Vedic pre-market tribal economy, gift-making had served more as a form of redistribution and exchange.[12] In the advanced food producing economy of later times, it appears that besides figuring as a means of creating a nexus between the rulers and priests, with the latter lending religious sanction to the power enjoyed by the former, *dāna* ritualism served as a mechanism of appropriating and controlling important means of production, especially land. In fact, in the context of the growing importance of landed economy and property rights, it is the property-based concept and status-conferring role of *dāna* which becomes more sharply focused. Thus, the growing importance and unprecedented extension of *śrāddha* ceremonialism in the early Purāṇas clearly reveals the property-oriented character of *dāna* rituals. This is evident from semantic studies as well as the analysis of the structural contexts in which *dāna* is known to occur.[13]

Status change affected through *dāna* would also seem to have a direct bearing on the question of social mobility, both vertical and horizontal, though upward mobility was always more difficult to achieve.[14] In its new aspect, *dāna* ritualism seemingly became central to the process of acculturation at work in peripheral tribal zones. Unless we assume that these areas were totally uninhabited by people engaged in some sort of food production, though based on the shifting mode of cultivation, we have to recognize the impact which the ritual gift-system must have had, no matter how indirectly, on the condition of the tribal peasantry.

Some impact exercised by *dāna* ritualism on the condition of peasantry can also be presumed in an earlier context, namely that of the transition from the Vedic pastoral tribal order to a *varṇa* stratified social order based on the intensive agriculture of post-Vedic times.

It was primarily by promoting *dāna* ritualism, which drew its strength from the principle of *ahiṁsā*, especially in the form of the non-killing of animals, that the sacrifice-based ideology of the Vedic period could be effectively negated. Cattle had become so vital for agricultural production by post-Vedic times that its decimation on a large scale, concomitant to the performance of Vedic sacrifices, was proving disastrous for agricultural growth. The substitution of sacrifices with *dāna*, therefore, must have directly safeguarded and promoted the interests of all those engaged in agricultural production.

In fact, it was during the post-Vedic period that the dynamics of *dāna* ritualism as an effective mechanism of validating new social norms came to be fully realized and exploited. This is amply borne out by the tenor of special *dāna*-making rules contained in the Smṛti texts, which began to be framed by contemporary Brāhmaṇical lawgivers. Through the introduction of new rites occasioning *dāna* and the revision and modification of the existent body of gift-making rules, the *dāna* ideology was explicitly aimed at achieving certain definite social and political ends. The process would seem to have continued during the subsequent phase when Purāṇa composers took on the task of further improvizing upon *dāna* ritualism by closely linking it with some prominent ritual practices such as *vratas*, *tīrthas*, temple-building, *pūjā*, etc. Those gained popularity mainly due to the ongoing process of the Brāhmaṇization of indigenous groups inhabiting regions far removed from the core cultural zone.

II

Although it is relatively easy to delineate some of the salient developments which marked the ritual gift-system up to the end of the first millennium AD, determining the structural composition of the peasantry as a social group may prove to be a more challenging task. Even ascertaining the social and economic status of this group is not possible for the simple reason that long before the beginning of the Christian era, it had ceased to be a homogeneous social entity. Its members had not only been drawn from a common *varṇa* stratum, namely vaiśya,[15] but had even owned the land and worked on the fields assisted by their family members, only occasionally employing hired or slave labour. However, the peasantry by early medieval period is found to bear an extremely heterogeneous character.[16] It had come to represent a multi-tiered economic order, exhibiting sharp social and economic variations. At the risk of adopting a rather simplistic framework, we may distinguish three distinct grades amongst those engaged in agricultural production. The first comprised the rich and influential landed gentry, who as proprietors of large landed estates did not actively participate in agricultural tasks. They enriched themselves by concentrating on land, the chief means of production within their group, as well as by using other's labour for production. The second segment consisted mainly of self-sufficient and self-cultivating peasants with proprietary rights on land. In contemporary sources, the terms used for them are *kṣetrasvāmin*, *kṣetrika*, or *kṣetrin*. It was a residual group which seems to have survived from pre-Gupta times but was almost marginalized by the fast-proliferating group of dependent peasantry,[17] although the practice of land grants would seem to have considerably augmented the size of such self-cultivating peasants exercising proprietary rights on land. In fact, Harbans Mukhia is inclined to treat it as the most dominant category of peasantry.[18] The lowest status within the peasant grouping was held by dependent farmers, namely seasonal share-croppers and agricultural labourers with very little or no land of their own. This class of tillers was mainly concomitant to the landed aristocracy and its members eked out a living by supplying their labour for the prosperity of the former. It may be noted, however, that the degree of servility of the peasants to the landlords must have considerably varied from region to region.

Yet another feature which characterized the land-system from the Gupta period onwards was that of graded controlling rights over land, created, to some extent, by the practice of land grants and sub-infeudation. The impact of these land grants, however, cannot be expected to have been uniform in all regions. According to one analysis, the maximum number of land grants (more than eighty) are recorded in western India during the sixth and seventh centuries AD.[19] Moreover, the entitlement of the beneficiaries to extract forced labour is mentioned less commonly in charters of eastern India than those of western and central regions.[20] What is even more significant is that the process of reclamation of forest and waste land must have also led to the large-scale assimilation of the tribal element into the peasant category. References to the gift of forest and waste land are forthcoming, especially from the sixth century AD onwards. The Ghugrahati copper plate from Bengal belonging to AD 560 records the donation of a land full of pits and infested with wild beasts.[21] The Tipperah copper plate of Lokanātha records the donation of forest land.[22] A sixth-century AD land grant[23] belonging to the Kadamba family entitled a brāhmaṇa to clear a patch of forest tract and cultivate it (*araṇya-karṣaṇa*). Similarly, the Goribidnur Taluk inscription of 762 refers to a Kāśyapa brāhmaṇa who received several allotments of different types of land together with a title over forest land, which formed the common boundary of all the four villages in which the lands were situated.[24] According to R.N. Nandi,[25] from the seventh century onwards, 'inscriptions begin to pour in information of the transfer of waste plots to brāhmaṇas and folk heroes'. Nandi further goes on to observe: 'The process of waste reclamation cannot be quantified to ascertain its impact on the overall progress of agriculture although it seems to have continued throughout the early middle ages.'

A more direct impact of the ritual gift-system on the agrarian economy was the rise of a class of big and small brāhmaṇa landowners. The emergence of a fairly large group of small landowners within the brāhmaṇa segment is indicated by frequent references to collective land grants made at times in favour of as many as a thousand brāhmaṇas, so that only very small pieces of land could be expected to have fallen to each recipient's share.[26] Sharp economic disparities existing within the brāhmaṇa *varṇa* is also suggested by Purāṇic evidence. In the *Nārada Purāṇa*, we get the story of a poor brāhmaṇa who, unable to maintain his family, went to Kauśāmbī and approached a wealthy brāhmaṇa for the gift of land measuring just 10 feet. The latter is said to have obliged by conceding the demand.

Another significant feature of such gifts of land to brāhmaṇas is that only the Vedapāraga or Śrotriyas amongst them came to be preferred as recipients. This practice further promoted segmentation within the brāhmaṇa grouping. In the *Matsya Purāṇa* (chapter 145, 35-40), Smārtta brāhmaṇas as beneficiaries of land grants are distinguished from their Śrauta counterparts. What is more significant is that by swelling the ranks of powerful landed gentry, these recipients of *brahmadeya* land further accentuated the fragmentary character of the peasantry as a social grouping. The irrevocable nature of these grants, manifest from such expressions as that they were to last as long as the sun, moon and stars existed,[27] combined with the important fiscal and administrative immunities and privileges which they carried,[28] transformed them into an important means of surplus extraction and exploitation.[29] The development, as adequately shown by R.S. Sharma[30] and B.N.S. Yadava,[31] was equally responsible for a large number of free peasants becoming relegated to the position of sharecroppers and dependents. That the changing character and composition of the peasantry was dialectically linked with the changing format of the Brāhmaṇical and non-Brāhmaṇical practice of ritual *dāna* has been effectively shown by Yadava. According to him, the Mahāyāna text, *Śrāvakabhūmi*[32] of Asaṅga (*c.* AD 340-415), 'represents a landmark in the development of the theory and practice of dāna' for 'it accords a clear sanction to the donation of slaves and gives a religious justification for giving non-slaves—dependent servants and workmen—also to śramaṇas and brāhmaṇas'. Since they were under the 'power (*aiśvarya*) and control (*vaśita*) of the donors', non-slaves, too, could be presented by the latter to the concerned donees.[33] As Yadava further points out, the evidence of the text is definitely corroborated by Fa-hsien[34] who has specifically referred to husbandmen and cattle being given to monasteries, along with fields which were to be cultivated by them. Even though Fa-hsien does not mention such gifts being made in favour of brāhmaṇas, the impact of these religious donations on the condition of the peasantry, especially in reducing them to a state of 'servile dependence', cannot be overemphasized.

Tribal accretions from acculturated zones must have also augmented the growing size of the subject peasantry. The development easily accounts for their impaired ritual status. *Kinasa* in earlier times denoted a free vaiśya peasant but by the early medieval period, his status appears to have declined and he came to be equated with the śūdras. Thus, the word *kinasa*, according to Asahāya's commentary on Nārada (I.181), means a śūdra. That the tilling of soil became the duty mainly of a śūdra is also evident from the *Parāśara Smṛti* (II.19) and the *Narasiṁha Purāṇa* (58.10-11), which recommend agriculture for the śūdras. Devala, quoted by the Mitākṣarā on the *Yājñavalkya Smṛti* (I.120), too, includes cultivation (*karṣaṇa*) in the list of duties to be performed by śūdras. The practice of *bhūmi-dāna*, therefore, on the one hand, raised the economic competence of a section of brāhmaṇas. On the other, it was equally responsible for the depressed social status of a sufficient majority of the peasant population to justify Hieun-Tsang's rather sweeping description of the latter as śūdras:[35] 'The fourth class is that of the śūdras or agriculturists. These toil at cultivating the soil and are industrious at sowing and reaping.' The *Mārkaṇḍeya Purāṇa*, as cited by Dānakhaṇḍa of the *Kṛtya-kalpataru* of Lakṣmīdhara and the *Nītivākyāmṛta* (17.364) of Jineśvara, reveal that a village was largely inhabited by 'śūdra-*karṣakas*'.

III

The role of the ritual gift-system, especially that of land grants, in affecting the condition of peasantry has long been acknowledged and the whole paradigm of the feudal formation seemingly rests upon it.[36] Yet the possibility of peasantry and the agricultural land to which it was attached, in its turn, changing the very complexion of the ritual gift-system has not been so well-explored. In order to do so, we need to bear in mind some dominant trends in the changing pattern of agricultural production. The first feature that strikes us is the continually ascending graph of the agrarian economy right from the later Vedic period onwards. A corollary to this development was the growing interest that came to be focused upon property rights, especially by brāhmaṇa lawgivers. Another directly affected area was that of agro-technology which showed unprecedented improvements. The development inevitably led to rural expansion, besides triggering off the processes of detribalization.

As already noted, another important feature that marked the agrarian economy, especially in the post-Gupta centuries, was the presence of a socially and economically oppressed class of husbandman tillers labouring under mounting fiscal pressure and social disabilities. Regarding the decline in the status of cultivators, no matter how scholars may differ over the optimal or minimal level of peasant exploitation during the early medieval period, the debilitating character and oppressive nature of fiscal dues and forced labour (*sarvapīḍaparihṛta*) attested by contemporary charters can scarcely be disregarded. Even if these charters did not carry any 'blanket authority' for the beneficiary, yet, as argued by Sharma, it seems difficult to believe that they did not in any way prove detrimental to the interests of the peasants or subvert their freedom to carry on agricultural operations in total disregard of the wishes of the assignee of the land. Available data, on the contrary, suggests that the cultivator's spatial mobility and access to agricultural resources such as wells, pasture lands and even pathways must have been seriously affected. Mass desertions of peasants under acute distress caused by excessive taxation and famine are described in the *Bṛhannāradīya Purāṇa* (38.87) as special features of the Kali age. Some idea of the extremely harsh conditions under which dependent farmers had to toil can be had from the fact that even brāhmaṇas devoid of Vedic learning were to be penalized, according to a stipulation contained in the *Devībhāgavata Purāṇa* (3.10.36; belonging to eleventh-twelfth-century Bengal), by being compelled to work as tillers of the soil like the śūdras.

Another important development related to the agrarian economy in the Gupta and post-Gupta period was the emergence of a dominant class of landowning brāhmaṇas and other religious beneficiaries of land grants, who became partly instrumental in the exploitation of the peasantry. In the Tipperah copper-plate inscription,[37] we get, reference to a feudatory brāhmaṇa described as *mahāsāmanta pradoṣaśarman*.

In any discussion of the role of peasantry in the restructuring of the ritual gift-system, we have to also take note of the specific circumstances that led to the sudden importance being attached to the gift of land from the period of the Sātavāhanas. Thus, it is remarkable how, from this time onwards, whole sections of Brāhmaṇical texts began to be devoted to the praise of the gift of land, a development that was bound to directly affect the peasantry. Sections devoted to *bhūmidāna praśaṁsā* are found contained in the *Yājñavalkya Smṛti* (IX.210), the Anuśāsana Parva (61.9; 11; 42; 58) of the *Mahābhārata* as well as the *Matsya Purāṇa* (283.1-19). Sufficient evidence is forthcoming both from contemporary literature and archaeology that throws light on the specific socio-economic conditions which compelled Brāhmaṇical lawgivers to rethink and redefine the parameters of the ritual gift-system.

Amongst the other circumstances which rendered innovative changes in the conceptual framework of the ritual gift-system imminent was the heightened importance of landed property. It was a development which, however, reaches back to a much earlier period. It was, in fact, a direct corollary of the agricultural advancement that followed in the wake of an improved iron technology. Irfan Habib,[38] citing Gordon Childe, points out how cheap iron tended to universalize peasant farming. Consequently, land rather than cattle or gold came to be valued as a form of wealth, and became the most powerful symbol of economic status and social prestige. During the NBPW cultural phase, even commercial magnates and rich merchants are known to have invested their capital in agricultural land. Thus, *seṭṭhīs* are very often described in the *Jātakas* as possessing land, which some of them may have held as absentee landlords.[39] Just as the *gahapati* who, derived social prestige through the ownership of landed property, sought to further augment his income by taking to money-lending and other industrial and commercial pursuits, the *seṭṭhī*, likewise, may have invested some of his capital earned through commercial enterprise in land, for purposes of acquiring greater social prestige and security. It is quite understandable, therefore, as to why contemporary Smṛti writers became so preoccupied with framing laws of inheritance and the partition of landed property.[40] Hence, the gift of land to religious beneficiaries inevitably came to represent a symbolic mode of begetting a superior social status and prestige. Its efficacy in securing the highest spiritual merit and an elevated ritual status began to be reiterated in all lawbooks.

More than being a source of prestige and social status, the receipt of land grants by brāhmaṇas and other religious beneficiaries lent religious endorsement and validation by implication to the nascent political power of the donor. The phenomenon gains special significance in the context of the appearance of a large number of foreign and ethnic groups on the political and social horizon. However, as pointed out by Romila Thapar,[41] it is significant that the newly-arisen ruling dynasties of the pre-Gupta period, though identically situated, are not known to have resorted to a similar subterfuge for gaining legitimacy. It is only from that post-Gupta period that land charters containing fabricated genealogies of donors become prolific. As suggested by Thapar, the most plausible explanation for this could be that land, particularly that meant for tillage, had still not become scarce and, therefore, as highly valued as an item of wealth as it was to become in later times. Consequently, land grants during the pre-Gupta phase could not have served as an effective mechanism of gaining legitimacy.

It is only after the advanced iron technology stepped up intensive field agriculture and made land reclamation possible at a faster pace that both the state and private individuals started taking an initiative in this direction. The extension of overseas trade during the Kuṣāṇa-Sātavāhana period promoted market-oriented agricultural production. This, too, must have contributed towards transforming land into a key factor in the contemporary economy. The developments also led to the substitution of collective rights of ownership over land by individual property rights.[42] The latter, in fact, proved to be an important factor in facilitating the practice of land grants by individual donors. More than anything else, the far-reaching importance of land as a gift-item was derived from the fact that not only had it longer lasting value for the donee but, from the Gupta period onwards, constituted the chief means of production in the dominant agrarian economic order. Its acceptance by learned brāhmaṇas, therefore, came to be imbued with deep symbolic importance, thus transforming such gifts into the most effective mode of conferring a superior ritual status and social rank upon the donor. The significance of *dāna* as an important instrument of conferring ritual status becomes manifest when considered in the light of an observation made by Thapar that the 'assertion of *varṇa* status as ritual status must have been important in a society where stratification was not based on economic control alone but also included ritual status'.[43]

IV

Besides the ascendance of the landed economy, the phenomenon of the rise of small regional kingdoms, particularly in those areas which had never witnessed the rise of full-fledged states, is found to lend further importance to the ritual gift of land. The rise of small states in outlying regions is amply attested by contemporary data. Thus, the Khoh copper-plate inscription of Saṁkṣobha[44] and Kanās plate of Lokavigraha[45] mention eighteen forest kingdoms (*aṣṭadaśa tavirājya*) located in central India. The Allahabad Pillar Inscription also refers to numerous forest states subjugated by Samudragupta.[46]

Therefore, along with the numerous alien groups thrown into the crucible of political power, there were also a large number of materially less advanced indigenous groups which, too, were seeking to enter the cultural mainstream and stake their claim to power. Martin Orans reports a relatively recent case of a Muṇḍa tribal who succeeded in establishing himself as a local *rājā*. His Rājpūt status acquired through the help of brāhmaṇa priests came to be acknowledged by other Rājpūts.[47] Although, till about the end of the Gupta period, there are hardly any instances of land grants being made by the above-mentioned category of political and social aspirants, considering the sacralizing role of rituals in general and of gift-making in particular, land grants as well as the performance of Vedic sacrifices entailing ostentatious gift-making must have opened to them a very effective means of achieving their goal.

Brāhmaṇa ideologues are known to have become willing collaborators in promoting this *dāna*/status equation. What reinforces such an impression is that it was from the Gupta period onwards that the Smṛtikāras began to expound and uphold the concept of royal ownership of all land, thereby lending a theoretical sanction to the royal practice of issuing land charters. The *Kātyāyana Smṛti* (V.16) refers to the king as the owner of all land.[48] Moreover, Nārada (XI.27; 42; XIII.51), Bṛhaspati (XIX.23; 30; V.119) and other authorities gave final accreditation to royal charters (*rājaśāsana*) over the religious right (*dharma*) and customary right (*vyavahāra*) in case of a dispute pertaining to tenure-related rights over land. The king-priest nexus would also seem to account for the introduction of *dāna*-related maxims that lent an irrevocable character to these grants. The latter development had, as noted above, major repercussions on the condition of the peasantry, especially in reducing them to a state of abject servility.

V

Moreover, though the growing hiatus between the owners of land and the actual cultivators is generally evident, we also come across, at this time, the rise of a large number of brāhmaṇas recipients of land grants who were themselves actively engaged in tilling their land. While the *Agni Purāṇa* (152.2) permits brāhmaṇas to take to cultivation, the *Garuḍa Purāṇa* (107.6) enjoins that a brāhmaṇa engaged in agriculture should not drive a tired bull. Such Purāṇic injunctions would seem to reflect the increasingly manifest contemporary situation marked by growing brāhmaṇa participation in agricultural pursuits. Even the *Bṛhatparāśara* (V.118), extolling the merit of the gift of goods, stipulates that the brāhmaṇas should take to cultivation with a view to growing grains. At another place in the same text (V.3), it is mentioned that a brāhmaṇa should practice agriculture along with his six main duties (*ṣaṭkarma sahita viprāḥ kṛṣi vṛtimsamāśrayet*).[49] Pushpa Niyogi has interpreted the term *kṣetrakaraṇabrāhmaṇan* occurring in some Bengal inscriptions to mean those brāhmaṇas who depended upon agricultural land as the mainstay of their livelihood.[50]

In fact, not all land grants would seem to be of a very large size. Since our data indicates the practice of intensive agriculture on small plots of land, especially in the eastern regions, a majority of these grants must represent small landholdings. Considering that many of them were made collectively to more than one and, at times, even to a group of as many as 1,000 brāhmaṇas, the actual size of land which fell to each individual donee's share could not have been uniformly very large. Thus, a Vākāṭaka charter records the endowment of 8,000 *nivartanas* of land to 1,000 brāhmaṇas.[51] Similarly, the Tipperah Copper Plate of Lokanātha belonging to AD 650 records the donation of forest land to a community of more than 100 brāhmaṇas.[52] Smaller landowners could not have wielded enough resources to engage hired labour or opt for sharecropping and must have, therefore, been forced to cultivate the land themselves. The *Bhaviṣyottara Purāṇa* assigned to the seventh-eighth century AD recounts the story of a poor but hardy brāhmaṇa agriculturist who was tired out by the work of cultivation. References to land being tilled by brāhmaṇas are forthcoming from the Kaman inscription as well as Hiuen Tsang's account in which he mentions noticing brāhmaṇa cultivators in the Takka region. As pointed out by Chitrarekha Gupta, whereas, of the Kanaujiyās, the Bhuinhar brāhmaṇas are agriculturists, among the Sārasvata brāhmaṇas, the tradition of cultivation still persists.[53] The emergence of a fairly large group of brāhmaṇa cultivators undoubtedly must have had a vital bearing on the ritual gift-system. Initially, such *kinasa* brāhmaṇas were held in rather low social esteem. They were placed by lawgivers in the category of people engaged in sinful acts and the gift of a cow to them was deemed as leading to *akṣaya naraka*. Subsequently, a more lenient stance was adopted towards brāhmaṇas engaged in cultivation. Not only were they permitted to practice agriculture[54] but special *dāna* maxims were introduced, ostensibly to accommodate the needs of this particular category of brāhmaṇas. Thus, the gift of a ploughshare along with bullocks came to be commended by Brāhmaṇical theorists.[55] Our sources record actual instances of such gift-making. The Ikṣavāku king, Chantamūla, is described as a donor of hundreds of kine and ploughshares.[56] As indicated by the *Bhaviṣyottara Purāṇa* (Chaps. 127-8), great emphasis also came to be laid on the donation of wells and tanks to brāhmaṇas living in arid zones. The introduction of new agricultural rites such as the *sīta-yajña*, *indra-yajña*, *śravaṇa* and *lāṅgala yajñas*, which entailed ritual *dāna* and were performed for obtaining good crops, was clearly due to the proximity of brāhmaṇas to agricultural pursuits in their dual role of cultivating peasants and ministrant priests of the tribal population undergoing acculturation. Similarly, the *aghrayām* rite was performed to ensure a good harvest, while *aśvayujī* and *kārtikī* were rites performed for the welfare of cattle.[57] We also get references to various other rites connected with agricultural operations such as the *halaropaṇa*, *muṣṭi-grahaṇa*, etc.[58] In fact, as pointed out by V.S. Agarwala many of these rites would seem to be directly drawn from local folk cults.[59]

Such a restructuring of the Brāhmaṇical gift-making ritual code by Purāṇa composers was seemingly meant to safeguard the interests of those brāhmaṇas who had come to be actively engaged in cultivation. The change in the Brāhmaṇical stance is reflected in the following statement of the *Bṛhatparāśara* (V.185): 'There is no religious duty other than cultivation, no profit other than that from cultivation and no happiness elsewhere if cultivation is done righteously.' The growing Brāhmaṇical propensity towards agriculture is amply proved by the detailed knowledge of agro-technology and allied subjects which came to be displayed by Brāhmaṇical writers during the post-Gupta centuries. The *Agni Purāṇa* (121.44-52) contains references to some astronomical considerations to be observed in connection with six agricultural operations such as *goṣṭhayātrā*, *kṛṣikarmasamācaraṇa*, *bījavāpana*, *dhānyaccheda*, *dhānyapraveśa*, and *dhānyaviṣkramaṇa*. The *Bṛhatsaṁhitā* deals with subjects such as the selection of land, the use of fertilizers, and the collection and treatment of seeds. The Amarakoṣa contains information on soil, irrigation and agricultural implements. The composition of texts such as the *Kṛṣi-Parāśara* and *Kṛṣi-Sūkta*, besides reflecting the growing importance and widespread knowledge of improved agricultural technology, might also indicate their authors' close familiarity and first-hand experience of farming techniques and processes.

However, some of the newly introduced agriculture-centric *dāna* rites would appear to be also due to the close interaction taking place between brāhmaṇa recipients of land grants situated in peripheral zones and the indigenous population there. The ritual of the *viśvajīt* sacrifice, which, according to the *Bhāgavata Purāṇa*,[60] required a temporary residence with the Niṣādas, would bear testimony to such close cultural interaction. In fact, many of the newly introduced rites would appear to be directly drawn from local folk cults. The assimilation of the latter into Purāṇic Brāhmaṇism is amply attested by the Purāṇas,[61] especially the Śākta Upa-Purāṇas, although the latter belong to a much later period. The Purāṇic texts contain numerous references to the ritual worship of tribal female deities, sometimes even for gaining protection against ferocious wild beasts and ghosts.[62] It was mainly such cultural interaction that led to ritual *dāna* to brāhmaṇas being recommended to members of pre-literate groups. A section of the *Devī Purāṇa* (Chap. 24) lists the good effects of making *dāna* on *saṁkrānti* by Cāṇḍālas, Pukkusas and others.

It is in this context that the role of brāhmaṇa peasants in pushing forward the forces of acculturation in peripheral zones has to be considered. K.S. Singh has, in fact, seriously doubted the role of brāhmaṇa ideologues in the diffusion of agricultural technology in tribal areas.[63] Instead, he emphasizes the role of peasants and artisans in promoting the acculturation process. Although Singh rightly maintains that such dissemination was not possible purely at a theoretical plane, it is worth considering how far the brāhmaṇa peasants, who, as recipients of smaller land grants and being well-versed in the latest agricultural techniques could have shared and imparted this knowledge to their tribal counterparts at a more basic level, and thus been instrumental in spreading dominant civilizational traits amongst the latter.

The brāhmaṇa-tribal peasant interaction at the grassroot level must have also led to cultural assimilation. Acceptance of *dāna* from members of tribal groups must have served as a form of recognition of the latter's integration into the mainstream social order. The newly devised *dāna* ritualism that prescribed ritual gift-making at *tīrthas* and at the time of purificatory and expiatory rites, especially by members of the lowest stratum, were clearly meant to maximize the scope for surplus extraction by the sacerdotal class under the conditions of agricultural expansion. It may be noted, in this context, that the concept of sin as the cause of impurity and, therefore, being regarded as a kind of contagion which could be removed by bodily contact with the pure and sacred, as well as by giving gifts to the deserving, are known to characterize the religious beliefs of most pre-literate societies and Brāhmaṇism. Hence, even though the concept had been integral to the Brāhmaṇical belief-system all along, under conditions of agricultural expansion and acculturation, the lawgivers seized it afresh to advocate numerous expiatory rituals, especially for the marginalized sections. The practice of both *dāna* and *tīrthas* were conceived as relatively easy measures for self-purification and sin-expiation and, therefore, were expected to hold greater appeal for the simple-minded peasant folk. According to a verse of the *Bṛhat Parāśara* (V.167), 'By performing the purificatory rites the cultivator is absolved of all sins even if they are endless, and goes to heaven.'

VI

Similar considerations seem to have also led to the restructuring of caste rules. Tribal and other alien elements were sought to be absorbed into the traditional caste order, although they were accorded a very low social status, mainly to ensure a large reserve force of agricultural labourers[64] and to extend the sphere of brāhmaṇa clientele. Besides promoting horizontal mobility, this development was directly responsible for an unprecedented proliferation in the number of lower caste groups.[65] The shift from tribal pole to caste pole proved to be a two-pronged process: admission into the caste hierarchy accompanied by their subsequent subjection through the use of extra economic means of coercion, thereby giving rise to a dominance-submission relationship.

It is in this context that the role of *dāna* ideology as a mechanism of social control gains in importance. In a feudal ethos, *dāna* ritualism, besides offering extra economic sanction to the ruling class for surplus extraction, also became one of the forms of exploitation of the producing classes. Once integrated into the Brāhmaṇical social order, the latter were naturally expected to submit to and observe the *dāna*-making rules, especially those pertaining to land grants. These rules were clearly conceived to buttress the vested interests of both the royal donors as well as the religious beneficiaries. This is sufficiently evident from the fact that the early medieval charters carried not only strictures against desertion by peasants residing over the land, but also strong invectives against those who tried to revoke the grants. Smṛti and Purāṇic stipulations connected with the recording of grants on permanent materials such as stone-slabs and copper plates were also meant to safeguard against any disruption of the ownership rights of the beneficiary over donated land.

Another religious belief which became central to the ritual gift-system from the beginning of the first millennium AD was that of pilgrimage. Gift-making at holy places was declared in the Purāṇas to be productive of maximum spiritual merit. Although there is no apparent linkage between this development and the peasantry, the sudden popularity gained by the institution of *tīrthas* at this particular time needs some explanation. Nandi's[66] postulate that decaying urban centres became transformed into *tīrthas* to buttress the interests of the affected sacerdotal class would not fully account for the phenomenon.[67] In fact, not all *tīrthas* are known to represent decaying settlements. Thus, the *Viṣṇu Smṛti* (Chap. 35) mentions, along with the more well-known *tīrthas* such as Puṣkar, Ayodhyā and Prayāga, some relatively new and lesser-known ones like Binduka and Kubjanīra, which have not been successfully identified so far.

Our study shows that more than the factor of urban decay and attempts on the part of jurists to stall the process by declaring the sites to be centres of pilgrimage, some other wider-ranging considerations popularized the concept of *tīrthas*. Additions to the Purāṇic lists of *tīrthas* refer to settlements that lay outside the pale of traditional Brāhmaṇical culture[68] and to how these holy places formed the congregating ground for brāhmaṇa families. This points to one major cause of this development, namely the need to provide a more popular base to the ritual gift-system. In order to mobilize the fairly expansive and widely distributed tribal peasantry as a potential client group, it became necessary for lawgivers to find some basis for the ritual gift-system which could both render *dāna* extraction easy as well as hold appeal for the common peasants. The concept of *tīrthas* seemed to fulfil both these requisites to a remarkable degree and hence began to be highly commended as a redemptory measure both for self-purification and for the salvation of one's ancestors. The *Matsya*, *Vāyu* and *Brahmāṇḍa Purāṇas* furnish long lists of *tīrthas* which are said to be especially profitable for the performance of *śrāddha* rites. In the *Vāyu Purāṇa* it is contended that by undertaking a pilgrimage, a non-brāhmaṇa *jajamāna* not only washes off all his sins but also obtains brāhmaṇa-hood.

The existence of a dialectical relationship, even if somewhat tenuous, between the changing structural composition of the peasantry and the ritual gift-system is, thus, revealed by our sources, especially by data pertaining to the Gupta/post-Gupta centuries. In fact, both the peasantry as a grouping and the institution of *dāna* are known to have undergone continual structural variations to meet the demands arising out of the changes besetting the other.

NOTES

1. Vijay Nath, *Dāna: Gift System in Ancient India*, Delhi, 1987, pp. 60-3.
2. Ibid., p. 61.
3. Ibid., p. 55.
4. Ibid., p. 62.
5. Ibid., pp. 168-90, 234-46.
6. A fact duly conceded by T.N. Madan in 'Gift of Food', *Culture and Society*, ed. B.N. Nair, Delhi, 1975, p. 85.
7. M. Marriott, 'Caste Ranking and Food Transactions: A Matrix Analysis', *Structure and Change in Indian Society*, ed. M. Singer & B.S. Cohn, Chicago, 1968, pp. 133-71.
8. Chitralekha Gupta, *The Brahmanas of India: A Study Based on Inscriptions*, Delhi, 1983, pp. 73-89; V.B. Mishra, 'The Remunerative Sequel of Dāna in the Epigraphs and Literature of Early Medieval India', *Prof. B.K. Barua Commemoration Volume*, ed. M. Neog and H.M. Sharma, Gauhati, 1966, pp. 207-11.
9. Erik Reenberg Sand, 'The Śrāddha According to Some Important Purāṇas', *South Asian Religion and Society*, ed. Asko Parpola & B.S. Hansen, Indian edn., Delhi, 1986, p. 98.

10. R.S. Sharma, *Indian Feudalism c.300-1200*, Calcutta, 1965; *The Feudal Order: State, Society and Ideology in Early Medieval India*, ed. D.N. Jha, Delhi, 2000.
11. Reference to the dedication of as many as six step wells by Dhruvasena I is recorded in Vivadia-Jogia Plate, *CII*, III, no. 14.
12. R. Thapar, 'Dāna and Dakṣiṇā as Forms of Exchange', *Ancient Indian Social History*, New Delhi, 1978.
13. Vijay Nath, 'Symbolic Content and Status Conferring Role of Dāna'.
14. *Social Mobility in the Caste System in India*, ed. James Silverberg, The Hague, 1968; R. Thapar, 'Social Mobility in Ancient India with Special Reference to Elite Groups', *Ancient Indian Social History*, New Delhi, 1978, pp. 124-49.
15. *Manusmṛti*, IX.326-33.
16. Irfan Habib, 'The Peasant in Indian History', General Presidential Address, PIHC, 43rd Session, Kurukshetra, pp. 3-54.
17. R.S. Sharma, 'How Feudal was Indian Feudalism?', *Feudal Social Formation in Early India*, ed. D.N. Jha, New Delhi, 1987, pp. 165-97.
18. 'Was There Feudalism in Indian History?' Presidential Address to Medieval India Section, PIHC, 1979.
19. Saroj Sharma, *Land System in Northern India*.
20. Ibid.
21. *EI*, XVIII, no. 11.
22. *EI*, XV, no. 19; D.C. Sircar, *Select Inscriptions*, vol. II, p. 28.
23. *EI*, XXXIII, no. 53.
24. *Epigraphia Carnatica*, X, Goribidnur, 47.
25. 'Agrarian Growth and Social Conflict', *The Feudal Order: State, Society and Ideology in Early Medieval India*, ed. D.N. Jha, New Delhi, 2000, p. 318.
26. *CII*, V.6.
27. *CII*, IV, no. 4; 5; *EI*, XXIII, no. 8; XXI, no. 13; XX, no. 5.
28. *CII*, no. 23; V, nos. 2 &3; *EI*, XXIII, no. 31.
29. R.N. Nandi, op. cit., p. 312.
30. Ibid.
31. 'The Problem of Emergence of Feudal Relations in Early India', *The Feudal Order*, ed. D.N. Jha, pp. 257-9.
32. Ed. K. Shukla, Patna, 1973, p. 151.
33. 'The Problem of Emergence of Feudal Relations', op. cit., p. 269.
34. Chinese Literature, 956, no. 3, 153; Yadava, op. cit.
35. T. Watters, I, p. 168.
36. V.K. Thakur, *Historiography of Indian Feudalism*, New Delhi, 1989.
37. Sircar, *Select Inscriptions*, vol. II, p. 28.
38. Ibid., pp. 3-54.
39. Jaimal Rai, *Rural Urban Economy and Social Changes in Ancient India, 300 BC-AD 600*), Varanasi, 1974, p. 342.

40. Shivaji Singh, *Evolution of Smṛti Law*, Varanasi, 1972, pp. 193-5.
41. Thapar, *Ancient Indian Social History*, p. 134.
42. Nath, *Dāna: Gift System in Ancient India*, pp. 165-6.
43. 'Legitimation by Descent: The Kṣatriya Varṇa in North Indian Society', in *Essays on Indian History and Culture*, ed. H.V.S. Murty et al., New Delhi, 1990, p. 80.
44. Sircar, *Select Inscriptions*, vol. I, p. 395.
45. *EI*, XXXVIII, p. 331.
46. Sircar, *Select Inscriptions*, vol. I, p. 265; also see D.N. Jha, 'State Formation in a Peripheral Region: The Case of Early Medieval Chamba', *The Feudal Order*, pp. 197-209.
47. Martin Orans, 'A Tribe in Search of a Great Tradition', *Man in India*, XXXIX, 1959, pp. 108-14.
48. For more references see R.K. Choudhary, *Some Aspects of Social and Economic History of Ancient India and Cambodia*, Varanasi, 1984, pp. 225-8.
49. Lallanji Gopal, *Aspects of the History of Agriculture in Ancient India*, Varanasi, 1980, p. 28.
50. *Contributions to the Economic History of Northern India*, Calcutta, 1962, pp. 17-18.
51. *CII*, V.6.
52. Ibid.
53. *The Brahmanas of India: A Study Based on Inscriptions*, Delhi, 1983, p. 41.
54. *Agni Purāṇa*, 152.2.
55. *Garuḍa Purāṇa*, 37.16-18; *Agni Purāṇa*, 211.7, 34-6.
56. Saroj Sharma, 'Land System in Northern India', Ph.D. thesis presented to the University of Delhi, 1986.
57. P. Arundhati, *Brahmanism, Jainism and Buddhism in Andhradesa*, Delhi, 1990, p. 67.
58. Gopal, *Aspects of History of Agriculture in Ancient India*, op. cit., Varanasi, 1980, p. 2.
59. *Matsya Purāṇa: A Study*, Varanasi, 1963, p. 280.
60. S.S. Dange, *The Bhāgavata Purāṇa: A Mytho-Social Study*, Delhi, 1984.
61. *Mārkaṇḍeya Purāṇa*, 92.25-7.
62. *Devī Purāṇa*,17-20; *Harivaṁśa Purāṇa*, 11.3.7-8.
63. 'Technology and Acculturation: The Brahmanical Model Reconsidered', *Social Science Probings*, vol. II, no. i, 1985.
64. Joan P. Mencher, 'Agricultural Labourers in Peasant Societies: The Case of South Asia', *Social Anthropology of Peasantry*, ed. Joan P. Mencher, Bombay, 1983, p. 292.
65. Bernard Barber, 'Social Mobility in Hindu India', *Social Mobility in the Caste System in India*, ed. James Silverberg, The Hague, 1968, p. 33.

66. *Social Roots of Religion*, Calcutta, 1986, p. 43. 'The concept of *tīrthas* represents an attempt to revive the prospects of gift-exchange in all the decaying settlements including towns'.
67. Vijay Nath, 'Tīrthas and Acculturation'.
68. Vijay Nath, 'Some Indigenous Tīrthas and Their Purāṇic Transformation'.

10

A New Form of Gift System as a Factor in Urbanization

Marcel Mauss's sociological study of gift-exchange, especially his observations on the subject of *dāna* in ancient India, not only caught the attention of many historians but has also evoked much debate and research.[1] Some of Mauss's formulations pertaining to the practice of the ritual gift-system in India have been questioned and even sought to be demolished. For instance, his contention that brāhmaṇas who lived solely by religious service 'refused to have anything to do with a national economy dominated by towns, money and market and remained faithful to the economy and morality of the Indo-Iranian shepherds',[2] can no longer be held tenable in the light of recent researches. Our own study shows that ritual gift-making, like any other social institution, was subject to constant variations and changed in consonance with the changing material milieu, be it pastoral, rural or urban.[3] Here, we may clarify that while focusing on the traditional ritual gift-system, we shall also be considering some of its other variations as they evolved under heterodox influences.

The two chief lines of argument adopted by scholars so far with regard to the Indian practice of ritual *dāna* are: (i) The traditional gift-system which developed during the Vedic period continued to retain its basic format and character, but was later transposed upon and adapted to changing socio-economic conditions such as urbanization; (ii) Such a transposition was the deliberate handiwork of Brāhmaṇical theorists with strong vested interests. The latter sought to achieve it by means of new rituals and an appropriate social theorization.[4]

We would like to posit that the new commerce and urban-dominated social order gave rise to a totally new form of gift system, which resembled its Vedic counterpart as a butterfly does a caterpillar or a frog a tadpole. Moreover, the emergence of the new gift-system was a phenomenon integral to the urbanization process and Brāhmaṇical lawgivers can, in no way, be held wholly responsible for affecting such a change. For existential reasons, they were merely giving formal sanction to changes which were absolutely inevitable.

I

Our study reveals that not one stereotype but several strands of gift-making which gained ascendancy at different points of time and in disparate material contexts can be discerned. Amongst the more easily discernible categories may be mentioned gifts made on the occasion of sacrifices (*yajña/sattra*), which were steeped in the pastoral tradition and, therefore, essentially had a non-urban base and character. Though, in the early Vedic phase, they might have served the purpose of the redistribution of tribal wealth,[5] yet, subsequently, they increasingly acquired the aspect of a 'potlatch', a form of contest among rival chiefs for their augmentation of their prestige and power.[6] Their relevance to the assertion of political authority during the nascent stages of state formation continued in later times, irrespective of urban or non-urban developments.

There was a considerable extension of sacrificial ritualism entailing ritual gift-making during the later Vedic period, when the former came to be classified under two broad heads, namely *nitya* or obligatory and *naimittika* or occasional. While the *nitya* category of sacrifices like *agnihotra* had to be performed without fail as their non-performance could bring about disaster, the latter were more in the nature of magico-religious rites meant to ensure a good harvest, numerous male progeny, family-well-being as well as to fulfil other temporal and spiritual needs and desires. A compulsory feature of all such performances was the payment of *dakṣiṇā* to the priests, for, according to the *Aitareya Brāhmaṇa* (6.30.9), 'Just as a cart without the bullocks harms the driver and is useless, likewise a sacrifice without the *dakṣiṇā* harms the sacrificer.' Similarly, the *Śatapatha Brāhmaṇa* (11.1.4.4) enjoins that 'the sacrificer should pay according to his means; the sacrifice must not go without the sacrificial fee'. However, the exact nature of *dakṣiṇā* to be paid to the priests remains somewhat ambiguous. The statements contained in the Brāhmaṇas do not clarify whether the payment was in the form of remuneration of services rendered or merely gifts given to augment the efficacy of the sacrificial offering. By the early medieval period, as the Purāṇas tell us, *dakṣiṇā* had definitely come to be understood in the latter sense.

Juxtaposed to these sacrificial offerings, which were later classified under the *iṣṭa* category of ritual *dāna*, were those made by householders to sages and priests for imparting education and performing other priestly duties such as interpreting stars and other occult signs and occurrences. To some extent, these represented the *jajamānī* mode of payment for services rendered and they mainly suited an agricultural-cum-rural milieu. Since the magical element appears to be strong in such a form of gift-making, as revealed by the *Atharvaveda* and the Brāhmaṇas,[7] a lot of emphasis came to be laid on the correct ritual performance, thereby causing considerable ritual complexity.[8]

The other major category of religious gift-making comprised *dāna* which accompanied sacramental rites performed at the time of child-birth, initiation, marriage, death and *śrāddha* ceremonies.[9] The former represented a *rite de passage* and essentially symbolized status-change.[10] Gift-making that formed part of purificatory and expiatory (*prāyaścitta*) ritualism constituted yet another form of *dāna*. Ritual gift-making was also practised on the occasion of religious festivals, eclipses and other important planetary conjunctions, as well as for the mitigation or aversion of natural calamities and personal misfortunes. The parameters of the religious gift system comprehended certain other forms of gift-making as well, such as benefactions to religious, charitable and educational institutions, alms to beggars, wayfarers and mendicants, and donations to temples, monasteries and other religious bodies. Most of these forms of gift-making are conspicuous by their absence in the pastoral or dominantly rural milieu of the Vedic times.

Yet another category of *dāna* singularly lacking in the Vedic period but which became a prominent feature of the subsequent urban ethos was that of consecrating tanks, wells, fruit-groves and gardens, as well as installing, images, pillars, gateways and other structural components of religious buildings and monuments.

II

Since our study reveals sharp variations in the ritual gift-system, as obtained at different stages of urban development, we would like to distinguish three stages of urban growth and decay, namely the period from *c.* 600 BC to the end of the Mauryan rule, which witnessed the beginning of the second urbanization and the culmination of the process of transition from a pre-market to market economy. The next stage, spanning a little over five centuries, epitomizes achievements in the field of urban development and commercial activities. The subsequent stage, roughly corresponding to the Gupta and post-Gupta times, is characterized by the reversal of the earlier process and the beginnings of feudal formations.

In order to fix the distinctive features and spirit of the religious gift-system as it generally evolved in a predominantly urban milieu, and the particular form it manifested at a definite stage of urban development, we need to consider the factors which gave rise to urbanism, such as a surplus economy combined with a ruling authority performing the task of organizing the surplus and a class-stratified social structure, as well as the important conditions and exigencies of urban life. The latter necessarily created the need for a flourishing trade hinged upon a money economy and organized commodity production, along with technological innovations including irrigational facilities and the construction of monumental buildings and highways. It also entailed the invention of the art of writing and a system of reckoning, as well as the development of other exact sciences.

Amongst the more auxiliary developments related to the urbanization process may be noted the emergence of craft and trade guilds, and the large-scale flow of traffic from one urban centre to another, giving rise to a vast floating population. Beggary is another phenomenon that characterizes the urban milieu. The latter shows a greater concentration of wealth in the hands of a few organizers and distributors of the surplus, thereby creating class disparities so that the number of the poor in cities is expectedly high. City life also undermines close kinship relations, so that destitutes, in the absence of an effective support system, are reduced to beggary. With growing hazards and the uncertainties of long-distance trade, instances of commercial catastrophes reducing rich magnates to a state of total bankruptcy or virtual beggary become quite common. The urban ethos is also marked by a spirit of individualism and competition,[11] which, however, could not have been as pronounced in pre-industrial societies as it became in their modern industrial counterparts.

III

Our sources reveal that by *c.* 600 BC, urbanization along with trade, craft-specialization and a monetary system appeared in not very advanced forms.[12] Consequently, whereas the demand for goods-exchange grew, the absence of standardized metal currency (punch-marked coins notwithstanding) hampered big commercial transactions.[13] The deficiency, therefore, appears to have been made up partly by the barter system and partly through gift-exchange. This is amply attested by the fact that whereas sacrificial gift-making receded into the background, religious gift-making in its other aspect of *dāna* and *dakṣiṇā* continued to serve as a means of payment in kind for important services rendered by teachers, philosophers, astrologers and priests. The exchange purpose of *dāna* in the new material context, may be inferred to some extent from the fact that commodities such as grain (*dhānya*), which tended to replace the cow as the media of exchange, now also became popular as common gift-items.[14]

A surplus-based urban economy, moreover, needs to support a large social stratum engaged in activities other than economic production. However, in the nascent stages of urban growth, as our sources clearly indicate, such a need was at least partially met through the development of a gift-system which directly sustained certain segments of the non-food producing class engaged in intellectual and spiritual pursuits.[15] In this context, it is remarkable that from *c.* 600 BC onwards, gifts were predominantly made by the affluent section amongst the producing and trading classes.[16] The *Illīsa Jātaka*[17] describes how a crier was once made to proclaim, by the beat of drums all through the city, that everyone who wanted gold, silver and the like were to come to the house of Illīsa, the treasurer. A large crowd soon assembled at the door carrying baskets and sacks.

These developments related to the gift-system are clearly reflected in the two distinct forms of unilateral gift-making, which make their appearance in contemporary literature and do not exactly fit into the *iṣṭa-pūrtta* structural framework. Thus, on the one hand, we come across elaborate Brāhmaṇical injunctions related to *dāna*-making at the time of sacramental rites,[18] and on the other, we get copious notices of alms attended with minimal ritual, made to newly-emergent donor categories such as monks, wayfarers, wanderers and beggars.[19] In the *Saṁyutta Nikāya* (I. 2.3.3), we get, reference to paupers, cripples, wayfarers and beggars as seekers of alms. Similarly, while the *Mahāsupīna Jātaka*[20] describes beggars and religious mendicants seated on the highway, at street corners and at the doors of the king's palace, the *Mahāvastu*[21] refers to alms being made to blind, helpless, poor and destitute. From the latter text,[22] we further learn how some young actors who had come from Takṣaśilā to Benares went to a merchant's house to beg for alms.

Significantly, both forms of gift-making (*dāna* accompanying sacramental rites and almsgiving to monks, beggars and wayfarers) were rooted in developments related to urbanization either as one of its by-products or as contributory factors. The *raison d'être* for the sudden popularity gained by *dāna* at the time of sacramental rites from *c.* 600 BC onwards can be found solely in the new spirit of individualism bred by urbanism. Manu (IV.240) gives expression to it when he states: 'single is each being born; single it dies, single it enjoys (the reward) of its virtue; single (it suffers the punishment) of its sins'. It tipped the scale in favour of the individual *vis-à-vis* the group, and emphasized the need to redefine a person's role and status both in the family and *varṇa* hierarchy. This was possible chiefly through the performance of sacramental rites, for which the services of priests had to be engaged and which could be remunerated in the form of *dāna*.[23] Similarly, amongst the new categories of alms recipients, monks (*bhikṣus*) and renouncers (*parivrājakas*) were evidently the products of the process of social alienation caused by the conflict-ridden urban mode of living. The class-fragmented structure of urban society was, likewise, responsible for precipitating the problem of beggary.[24] In fact, it necessitated the development of some mechanism, such as building of hospices and organizing the regular distribution of alms, through which suffering arising from sharp fluctuations in fortune could be partly alleviated.

The gift-system in an urban setting also served to cater to the needs of an ever-expanding floating population resulting from the commercial and religious traffic from one urban centre to another.

The absence of adequate boarding and lodging facilities in strange cities and towns could be made up mainly through the extension of the existent gift-system. It accounts not only for the emergence of a new category of alms recipients, namely wayfarers and wanderers who find frequent mention in contemporary Buddhist literature,[25] but also for the emphasis which, henceforth, came to be laid, in both Brāhmaṇical and non-Brāhmaṇical systems, on hospitality as a cardinal virtue integral to gift-making.[26] References in contemporary literary and epigraphic records to the construction of rest-houses and hospices[27] by religious benefactors acquire special significance in the emergent urban context, and underline the changing role and dimensions of the new gift-system.

Some other indispensable contributory factors to urban growth, if secondary in nature, such as the art of writing and a system of reckoning along with other exact sciences, would also seem to owe their origin and development to the gift-system. In fact, in its aspect of *dāna* and *dakṣiṇā*, the latter was entirely responsible for supporting the teaching community and for the development and dissemination of education and learning. This is equally true of the munificent benefactions that came to be made in favour of Buddhist monasteries, which turned out to be major centres of imparting education.

The gift system reflected by our sources for the earlier phase is, thus, found to be both seminal to as well as the intrinsic product of a series of developments in material culture, which culminated in the centuries following *c.* 600 BC. Besides serving as an effective stop-gap measure to meet the demands for goods-exchange in the absence of a standardized and technically advanced metal currency, it now came to bear a unique aspect. While the practice of gift-distribution at the time of sacrifices became marginalized, representing merely the residual element in the new gift-system, the latter now came to be characterized by certain novel features. For instance, there is remarkable diversification in the occasions for making *dāna*. More than sacrifices, sacramental rites, the inauguration of trade and business ventures,[28] and the beginning of construction activities figured prominently amongst the important occasions for ritual gift-making, along with daily or periodical alms distribution to monks and beggars.[29] Thus, we learn from the *Dhammapada* (17.5; 26.1) how a 'brāhmaṇa thereafter gave food regularly to sixteen monks at his house'.

Similarly, the donor category, besides displaying new elements, also became more variegated and broadbased. Royal princes and chieftains were now no longer the sole or even predominant donor grouping. Instead, urban-based sections of society such as the *gahapatis*,[30] *seṭṭhīs*,[31] bureaucratic functionaries,[32] and members of artisanal[33] and other professional groups such as moneylenders and prostitutes[34] emerged as major donor categories from *c.* 600 BC, lending a totally new complexion to the religious gift system. In fact, some brāhmaṇas who had accumulated wealth also figure as donors. In the *Peṭavatthu* (II.2), we get a reference to a wealthy brāhmaṇa of Benares who was 'a well unto recluses and brāhmaṇas, indigents, tramps, wayfarers and beggars'.

Consonant with the demands of an urban mode of living, there is a striking metamorphosis in the donee category as well. Brāhmaṇas *per se* were no longer considered worthy recipients of *dāna*. Instead, preference came to be shown towards the more learned and morally upright (*śrotriya/vedapāraga*) brāhmaṇas as befitting subjects of religious gifts.[35] The new thrust upon high ethical values was, in fact, a typical manifestation of the commercial ethos,[36] which is conspicuous by its absence in the predominantly tribal Vedic culture. Developments in the sphere of trade and commerce seem to have necessitated the growth of an effective code of business ethics, underlining virtues such as truth, honesty and fair play. We notice a new moral climate which directly affected the institution of *dāna*. Moral considerations became more important in the selection of the donor and donee. The economic need alone did not determine the worthiness of a donee. The possession of moral virtues and high learning seemed to be more important as is also evident from the writings of heterodox orders. This development in the case of brāhmaṇas not only caused a split within their ranks but also lent a new dimension to the Brāhmaṇical mode of gift-making. During the subsequent post-Mauryan period, the qualifications of the brāhmaṇa donee became the subject of detailed rulings in the Dharmaśāstras.[37] A certain amount of fragmentation within the brāhmaṇa ranks was also caused by a fairly large segment forsaking its traditional pursuits and adopting urban-based occupations, a development that was bound to erode the high social esteem to which brāhmaṇas had laid undisputed claim till then. It was largely in response to such a development that Brāhmaṇical lawgivers, gradually coming to terms with the emergent urban situation, formally allowed brāhmaṇas to take up some of these urban-based occupations including trade and money-lending during times of distress.[38] Moreover, the purview of religious gift-making now also comprehended a variety of non-Brāhmaṇical recipient groupings, especially monks, wayfarers and beggars.

An equally characteristic change, clearly in response to the urban development, is also evident in the nature of popular gift-items. The gift of cattle and slaves in very large numbers which was so popular in the preceding period continued to find mention in Brāhmaṇical texts, yet they were being fast superseded by a multitude of new gift-items bearing relevance mainly to an urban society. Thus, we get overwhelming evidence, in contemporary Buddhist and Jaina literature, of cooked food being given in alms.[39] Brāhmaṇical law-givers, overcoming their initial prejudice against the urban mode of living, are known to prescribe the offering of cooked food to brāhmaṇas as a necessary accompaniment to all sacramental rites.[40] Other items figuring in the list of popular gift articles included finished goods[41] such as items of clothing,[42] bedding,[43] furniture,[44] utensils,[45] medicine, etc.[46]

Besides these, our sources also reveal an altogether new form of gift-making epitomized in the shape of religious endowments made for the construction of wells (*kūpa*), tanks (*udapanas*, *taḍāga*) and roads.[47] Although the latter may also bear relevance to a rural land-scape, their significance in an emergent urban context cannot be overemphasized. The sudden popularity gained by this form of gift-making from *c.* 600 BC would point to its being seminal to urban growth.

The striking resemblance between the measures adopted by Aśoka to promote *dhamma* and the gift-system as it obtained at that time deserves some mention in this context. It is significant how both comprehend not only common donee categories[48] but also recommend similar kinds of charitable acts such as planting trees, constructing roads, digging wells, providing of medical facilities, etc.[49] Aśoka's Kalsi Rock Edict V[50] and the Delhi-Topra Pillar Edict VIII[51] contain references to the measures adopted by the emperor to provide relief to the orphans, aged, poor and miserable. To some extent, it reinforces the impression that, like Aśoka's *dhamma*, the gift-system, as it evolved by this time, developed largely in response to the needs and conditions of an urban-dominated social order.

Perhaps the maximum contradistinction between the Vedic and post-Vedic gift-system is to be found in their respective gift-making procedures. From *c.* 600 BC, sources reveal two sharply juxtaposed but parallel modes of gift-making procedures. While, on the one hand, we come across gift-making accompanied by elaborate ritual performance, on the other, we get notices of gift-making popularized by non-conformist systems which represented a better organized and more efficient mode of gift-distribution. Buddhist literature, particularly, furnishes evidence for an organized form of gift-making, which was quite unheard of in the preceding period. We come across notices of the construction of hospices and alms-halls,[52] where arrangements for the distribution of food, medicine, etc., were made on a regular basis. We also get references to some novel measures such as the ticket-system,[53] which were adopted in order to make gift-distribution more orderly and efficient. Such attempts at organized gift-distribution seem to manifest a singularly urban spirit.

Amongst other new features of the gift-making procedure which seemingly arose out of an urban contingency, we may especially take note of the Buddhist and Jaina alms-giving rules.[54] The latter appear to have been framed entirely to suit the convenience of city-dwelling householders. We learn from the *Pīṭha Jātaka* (vol. III, no. 337, p. 79) how a lay donor, saluting the monk, 'took his alms-bowl and led him to his house, where he offered him a seat'. In the *Majjhima Nikāya* (CX, Cula Punnama Sutta, III.22), we get a description of a person who does not distribute alms properly: 'He is casual in his giving, gives neither with his own hand nor with consideration, gives only the scraps away, heedless of retribution to come'. The *Cullavagga* (IV.4-6) refers to a certain householder who, along with his wife and children, used to stand at the place of alms and serve. According to the *Majjhima Nikāya* (XXXV, Cula Saccaka Sutta, I.286), Saccaka, with his own hands, served the cofraternity headed by Buddha 'with that excellent meal without stint till all had eaten their full'.

IV

In the ensuing period from the end of Maurya rule to the beginning of that of the Guptas, material conditions underwent significant changes. Literary sources backed by archaeology make it evident that India under the Kuṣāṇas and Sātavāhanas witnessed the 'highest peak'[55] of not only urbanization[56] and trade[57] but also of craft organization and a monetary economy.[58] Besides the more well-known sites of Taxila, Hastināpur, Ahicchatra and Mathurā,[59] material remains of Kuṣāna townships have been discovered at Kurukṣetra, Noh, Vaiśālī, Chirand, Buxar, Kumrahār and Sonpur. Significantly, most of these sites are known to be situated on the northern trade route.[60] A great spurt in internal and external trade, especially with Rome and China, is amply borne out by our sources.[61] The discovery of coin-moulds and large hoards of gold and copper coins from Kuṣāna sites, likewise, testify to the presence of a developed metallic currency. Our sources further affirm the large-scale inflow of Roman gold coins at this time. Western Deccan under the Sātavāhanas also experienced a similar economic growth, especially in the field of trade and commerce, accounting for the prosperity of the region in general and of the mercantile community in particular.[62] Another prominent feature of the contemporary economy was the guild system, which played a key role in organizing industry and trade. Consequently, the gift-system as it prevailed in the post-Vedic centuries shed some of its former aspects, and acquired new features and a considerably altered format.

With the development of advanced metallic currency under the aegis of the Indo-Bactrians, Kuṣāṇas, Śakas and Sātavāhanas, the earlier purpose of goods-exchange, partly served by the gift-system, now became, especially in a purely urban context, completely redundant. Payment for services of a sacerdotal nature could now be made directly in coins, which perhaps explains why money suddenly gained in popularity as an important gift-item.[63]

The need for goods-exchange, however, was almost immediately replaced by a fresh need to step up the demand for craft-goods, especially luxury articles, in order to keep up with the spurt in commodity production resulting from technological advancements. An unprecedented proliferation of artisanal groupings is sufficiently attested by our sources. Thus, whereas the *Jātakas* and the *Dīgha Nikāya* (II.50) mention only 18 and 24 kinds of guilds, the *Mahāvastu* (III.442-30) and the *Milindapañho*[64] refer to as many as 36 and 75 types of artisans and crafts. The gift-system helped to provide the necessary inducement by creating demand and a ready market for surplus goods. This accounts for the prominence gained by luxury articles and other craft-products such as ivory goods in the list of popular gift-items.[65]

Inscriptions attest another innovative form of gift-making which can be directly linked with developments in the field of stone technology, namely the consecration of images, pillars (*stambhas*), doorways (*toraṇas*) and other structural components of religious monuments. Such gifts are conspicuous by their absence in the preceding period and underline the changed aspect of the gift-system under advanced urban conditions. The efflorescence of the Gandhāra, Mathurā, Sāñcī and Amarāvatī schools of sculpture, and the prolific production of the images of the Buddha and other Buddhist, Jaina and Hindu deities by the sculptors of both northern as well as Deccan regions, may account for the extensive popularity gained by the practice during this period. The easy and extensive supply of raw materials like stone could have been facilitated only by an advanced means of transportation, which had apparently come to exist by this time. The large-scale carving of stone images, pillars, etc., would suggest the greater availability of finer quality tools used by the sculptors.

The growing popularity, during the post-Mauryan period, of the practice of dedicating wells and tanks would reflect a changed topography in which an artificial source of water supply for the purposes of irrigation and domestic use was gaining importance over river water. It is significant that whereas in the PGW and NBPW periods, settlements were usually adjacent to river courses, in the Śuṅga-Kuṣāṇa periods, several sites were not near any natural water source.[66] Some idea of the extent to which the practice of dedicating tanks had become popular by the Kuṣāṇa period can be obtained from the numerous epigraphic notices of the construction of tanks, which are forthcoming mostly from drier tracts such as the sites of Kal,[67] Chargāon,[68] Maholi,[69] Jamālpur, etc. The tiny clay tanks that have been discovered in large numbers from many sites[70] reinforce the evidence regarding tank-digging. The deposition of votive tanks would clearly show that the belief in the spiritual merit accruing from the gift of a tank had become so strong that all those who could not afford to build and donate an actual tank began substituting it by a votive one.

Perhaps the most significant addition to the list of gift-items was land, both residential and agricultural.[71] Inscriptions belonging to the Sātavāhana times furnish the earliest epigraphic notices of land grants to religious beneficiaries in parts of western India, which became the epicentre of commercial activities during this period.[72] Residential land was used mostly for the construction of *caityas*, *vihāras*, rest-houses, alms halls, etc. Thus, on the one hand, we come across a reference to a Pravarika-vihāra built by cloakmakers.[73] On the other, we learn from an epigraph dated in the year 28 of the time of Huviṣka about the construction of a *puṇyaśālā* at Mathurā for the feeding of 100 brāhmaṇas.[74] Our sources further reveal that commercially viable land strategically situated near main highways was generally granted by royal princes and commercial entrepreneurs for the construction of religious monuments and monastic establishments.[75] The latter are known to provide boarding and lodging facilities to passing merchants and other wayfarers. They also encouraged religious traffic and were, to some extent, instrumental in promoting trade links with far-off urban centres.[76] In the new urban context, the gift-system in its aspect of land grants, therefore, was largely responsible for the close nexus which is apparent between trading and monastic centres during the Śaka-Sātavāhana times.[77]

Integral to the same development were several features which came to characterize the contemporary gift-system. Large monetary endowments[78] to collective groups and institutions such as monasteries, hospices and rest-houses now gained ascendancy over smaller gifts to individual donees. The former were not only instrumental in catering to the needs of alienated segments of society but also underlined the growing importance of organized charity.

Perhaps the most significant addition to the mode of gift-making was the role which now began to be played by trade and craft guilds. Making permanent endowments of large sums of money with guilds for the construction or regular maintenance of religious or charitable institutions out of the interest accruing from the originally deposited amount became common practice during this period.[79] Such a development was possible only in the commerce-oriented milieu of the post-Mauryan times. The practice not only made available liquidity which could be invested in commercial enterprises but also checked the tendency to hoard wealth, which had been so strongly decried by Aśoka in his edicts.[80]

Another salient feature of the new gift-system was the practice of making collective donations by corporate bodies, especially guilds.[81] The chief purpose of this gift-making could have been to establish the latters' bona fides by associating them with religious activities. It was, in fact, the only way by which confidence and trust in guilds could be developed amongst the people, especially in the more affluent sections, in order to make them invest larger sums of money with them. Such a purpose was realized to a great extent. Guilds came to be regarded as a stable factor in the contemporary economy and less of an investment hazard than the state itself. This is evident from the fact that even royal personages like Uṣavadāta, the son-in-law of Śaka-Kṣatrapa Nahapāna,[82] preferred to invest their money with these corporate bodies rather than run the risk of putting it for safekeeping in the royal treasury.

Our sources, moreover, reveal that the expanding commercial ethos encouraged competition and striving after material wealth, thus giving rise to a new spirit of individualism.[83] Personal considerations inevitably took precedence over collective welfare. Consequently, *dāna* was now inspired more by motives of self-interest such as the acquisition of temporal gain and spiritual merit by the donor. It was the growing desire on the part of the individual to earn lasting fame which perhaps explains why the gift of land, pillars, images, *caityas*, caves and other endurable items became more common in the post-Christian era centuries. Similarly, the economic and emotional insecurities created by trade and commercial hazards seem to have bred a superstitious fear in the people's mind. The degree of risk involved in commercial ventures proved to be the biggest incentive for *dāna* made by merchants and financiers. Votive inscriptions found at Mathurā and Śañcī frequently allude to gifts made by bankers (*śreṣṭhin*), treasurers (*heraṇaka*), caravan leaders (*sārthavāha*), merchants (*vaṇija* or *vaṇika*, *nigam*), as well as by their close relations.[84] Similarly, members of those craft-groupings which boasted of a more thriving inland and overseas trade, e.g. goldsmiths (*suvarṇakāra*), perfumers (*gandhaka*), weavers (*sautrika*), sculptors (*rūpakāraka*) and ivory-workers (*dantakāra*), figure prominently in votive inscriptions.[85]

The overall increase in commercial activities would seem to have added not only to the prosperity of merchants and craftsmen but to that of all professional groupings living in towns. The growing prosperity of towns is reflected by the increasing dominance of the urban section within the donor class during the post-Mauryan period. An analysis of *Luder's List* of inscriptions shows that while the majority do not disclose the place of residence of the donor, as many as 305 records specifically mention the name of the town to which the donor belonged. The fact that donors are known to have come from distant regions to make donations at Mathurā and Śañcī indicates a greater inter-regional mobility. Thus, donors came all the way from Uḍḍiyāna (situated to the north of Punjab) and Dadhikarṇa to make gifts at Mathurā. Similarly, the Śañcī inscriptions record donations by the residents of Ujjayinī, Nandinagar, Vidiśā, Kurāragṛha and Puṣkara. Most of these towns were not only important centres of trade but were situated on the main highways.

Though the accelerated pace of commodity production, commercial activities and urban growth had given rise to a prosperous and thriving mercantile and artisanal class, in the traditional *varṇa* system the latter were accorded a ritual status not quite at par with their newly-acquired economic status. This holds true also of members of other professional groupings such as courtesans and moneylenders. They were, therefore, forced to exploit the opportunity offered by the gift-system to gain recognition for their improved economic status. If the Brāhmaṇical lawgivers were initially reluctant to extend to them such validation, then they eagerly turned to alternative religious systems to gain the necessary recognition. This explains why brāhmaṇa ideologues, for the sake of existential reasons, were forced to come to terms with the new situation, retract their earlier stand and make suitable amendments in the Brāhmaṇical gift-making rules to accommodate new donor groupings.[86] The gift-system, therefore, fulfilled an important need of the newly-emergent urban-based social groups. It also accounts for the shift in the Brāhmaṇical stand with regard to gift-making rules, which now acquired a distinct urban orientation. Thus in the *Mahābhārata* (Anuśāsana Parva, 118.18.26), gift-making for the śūdras, who served mostly as artisans and field workers, is especially praised. It is deemed the most meritorious act through which they could achieve all their ends and even attain brāhmaṇahood in their next lives. The same considerations would seem to have led the lawgivers to adopt a more accommodating stance towards donors of foreign origin, who constituted a substantial portion of the affluent urban society. *Dāna* served as an important means of diverting some of their wealth towards religious beneficiaries. This is affirmed by the Nasik inscription, the recording munificent gifts made by Nahapāna's son-in-law, Uṣavadāta, and his wife, Dakṣamitrā.

The changed format of the religious gift-system is also evinced by the fact that besides the accompanying sacramental rites, *dāna* now also became integral to the purificatory and expiatory rituals.[87] The need for the latter arose mainly due to the urban contingency. The urban mode of living exposed members of the higher *varṇa* stratum to greater possibilities and risks of ritual pollution and transgressions of *varṇa* regulations, for which the performance of purificatory and expiatory rites became imminent. Moreover, the total breakdown of close kinship bonds in the expanding urban milieu must have not only fostered a feeling of self-alienation in the individual but also heightened his sense of guilt. This indirectly strengthened the concept of moral sin and the need for its atonement. Significantly, in the early Smṛtis such as the *Manusmṛti* (XI.130-1, 134, 140, 142, 228), *dāna* figures prominently in the section dealing with *prāyaścitta* or expiation. *Dāna* made for expiatory purposes not only proved to be an additional source of income for the priestly class but also greatly expanded the purview of ritual *dāna*.

The gift-system in the advanced stage of urbanization during the Kuṣāṇa-Sātavāhana times thus manifested altogether new aspects and features not found in its counterpart, either in the predominant pastoral milieu of the Vedic age or during the formative stages of urbanization in the post-Vedic period. A more effective way of highlighting its unique contours would be to compare it with the gift-system in the subsequent period of urban decline in the Gupta and post-Gupta times.

V

That the decline of urban centres during the Gupta and post-Gupta centuries was a pan-Indian phenomenon is duly affirmed, as shown by R.S. Sharma,[88] both by literary and archaeological data. The latter reveals that many prosperous cities and towns of the preceding period were either decaying or had already disappeared during this period. According to Sharma, 'the material remains of early medieval levels, when compared with those from early historic layers, appear to be generally non-urban in character'.[89] Some of the important features that marked this process of de-urbanization were the paucity of coins and coin-moulds, the absence of artisanal and commercial seals, a decrease in craft tools and craft-goods, a decline in the volume of internal and external trade, and the decay or disappearance of urban-styled structures. Amongst the causative factors that led to urban decay would appear to be the decline in long-distance trade, especially with Rome and China, as well as the fragmentation of political power in which foreign invasions seemingly played an important role. This naturally must have encouraged centrifugal tendencies. The chief impact of this development was evident on craft production and commercial enterprise. The latter severely affected the condition of traders and artisans, many of whom were forced to either give up their traditional vocation or shift to the countryside to eke out a living, as also the money economy and state resources in the form of revenue generated by towns and cities. Consequently, a land-based closed economic order characterized by a strong feudal ethos came to replace the dynamic and vibrant commercial economy of the earlier period.

Our sources reveal that the ritual gift-system was central to many of these developments. Thus, the breakdown of a commercial order raised the importance of agricultural land to an unprecedented degree, turning it into a most coveted item of gift. The practice of making land grants, which came to represent a new form of gift-making, also led to certain remarkable feudal developments. Though the beginnings of the practice go back to the preceding period, it was only under regressive urban conditions, marked by withdrawal of the large-scale circulation of metal currency, sluggish trade and sag-ging commodity production, that land grants emerged as a catalytic factor in the contemporary economy. It became an important means of coping with some of the problems besetting the monarchical states such as dwindling fiscal resources, retrenchment of military force and administrative machinery. It also became instrumental in re-inforcing claims to political power in a continually changing power configuration. Moreover, the special fiscal privileges and other forms of immunity granted along with land by royal donors created conditions of a feudal relationship between the beneficiaries of land grants and the actual tillers of soil. Another important feature of the feudal ethos, namely the element of ostentation, pomp and pageantry, is known to find expression in the sixteen great gifts or *mahadānas*, which, for the first time, are heard of in the Purāṇas. It was an innovative concept introduced by the composer of the *Matsya Purāṇa* (Chaps. 271-89), mainly to meet the demands of a prestige-based feudal milieu. *Mahādānas* such as the *hiraṇyagarbha*, *brahmāṇḍa*, *mahābhūtaghaṭa* and *tulāpuruṣa*, by serving as an effective validating mechanism, also became instrumental in encouraging royal aspirants with tribal antecedents to stake their claim to power.[90] The ritual gift-system, moreover, became auxiliary to the process of acculturation, which had been precipitated at this time by the accelerated pace of agricultural expansion. The latter was, to a great extent, the outcome of land grants issued in large numbers, particularly in peripheral zones representing cultural backwaters and inhabited mainly by indigenous tribal groups.

Though we get notices of the gift of residential and other kinds of land for the construction of *caityas*, *vihāras*, alms-halls, etc., even in the Kuṣāṇa-Sātavāhana period, the issue of land charters in very large numbers permanently bequeathing villages, agricultural fields and waste land was a phenomenon not quite in consonance with the urban milieu and is met with mainly in the subsequent Gupta/post-Gupta period. The Purāṇas are known to especially recommend the establishment and maintenance of rural settlements. According to the *Bṛhannāradīya Purāṇa* (13.44; 13.54), one who maintains a village gains a hundred times more piety than one who creates it. The unprecedented popularity gained by the practice of making land grants during this period led to certain new features being added to the gift-making ritualism. The permanent nature of the land grant had long-term implications, for it directly affected not one but several generations of both the donor and the donee. The former was specifically enjoined by lawgivers[91] to not only get the grant formally recorded on some durable material such as a copper plate or stone slab but also duly specify the date, the name and the family antecedents of the donor, donee and the king in whose time it was made, the size and other details about the donated land, the exact terms of the grant, and, finally, to clearly acknowledge its irrevocable nature by declaring it to last as long as the sun and the moon.

The effect of urban decline on the ritual gift-system is clearly revealed by the fact that several features that had characterized it during the prosperous commercial phase under the Kuṣāṇas and Sātavāhanas disappeared completely. Urban donors now receded into the background and some of the organized modes of gift-distribution are no longer heard of in literary and epigraphic records belonging to the early medieval period. Traders, artisans and other urban-based professional groupings such as courtesans figure only marginally in prominent donor categories, which now came to be dominated mainly by kings and their kinsmen, administrative functionaries and the landed gentry enjoying a feudal status. However, with gift-ritualism acquiring a more popular aspect and broader base, the lower segments of society now emerged as the principal and much larger donor category, the modest scale of their gifts notwithstanding. We also do not come across many notices of large sums of money being deposited with guilds for benefaction purposes, just as we do not hear of any instance of alms distribution through the ticket system.

The maximum impact of urban decay is perceptible on the waning or soaring popularity of gift-items. Thus, metallic currency now faded into the background as a popular gift-item; instead, gold and silver in various forms began to be preferred. Moreover, whereas the popularity of the practice of consecrating wells and tanks remained unaffected by the growing shift towards a closed agrarian economy, the latter development was responsible for making agricultural products, especially cereals as well as agricultural equipment such as ploughshares, extremely popular as gift-items, next only to land. Thus, amongst the sixteen *mahādānas* listed in the *Matsya Purāṇa* (Chap. 283), we come across the *pañcalāṅgalaka mahādāna*, which fitted perfectly into the agrarian mould and entailed the gift of five ploughs made of wood of the finest quality, along with a plot of land and five pair of oxen with their horns covered with gold. The donor was also required to gift five ploughs made of 5 to 1,000 *palas* of gold. The popularity of cereals as gift-items is very effectively reflected in the Purāṇas. In the *Matsya Purāṇa* (Chaps. 82 *gūḍadhenu*, 83 *dhānyaśaila*, 87 *tila-parvata* and 92: *dhānya-parvata*), we come across references to gifts such as *dhenu-dāna* and *meru-dāna* in which a prescribed quantum of food items such as cereals, *tila*, salt, sugar, *ghṛta*, etc., had to be arranged in the shape of a hillock or a cow before being given away to ministrant brāhmaṇas. Food, moreover, became an even more popular item of *dāna* at the time of performing sacramental rites, *vratas* and *pūjā*, as also at places of pilgrimage or *tīrthas*.

The sudden popularity gained by the practice of *tīrthas*, which became closely associated with ritual gift-making, has also been linked by scholars with the phenomenon of urban decay. Thus, according to R.N. Nandi,[92] the rise of *tīrthas* in the early medieval period was the result of the attempt on the part of brāhmaṇa ideologues to transform many of the decaying urban centres into places of pilgrimage. To quote Nandi:

> Significantly the lists of 'holy places' in the *Viṣṇusmṛti* and the subsequent Purāṇas enumerate a large number of important ancient towns which are found to have been, on the basis of archaeological evidence, in a state of decline during the early medieval period. Some of these settlements were picked up for systematic glorification as *tīrthas*. . . . The places which can be clearly identified as important ancient towns are Varanasi (Rājghāṭ), Gayā (probably represented by Sonpur), Prayāga (Bhītā), Ayodhyā, Prabhāsa (Dwārkā), Vidiśā (Bhilsā) and Sūrpāraka (Sopārā) on the west coast.

The attempt at glorification is especially evident from the *Matsya Purāṇa*, for instance, which has 10 chapters on Prayāga, and the *Varāha Purāṇa*, which pays special attention to Mathurā. Nandi's chief contention is that the decay of towns and the subsequent proclamation of a large number of them as places of pilgrimage and gift-making were not isolated phenomena 'for the town and the *tīrtha* refer to two different types of settlement and represent two different but causally related social economies'. Whereas the towns represented 'a flourishing market economy and the incidental *saṁskāra*-based gift-exchange system which thrived on the affluence of urban householders', the concept of *tīrtha* was more 'an attempt to revive the prospects of gift-exchange in all the decaying settlements including towns'.

The main line of argument adopted by Nandi is that the decay of towns must have affected the prosperity of the city-based *jajamānas* who had been chiefly patronizing the priestly class, so that it eventually resulted in 'the decline of the *saṁskāra* religiosity in towns and cities'. We do not entirely agree with some of Nandi's contentions such as the rise of the institution of *tīrthas* being a direct corollary of the phenomenon of urban decay,[93] or the institution of *tīrthas* having been promoted by brāhmaṇas mainly to make up for 'the decline of *saṁskāra* religiosity in towns and cities'. Yet there is no denying the fact that the resurfacing, in the Purāṇas, of many prosperous cities of the earlier period as popular *tīrtha* sites does suggest a definite attempt on the part of the brāhmaṇas to try and confer the *tīrtha* status upon them in order to revive some of their lost importance, and make them into a lucrative source of income. The point has been quite effectively put across by Nandi.[94] In fact, there is enough evidence forthcoming from the later Smṛtis and Purāṇas to show that their composers, realizing the importance of these texts as potential mediums of ideological propaganda, made them instrumental in resuscitating and transforming many of the cities and towns that had lost their former eminence as commercial centres and were almost on the verge of decline into popular pilgrimage sites. Besides weaving elaborate mythological tales around them, such a transformation was invariably attended by vehement proclamation by the authors of the Purāṇas that *dāna* made to brāhmaṇas at these sites was imbued with the highest spiritual merit.

A practice which might have, to some extent, revived the importance of these decaying towns, turning them into popular *tīrthas*, could have been that of constructing temples and other imposing religious monuments and structures there. Both archaeological and Purāṇic *dātā* affirm that the practice of building temples, *stūpas* and large monastic establishments by aspirant rulers and their kinsmen gained unprecedented popularity from the time of the Guptas. However, it has to be admitted that most of these monuments are known to have come up not in the core Brāhmaṇical zone in the north but in regions far removed from it.[95] Moreover, considering the magnificent scale of such temple-building activities, the practice would appear to be more in consonance with the emergent feudal spirit than with the fast-fading urban ethos. Hence, aspects of the ritual gift-system which were directly impacted by urbanization would include not merely the nature of gift-items but also the categories of donor and donee, as well as the procedure accompanying such gift-making.

Our study, thus, reveals that more than its ritual import, the dynamics of the gift-system lay in its essentially being a socio-economic mechanism. The specific form in which it was found in a particular material milieu was largely in response to the definite needs and exigencies of that society. *Dāna*, as it prevailed in the dominant urban social order in the post-Mauryan centuries, was, therefore, an altogether new form of gift-system, manifesting totally unique dominant traits and format, though many residual elements continued to survive in the shape of secondary features.

NOTES

1. Romila Thapar, '*Dāna* and *Dakṣiṇā* as Forms of Exchange', *Ancient Indian Social History*, New Delhi, 1978, pp. 105-21.
2. Marcel Mauss, *The Gift*, tr. I.A.N. Cunnison, London, 1954, p. 57.
3. Vijay Nath, *Dāna: Gift System in Ancient India*, Delhi, 1987.
4. R.N. Nandi, *Social Roots of Religion in Ancient India*, Calcutta, 1986, p. 11.
5. R.S. Sharma, 'Conflict, Distribution and Differentiation in Ṛgvedic Society', Proceedings of the Indian History Congress, 1977, p. 183.
6. C. Drekmeier, *Kingship and Community in Early India*, Bombay, 1962, p. 47.
7. *Śatapatha Brāhmaṇa*, VI.2.137.
8. Jogiraj Basu, *India of the Age of the Brāhmaṇas*, Calcutta, 1969, p. 147.
9. R.N. Nandi, 'Client, Ritual and Conflict in Early Brāhmaṇical Order', *Indian Historical Review*, vol. V, nos. 1-2, 1979-80.
10. Vijay Nath, 'Ritual Symbolism and Status Conferring Role of Dāna', Proceedings of the Indian History Congress, 1989.
11. G.S.P. Mishra, 'A Study of Philanthropy in Early Buddhist Ethics', *Indica*, vol. XVIII, no. ii, 1981, p. 81.
12. V.K. Thakur, *Urbanization in Ancient India*, New Delhi, 1981, pp. 66-71.
13. Upendra Thakur, 'The First Coins: A Study in Evolution and Growth', *Early Indian Indigenous Coins*, ed. D.C. Sircar, Calcutta, 1970.
14. Nath, *Dāna*, op. cit., p. 173; Md. Aquique, *Economic History of Mithila*, Delhi, 1974, p. 168.
15. Nath, *Dāna*, op. cit., p. 101.
16. Ibid., pp. 54-66.
17. *Illīsa Jātaka*, vol. I, no. 78, p. 199; *Jātakas*, ed. V. Fausboll, 6 vols., London, 1877-98; tr. E.B. Cowell, Cambridge, 1895-1913.
18. *Pāraskara Gṛhyasūtra*, I.10.5; *Āśvalāyana Gṛhyasūtra*, IV.7.17; *Sāṅkhyāyana Gṛhyasūtra*, III.11.16; *Āpastamba Gṛhyasūtra*, VI.16.4.
19. *Mahāvagga*, I.22; *Saṁyutta Nikāya*, I.II.3.3.
20. *Mahāsupīna Jātaka*, vol. I, no. 77, p. 191.
21. *Mahāvastu*, tr. J.J. Jones, vol. I, SBB, vol. XVI, London, pp. 76-7.
22. Ibid., p. 169.
23. Nath, 'Ritual Growth in Later and Post-Vedic Times', op. cit.

24. Nath, *Dāna*, op. cit., p. 113.
25. *Mahāvagga*, VIII.1.8; 34.21; *Milindapañho*, I.32.
26. *Baudhāyana Dharmasūtra*, II. 3.5.17-18; *Manusmṛti*, IV.32; *Therigāthā*, XXX, *Uttama*; *Vinaya* (Nissaggiya), VIII.1.
27. *Khadiraṅga Jātaka*, vol. I, no. 40; *Visayha Jātaka*, vol. III, no. 340; *Milindapañho*, I.2.
28. *Vinaya* (Nissaggiya) XXVIII.1; *Jarudapana Jātaka*, vol. II, no. 256; *Mahāvaṇija Jātaka*, vol. II. no. 493; *Vimānavatthu*, Serisaka's Mansion, VI.9.83.
29. *Vinaya* (Nissaggiya), VIII.1; *Milindapañho*, I.30.
30. *Kimi Jātaka*, vol. VI, no. 541.
31. *Visayha Jātaka*, vol. III, no. 340; *Mayhaka Jātaka*, vol. III, no. 390; *Gaṅgamāla Jātaka*, vol. III, no. 421.
32. Junnar Buddhist Cave inscription, *Luder's List*, no. 1174; Kanheri Buddhist Cave Inscription, *Luder's List*, no. 994; H. Luders, *A List of Brahmi Inscriptions from the Earliest Times to about* AD *400 with the Exception of Those of Aśoka*, Appendix to Epigraphia Indica and Record of the Archaeological Survey of India, vol. I, X, 1909-19; 'Gunda Stone Inscription', *Select Inscriptions*, D.C. Sircar, vol. I, bk. II, no. 69, p. 181.
33. *Vinaya* (Nissaggiya), XXII; *Hatthipāla Jātaka*, vol. IV, no. 509.
34. *Mahāparinibbāna Sutta*, II.19; *Mahāvagga*, VI. 30.5.
35. *Baudhāyana Dharmasūtra*, ii.3.5.19.
36. Vijay Nath, 'Dāna in the Context of Commerce and Urbanization in Kuṣāṇa Times', *Journal of Bihar Research Society*, vol. LXV-LXVI, pts.1-4, 1979-80, p. 175.
37. *Manusmṛti*, VII.133-4.
38. *Āpastamba Gṛhyasūtra*, I.7.20.11-16; *Gautama Gṛhyasūtra*, X.5-6; *Manusmṛti*, X.115-116.
39. *Bilāri Kosīya Jātaka*, vol. IV, no. 450; *Vessantara Jātaka*, vol. I, no. 69.
40. *Pāraskara Gṛhyasūtra*, I.2.13; *Gobhila Gṛhyasūtra*, I.6; IV.2.33.
41. Nath, *Dāna*, op. cit., p. 151.
42. *Dīgha Nikāya*, III.1.160; *Mahāvagga*, VIII.3.1.
43. *Mahāvagga*, V.10.3; V.13.6.
44. *Cullavagga*, VI.2.4; *Vasiṣṭha Dharmasūtra*, XXIX.12.
45. *Cullavagga*, V.16.2.
46. *Dīgha Nikāya*, III.2.259; *Apannaka Jātaka*, vol. I, no.1; *Gandhāra Jātaka*, vol. III, no. 406.
47. *Mahābhārata*, XIII, 145; *Saṁyutta Nikāya*, I. 5.7, tr., p. 46.
48. 'Aśoka's eleventh Major Rock Edict', *Select Inscriptions*, D.C. Sircar, vol. I, bk. I, p. 31.
49. 'Major Rock Edict II', *Select Inscriptions*, vol. I, bk. I, p. 18; Pillar Edict VII, ibid., vol. I, bk. I, p. 62.
50. D.C. Sircar, *Select Inscriptions*, vol. I, bk I.

51. Ibid.
52. *Dīgha Nikāya*, III, *Ambattha Sutta*, II.4; *Dhammapada*, III.16.9; *Kurudhamma Jātaka*, vol. II, no. 276.
53. *Dhammapada*, II.1; *Mahāsutsoma Jātaka*, vol. V, no. 537; *Vimānavatthu*, Sirima's Mansion, I.17.
54. *Uttarādhyayana Sūtra*, II.30; *Majjhima Nikāya*, LXIX.1.470; *Dhammapada*, III.19.8; S.B. Deo, *History of Jaina Monachism*, p. 308.
55. R.S. Sharma, 'Decay of Gangetic Towns in Gupta and Post-Gupta Times', *Journal of Indian History*, Golden Jubilee volume, p. 137.
56. Thakur, op. cit.
57. B. Gafurov, 'Kuṣāna Civilization and World Culture', *Kusana Studies in USSR*, Calcutta, 1970.
58. B. Chattopadhyaya, *The Age of the Kusanas: A Numismatic Study*, Calcutta, 1967, p. 189; Upendra Thakur, 'Economic Data from the Early Coins of India', *JESHO*, 1971.
59. Y.D. Sharma, 'Remains of Early Historical Cities', *Archaeological Remains, Monuments and Museums, ASE*, 1964, pp. 48-54.
60. Motichandra, *Trade and Trade-routes in Ancient India*, New Delhi, 1977.
61. B.N. Mukherjee, *The Economic Factors in Kusana History*, Calcutta, 1970, p. 16.
62. H.P. Ray, *Monastery and Guild: Commerce Under the Satavahanas*, Delhi, 1986.
63. *Rāmāyaṇa*, I.14.51; 'Nasik Buddhist Cave Inscription', *Select Inscriptions*, ed. D.C. Sircar, vol. I, no. 82; *Mathura Stone Inscription of Huviṣka*, ibid., no. 49.
64. *Milindapañho*, ed. V. Trenckner, London, 1928; tr. T.W. Rhys Davids, Sacred Books of the East, Oxford, 1890-4, p. 331.
65. Nath, *Dāna*, op. cit., p. 152.
66. Roshan Dalal, 'The Historical Geography of the Mathurā Region', *Mathurā: The Cultural Heritage*, ed. D.M. Srinivasan, New Delhi, 1989, p. 6.
67. *EI*, vol. VII, 1923-4, p. 13.
68. *Journal of U.P. Historical Society*, vol. XXII, 1949, p. 199.
69. Ibid., XXIII, 1950.
70. *ASI Annual Report, 1924-25*, Pl. XXIII, p. 50.
71. D.C. Sircar, *Select Inscriptions*, vol. I, pp. 146, 157.
72. Ray, op. cit.
73. *EI*, XIX, 1928.
74. Sircar, *Select Inscriptions*, p. 152.
75. J. Burgess, 'Report on the Ellora Cave Temples and the Brahmanical and Jaina Caves in Western India', *ASWI*, vol. V, 1883, London, p. 81; Ray, op. cit., p. 102.
76. D.D. Kosambi, 'Dhenukakata', JASB, XXX, 1955, p. 53.
77. Ray, op. cit., p. 183.

78. 'Nasik Buddhist Cave Inscription', *Select Inscriptions*, vol. I, bk. II, no. 82; *Mathura Stone Inscription of Huviska*, ibid., vol. I, bk. II, no. 49.
79. *Luder's List*, nos. 1133, 1137, 1165; 'Nasik Buddhist Cave Inscription', *Select Inscriptions*, vol. I, bk. II, nos. 49, 58; B.D. Chattopadhyaya, 'Mathurā from the Śuṅga to the Kuṣāna Period', op. cit., p. 13.
80. 'Major Rock Edict III', *Select Inscriptions*, vol. I, bk. I, p. 18.
81. Nath, *Dāna*, op. cit., p. 67.
82. 'Nasik Cave Inscription', *Select Inscriptions*, vol. I, bk. II, no. 59, p. 169.
83. G.S.P. Mishra, 'A Study of Philanthropy in Early Buddhist Ethics', *Indica*, vol. XVIII, no. 2, 1981, p. 81.
84. *Luder's List*, nos. 15, 30, 31, 105, 184, 207, 208, 220, 246, 248, 255, 269, 283, 339, 355, 363, 379, 422, 423, 470.
85. B.D. Chattopadhyaya, 'Mathura from the Sunga to the Kusana Period: An Historical Outline', *Mathura: The Cultural Heritage*, ed. D.M. Srinivasan, New Delhi, 1989, pp. 23-4.
86. Nath, *Dāna*, op. cit., p. 99.
87. *Manusmṛti*, XI.73-87.
88. *Urban Decay in India (c. 300-c.1000)*, New Delhi, 1987.
89. Ibid., p. 122.
90. Vijay Nath, 'Mahādāna: The Dynamics of Gift-economy', *The Feudal Order*, ed. D.N. Jha, New Delhi, 2000, pp. 411-40.
91. *Viṣṇusmṛti*, III.82.
92. Nandi, *Social Roots of Religion in Ancient India*, Calcutta, 1986, p. 47.
93. Vijay Nath, 'Tirthas and Acculturation', *Pilgrimage Studies: The Power of Sacred Places*, ed. D.P. Dubey, Allahabad, 2000.
94. Nandi, *Social Roots*, op. cit., pp. 51-4.
95. Vijay Nath, 'Tīrthas and Acculturation', op. cit., pp. 85-6; Vijay Nath, 'Purāṇic Tīrthas: A Study of Their Indigenous Origins', *Indian Historical Review*, XXXIV, no. i, 2007, pp. 14-15.

Bibliography

A. ORIGINAL SOURCES

Agni Purāṇa, tr. M.N. Dutt, Calcutta, 1901.

Aitareya Brāhmaṇa of the Ṛgveda, tr. Martin Haug, Bombay, 1863.

Amarakośa, with Hindi comm. by Hargovinda Astir, Haridas Sanskrit Series, no. 30, 4th edn., Varanasi, 1978.

Aṅguttara Nikāya, ed. R. Morris and E. Hardy, 5 vols., *PTS*, London, 1885-1900; tr., *The Book of the Gradual Sayings*, I, II and V by F.L. Woodward and III and IV by E.M. Hare, *PTS*, London, 1932-6.

Āpastamba Dharmasūtra, ed. G. Bühler, Bombay Sanskrit Series, Pune, 1932; tr. SBE, II, rpt., Delhi, 1965.

Āpastamba Gṛhyasūtra, ed. U.C. Pandey, Kashi Sanskrit Series, no. 59, Varanasi, 1971.

Āpastamba Śrautasūtra with comm. by Dhrutta Svami, ed. A.C. Shastri, Gaekwad's Oriental Series, CXXI, Baroda, 1955.

Aṣṭādhyāyī of Pāṇini, ed. and tr. S.C. Vasu, 2 vols., rpt., Delhi, 1962.

Āśvalāyana Gṛhyasūtra with the comm. of Haradattacharya, ed. T. Ganpati Sastri, Trivandrum, 1923.

Āśvalāyana Śrautasūtra with the comm. of Narayana, ed. H.N. Apte, Anandasrama Sanskrit Series, no. 81, Poona, 1917.

Baudhāyana Dharmasūtra with the *'Vivaraṇa'* comm. by Sri Govinda Svami, ed. U.C. Pandey, Kashi Sanskrit Series, no. 104, Varanasi, 1972.

Baudhāyana Dharmasūtra, ed. E. Hultzsch, Leipzig, 1884.

Baudhāyana Gṛhyasūtra, ed. R. Shamasastry, Mysore, 1927.

Beal, S., *The Life of Hiuen-Tsang*, London, 1888, rpt., New Delhi, 1973.

Buddhacarita or Acts of the Buddha, ed. and tr. E.H. Johnston, Delhi, 1972.

Buddhist Legends, tr. from the original Pāli text of the *Dhammapada* commentary by E.W. Burlingame, 3 pts., Harvard Oriental Series, Cambridge (Mass.), 1921.

Cullavagga, ed. Bhikkhu J. Kashyap, Nālandā-Devanāgarī-Pāli Series, Nalanda, 1956, tr. T.W. Rhys Davids and H. Oldenberg, SBE, XVII and XX, rpt., Delhi, 1965.

Dhātupāṭha of Pāṇini, Haridas Sanskrit Granthmala, no. 281, Banaras.

Dānakriyā Kaumudī of Govindānanda, *Bibliotheca Indica*, Calcutta, 1903.

Dharmaśāstras or Hindu Law Codes, tr. M.N. Dutt, Calcutta, 1908.

Dīgha Nikāya, ed. T.W. Rhys Davids and J.E. Carpenter, 3 vols., PTS, London, 1890-91; tr. T.W. Rhys Davids, 3 vols., SBB, London, 1899-1921.

Divyāvadāna, ed. P.L. Vaidya, Buddhist Sanskrit Texts, no. 20, Darbhanga, 1959.

Gautama Dharmasūtra, with the Mitākṣarā Sanskrit comm. of Hardatta, ed. U.C. Pandey, Kashi Sanskrit Series, no. 172, Varanasi, 1966.

Gobhila Gṛhyasūtra, with comm. by Bhaṭṭanārāyaṇa, ed. C. Bhattacharya, Calcutta, 1936.

The Gṛhya-Sūtras, tr. of the *Gṛhyasūtras* of Sāṅkhyāyana, Āśvalāyana, Pāraskara, Khadira, Gobhila, Hiraṇyakeśin, and Āpastamba by H. Oldenberg, SBE, XXIX and XXX, rpt., Delhi, 1964.

The Hymns of the Ṛgveda, tr. Ralph T.H. Griffith, new rev. edn., ed. J.L. Shastri, Delhi, 1973.

Hitopadeśa of Nārāyaṇa Paṇḍit, ed. Nārāyaṇa Rām Acharya, Bombay, 1955; tr. *The Book of Good Counsels* by Edwin Arnold, London, 1924.

The Institutes of Viṣṇu, tr. J. Jolly, SBE, VII, rpt., Delhi, 1965.

Jaina Sūtras, tr. Hermann Jacobi, SBE, XXII, XLV, rpt., Delhi, 1965.

Jātakas, ed. V. Fausboll, 6 vols., London, 1877-98; tr. E.B. Cowell, Cambridge, 1895-1913.

Jātaka-Mālā of Ārya Sura, ed. P.L. Vaidya, Buddhist Sanskrit Texts, no. 21, Darbhanga, 1959; tr. J.S. Speyer, 1895, rpt., Delhi, 1971.

Kalpasūtra, tr. Mahopadhyaya Vinaya Sagar, Prakrit Bharati, Jaipur, 1977.

Kātyāyana Smṛti, ed. with reconstituted text and tr. P.V. Kane, Bombay, 1943.

Kauṭilya's Arthaśāstra, ed. and tr. R. Shamasastry, Mysore, 1923; ed. and tr. R.P. Kangle, 3 pts., Bombay, 1970-5.

Khuddaka Nikāya, ed. Bhikkhu J. Kashyap, 7 vols., Nālandā-Devanāgarī-Pāli Series, Nalanda, 1959.

(i) *Khuddakapāṭha, Dhammapada, Udāna, Itivutthaka, Suttanipāta.*
(ii) *Vimānavatthu, Petavatthu, Theragāthā, Therigāthā.*
(iii) *Jātaka*, 2 pts.
(iv) *Mahāniddesa, Cullaniddesa.*
(v) *Apadāna*,
(vi) *Buddhavaṁśa*,
(vii) *Cariyāpiṭaka.*

Khuddakapāṭha, tr. *The Minor Readings* by Bhikkhu Nanamoli, PTS, no. 32, London, 1960.

Kātyāyana Śrautasūtra, ed. A. Weber, Chowkhamba Sanskrit Granthmala, no. 104, Varanasi, 1972.

Kṛtyakalpataru of Bhaṭṭa Lakṣmīdhara, vol. 5, Dāna Kāṇḍa, ed. K.V. Rangaswami Aiyangar, Baroda, 1941.

Legge, James, *A Record of the Buddhistic Kingdoms*, Being an Account of the Chinese Monk Fa-hsien's Travels, rpt., New Delhi, 1982.

Mahābhārata, text as constituted in its critical edition, ed. various hands, BORI, Poona, 1971-5; tr. K.M. Ganguly, 3rd edn., 12 vols., Delhi, 1975.

Mahābhāṣya by Patañjali, ed. F. Kielhorn, 3 vols., Bombay, 1892-1909.

Mahāvagga, ed. Bhikkhu J. Kashyap, Nālandā-Devanāgarī-Pāli Series, Nalanda, 1956; tr. T.W. Rhys Davids and H. Oldenberg, SBE, XIII, XVII, rpt., Delhi, 1965.

Manusmṛti, ed. Hargovinda Shastri, Haridas Sanskrit Granthmala, no. 226, Varanasi; tr. Ganganath Jha, Calcutta, 1920-6.

Mahāvastu, ed. E. Senart, 3 vols., Paris, 1882-97; tr. J.J. Jones, 2 vols., SBB, vol. XVI, London.

Majjhima Nikāya, ed. V. Trenckner and R. Chalmers, PTS, 3 vols., London, 1886-96; *The Collection of the Middle Length Sayings*, tr. I.B. Horner, PTS, no. 29, London, 1954.

Milindapañho, ed. V. Trenckner, London, 1928; tr. T.W. Rhys Davids, SBE, Oxford, 1890-4.

Mīmāṁsā Sūtras of Jaimini, tr. M.L. Sandal, SBH, XXVII, Allahabad, 1928.

Nārada Smṛti, with extracts from the comm. of Ashaya, ed. J. Jolly, Calcutta, 1885; tr. J. Jolly, SBE, XXXIII, rpt., Delhi, 1965.

The Nighaṇṭu and the Nirukta, ed. Laksman Sarup, rpt., Delhi, 1962.

Pacittiya Bhikkhu Vibhaṅga, pt., II and *Bhikkunī-Vibhaṅga*, ed. Bhikkhu J. Kashyap, Nālandā-Devanāgarī-Pāli Series, Nalanda, 1958.

Pañcatantra of Viṣṇuśarman, ed. Johannes Hertel, *Harvard Oriental Series*, Cambridge (Mass.), 1908; tr. Franklin Edgerton, London, 1965.

Pāṇini Sūtra-Pāṭha and Pariśiṣṭas, with work index, compiled by S. Pathak and S. Chitrao, Poona, 1935.

Pāraskara Gṛhyasūtra, Bombay, 1917.

Petavatthu: Stories of the Departed, tr. Henry Synder Gehman, London, 1962.

Paumcariyam of Vimala Sūri, ed. H. Jacobi, tr. S.M. Vohra, Banaras, 1962.

The Ṛgveda Saṁhitā, tr. H.H. Wilson, London, 1850-7.

The Sacred Law of the Āryas, tr. of the *Dharmasūtras of Āpastamba, Gautama, Vasiṣṭha and Baudhāyana* by G. Bühler, SBE, II and XIV, rpt., Delhi, 1964.

Saṁyutta Nikāya, ed. Bhikku J. Kashyap, Nālandā-Devanāgarī-Pāli Series,

Nalanda, 1959; *The Book of the Kindered Sayings*, tr. Mrs. Rhys Davids, 5 vols., PTS, London, 1950-6.

Sāṅkhyāyana Gṛhyasūtra, ed. S.R. Sehgal, Delhi, 1960.

Sāṅkhyāyana Śrautasūtra, tr. W. Caland, rpt., Delhi, 1980.

Śrī Bhagwatī Sūtram, ed. Muni Kanhaiyalal Ji, Rajkot, 1965.

Sumaṅgala Vilāsinī of Buddhaghoṣa, ed. T.W. Rhys Davids and J.E. Carpenter, PTS, London, 1886.

Theragāthā, tr. *Psalms of the Brethren* by Mrs. Rhys Davids, PTS, London, 1951.

Therigāthā, tr. *Psalms of the Sisters* by Mrs. Rhys Davids, PTS, London, 1909.

The Travels of Fa-hsien (AD 399-414), or *Record of the Buddhistic Kingdoms*, tr. H.A. Giles, rpt., London, 1959.

Udāna, tr. *Verses of Uplift* by F.L. Woodward, SBB, Oxford, 1948.

Vajrasūci of Aśvaghoṣa, ed. and tr. Sujit Kumar Mukhopadhyaya, Shantiniketan, 1950.

The Vālmikī-Rāmāyaṇa, Critical edition, ed. G.H. Bhatt, 7 vols., Baroda, 1960; tr. Hari Prasad Shastri, 3 vols., London, 1952.

Vimānavatthu, tr. E.R. Gooneratne, PTS, London.

Vimuttimagga of Upatissa, tr. *The Path of Freedom* by Sona Thera, Colombo, 1961.

Vinaya Piṭaka, ed. H. Oldenberg, 5 vols., London, 1879-83; *The Book of Discipline*, tr. I.B. Homer, 5 pts., SBB, London, 1938-52.

Yājñavalkya Smṛti, with the *Mitākṣarā* comm. of Vijñāneśvara, ed. Narayan Ram Acarya, Bombay, 1949.

Yāska's *Niruktam*, with comm. by Chajjuram Sastri and Devasarma Sastri, Delhi, 1963.

On Yuan Chwang's Travels in India, Thomas Watters, ed. T.W. Rhys Davids and S.W. Bushell, 2 vols., rpt., New Delhi, 1973.

B. INSCRIPTIONS

Barua, B.M., *Aśoka and His Inscriptions*, Calcutta, 1955.

———, *Old Brahmi Inscriptions in the Udaygiri and Khandagiri Caves*, Calcutta, 1929.

Burgess, Jas, *Inscriptions from the Cave Temples of Western India*, with descriptive notes by Bhagwanlal Indraji, rpt., Delhi, 1976.

Cunningham, A., *The Bhilsa Topes, or Buddhist Monuments of Central India*, London, 1854.

Hultzsch, E., *Inscriptions of Aśoka*, vol. 1, *Corpus Inscriptionum Indicarum*, ed., rpt., Varanasi, 1969.

Kant, Shashi, *The Hathigumpha Inscription of Kharavela and the Bhabru Edict of Asoka: A Critical Study*, Delhi, 1971.

Konow, Sten, *Kharoshti Inscriptions*, vol. 3, pt. I, *Corpus Inscriptionum Indicarum*, London, 1929.

Luders, H., *A List of Brahmi Inscriptions from the Earliest Times to about AD 400 with the Exception of those of Aśoka*, Appendix to Epigraphia Indica and Record of the Archaeological Survey of India, vol. I, X, 1909-19.

———, *Bharhut Inscriptions*, vol. 2, pt. II, *Corpus Inscriptionum Indicarum*, rev. edn., New Delhi, 1963.

Sircar, D.C., *Select Inscriptions Bearing on Indian History and Givilization*, vol. I, Calcutta, 1965.

———, *Indian Epigraphical Glossary*, Delhi, 1966.

C. DICTIONARIES AND REFERENCE BOOKS

Anderson, Dines et al., *A Critical Pali Dictionary*, Copenhagen, 1924-48.

Brandon, S.G., *A Dictionary of Comparative Religion*, London, 1970.

Cappeller, Carl, *A Sanskrit-English Dictionary*, Varanasi, 1972.

Gode, P.K. and C.G. Karve, *Vaman Shivram Apte's The Practical Sanskrit-English Dictionary*, 3 vols., rev. edn., Poona, 1958.

Hastings, James, ed., *Encyclopedia of Religion and Ethics*, Edinburgh, 1908-21.

Katre, S.M., *Dictionary of Panini*, Poona, 1968.

Macdonald, A.M., *Chamber's Twentieth Century Dictionary*, London, 1972.

Macdonell, A.A., *Saskrit-English Dictionary*, London, 1893.

Malalasekera, G.P., ed., *Encyclopedia of Buddhism*, Colombo, n.d.

Monier-Williams, M., *A Sanskrit-English Dictionary*, rpt., Delhi, 1976.

Muir, J., *Original Sanskrit Texts on the Origin and History of the People of India, their Religion and Institutions*, 5 vols., rev. 2nd. edn., rpt., Delhi, 1972.

Rhys Davids et al., *Pāli-English Dictionary*, rpt., New Delhi, 1975.

Sen, Chitrabhanu, *A Dictionary of the Vedic Rituals based on the Śrauta and Gṛhya Sūtras*, Delhi, 1978.

Simpson, D.P., *Cassell's New Latin Dictionary*, London, n.d.

Shastri, M. Sripathi, *A Dictionary of Sanskrit Roots*, n.d.

Tarkavachaspati, Taranath, *Vācaspatyam, A Comprehensive Sanskrit Dictionary*, 5 vols., Varanasi, 1962.

Whitney, W.D., *The Roots, Verb Forms and Primary Derivatives of the Sanskrit Language*, Delhi, 1963.

D. HISTORY OF INDIAN LITERATURE

Dasgupta, S.N. and S.K. De, eds., *A History of Sanskrit Literature*, vol. I, *Classical Period*, Calcutta, 1947.

Keith, A.B., *A History of Sanskrit Literature*, Oxford, 1928.

Law, B.C., *A History of Pāli Literature*, 2 vols., London, 1933.

Macdonell, A.A., *A History of Sanskrit Literature*, rpt., Delhi, 1972.

Macdonell, A.A. and A.B. Keith, *Vedic Index of Names and Subjects*, 2 vols., rpt., Varanasi, 1958.

Weber, A.A., *A History of Indian Literature*, London, 1914.

Winternitz, M., *A History of Indian Literature*, 2 vols., rpt., Delhi, 1972.

E. SECONDARY WORKS

Adhya, G.L., *Early Indian Economics: Studies in the Economic Life of Northern and Western India (c. 200 BC-AD 300)*, Bombay, 1966.

Agarwal, D.P., *The Copper Bronze Age in India*, Delhi, 1971.

Agarwal, Pratap C., *Caste, Religion and Power: An Indian Caste Study*, Delhi, 1971.

Agnihotri, P.D., *Patañjali Kālīna Bhārata*, Patna, 1963.

Agrawala, V.S., *India as Described by Manu*, Varanasi, 1970.

———, *India as Known to Pāṇini*, Varanasi, 1963.

———, 'The Bhakti Cult in Ancient India', *The Bhakti Cult and Ancient Indian Geography*, ed. D.C. Sircar, 1970, pp. 11-23.

Aiyangar, K.V.R., *Aspects of Ancient Indian Economic Thought*, Varanasi, 1965.

———, *Some Aspects of the Hindu View of Life According to Dharmaśāstra*, Baroda, 1952.

Aiyar, P.S.S., *Evolution of Hindu Moral Ideas*, rpt., Delhi, 1976.

Allchin, F.R., 'Upon the Antiquity and Methods of Gold Mining in Ancient India', *JESHO*, V, 1962, pp. 195-211.

Altekar, A.S., *Sources of Hindu Dharma: In its Socio-Religious Aspects*, Sholapur, n.d.

———, *Education in Ancient India*, Varanasi, 1965.

———, *The Position of Women in Hindu Civilisation, from Pre-historic Times to the Present Day*, Delhi, 1962.

Apte, V.M., *Social and Religious Life in the Grihya Sutras*, Bombay, 1954.

Aquique, Md., *Economic History of Mithila (c. 600 BC-AD 1097)*, Delhi, 1974.

Auboyer, J., *Daily Life in Ancient India, from 200 BC to 700 AD*, tr. S.W. Taylor, London, 1965.

Bailey, F., 'Spiritual Merit and Morality', *Culture and Morality: Essays in*

Honour of Christoph Von Furer-Haimendorf, ed. A.C. Mayer, Delhi 1981.

Bailey, F.G., ed., *Gifts and Poison (the Politics of Reputation)*, Oxford, 1971.

Baird, Robert D. and Alfred Bloom, *India and Far Eastern Religious Traditions*, New York, 1972.

Bandyopadhyaya, N.C., *Economic Life and Progress in Ancient India*, rpt., Allahabad, 1980.

Bandyopadhyaya, S., *Early Foreigners on Indian Caste System*, Calcutta, 1974.

Banerjee, B.N., *Hindu Culture Custom and Ceremony*, Delhi, 1979.

Banerjee, Gooroo Dass, *The Hindu Law of Marriage and Strīdhana*, Calcutta, 1923.

Banerjee, N.R., *The Iron Age in India*, Delhi, 1965.

Banerjee, N.V., *Studies in the Dharmaśāstra of Manu*, Delhi, 1980.

Banerji, S.C., *Dharma Sūtras: A Study in Their Origin and Development*, Calcutta, 1962.

———, *Indian Society in the Mahābhārata* (*Based on Smṛti Material in the Mahābhārata*), Varanasi, 1976.

Banerjee, S.C., *Aspects of Ancient Indian Life from Sanskrit Sources*, Calcutta, 1972.

Bapat, P.V., *Vimuttimagga and Viśudhimagga: A Comparative Study*, Poona, 1937.

Barua, D.K., *An Analytical Study of the Four Nikāyas*, Calcutta, 1971.

———, *Vihāras in Ancient India: A Survey of Buddhist Monasteries*, Calcutta, 1969.

———, 'Buddda's Ethical Discourses to the Laity', *MB*, 1967, pp. 39-41.

Barua, P.R., 'Brahmin Doctrine of Sacrifice and Rituals in the Pāli Canon', *JASP*, I, 1956, no. 1, pp. 87-108.

Basak, R.G., 'Indian Life as Revealed in the Buddhist Work, the *Mahāvastu Avadāna*', *J.N. Banerjee Volume*, Calcutta, 1960, pp. 1-70.

Basham, A.L., *The Wonder That Was India*, London, 1954.

———, ed., *Cultural History of India*, Oxford, 1975.

Basu, Jogiraj, *India of the Age of the Brāhmaṇas*, Calcutta, 1969.

Basu, P.C., 'Social and Religious Ceremonies of the Chakmas', *JASB*, NS, XXVII, 1931, pp. 213-23.

Basu, S.N., 'Slavery in the *Jātakas*', *JBORS*, 1923, pt. II, pp. 263-78.

Beattie, J., *Other Cultures: Aims Methods and Achievements in Social Anthropology*, New York, 1964.

Bedekar, D.K., 'Primitive Society and *Yajña*', *ABORI*, XXXI, 1951, pp. 70-90.

Bedi, R., 'Garlic', *Professor P.K. Gode Commemoration Volume*, ed. H.L. Hariyappa and M.M. Patkar, Poona, 1960, pp. 9-14.

Beidelman, T.O., *A Comparative Analysis of the Jajmānī System*, New York, 1959.

Bhagat, M.G., *Ancient Indian Asceticism*, New Delhi, 1976.

Bhandarkar, D.R., *Some Aspects of Ancient Indian Culture*, Madras, 1940.

Bhargava, D.V., *Jaina Ethics*, Delhi, 1968.

Bhargava, R.L., *India in the Vedic Age: A History of Aryan Expansion in India*, Lucknow, 1971.

Bhattacharjee, A.K., 'Agriculture in the Vedic Age', *BV*, XXXVIII, 1978, pp. 47-51.

Bhattacharya, B., *Urban Development in India (Since Pre-Historic Times)*, Delhi, 1979.

———, 'Treatment of Dāna by Kane and Rangaswami Aiyangar', *PO*, XIII, 1948, pp. 7-18.

Bhattacharya, J.N., *Hindu Castes and Sects*, Calcutta, 1896.

Bhattacharya, N.N., *Ancient Indian Ritual and their Social Contents*, Delhi, 1975.

———, *Jain Philosophy: Historical Outline*, Delhi, 1976.

Bhattacharya, S.C., *Some Aspects of Indian Society: From c. 2nd Century BC, to c. 4th Century AD*, Calcutta, 1978.

Bhattacharya, V., 'The Evolution of Bhakti Cult in Āryavarta', *S.K. De Memorial Volume*, Calcutta, 1972, pp. 156-63.

Bingley, A.H. and A. Nicholas, *Brāhmaṇas*, Simla, 1897.

Bloomfield, M., *The Religion of the Veda: The Ancient Religion of India (From Rig-Veda to Upanishads)*, rpt., Varanasi, 1972.

Blunt, E.A.H., *The Caste System of Northern India*, Delhi, 1969.

Bohannan, P., *Social Anthropology*, New York, 1963.

Bongard-Levin, G.M., *A Complex Study of Ancient India*, New Delhi, 1986.

———, *Mauryan India*, Delhi, 1985.

———, 'Studies in Ancient India and Central Asia', *Soviet Indology*, no. 7, Calcutta, 1971.

———, 'Some Problems of the Social Structure of Ancient India', *History and Society: Essays in Honour of Professor Niharranjan Ray*, ed. D.P. Chattopadhyaya, Calcutta, 1978, pp. 199-227.

Bose, A.N., *Social and Rural Economy of Northern India, 600 BC-AD 200*, Calcutta, 1961-7.

Bose, Devabrata, *The Problems of Indian Society*, New York, 1968.

Bose, N.K., *The Structure of Hindu Society*, Delhi, 1975.

———, *Cultural Anthropology*, Bombay, 1961.

———, 'Class and Caste', *MI*, XLV, 1965, pp. 265-74.

Bougle, Celestin, *Essays on Caste-System*, Cambridge, 1971.

Bremner, Robert, 'Modern Attitudes towards Charity and Relief', *Comparative Studies in Society and History*, vol. I, 1958-9.

Brockington, J.N., 'Religious Attitudes in Vālmīki's *Rāmāyaṇa*', *JRAS*, 1976, no. 1, pp. 108-29.
Buch, M.A., *Economic Life in Ancient India*, 2 vols., Allahabad, 1979.
Buck, C.H., *Faith, Fairs and Festivals of India*, rpt., Delhi, 1977.
Buddha Prakash, 'Landed Aristocracy in India', *JESHO*, XIV-XV, 1971-2, pp. 196-220.
———, 'Some Aspects of the Socio-Economic System of the Maurya Empire', *JBRS*, LIV, 1968, pp. 51-4.
Bühler, G., 'Further Votive Inscriptions form the Stupas at Sanchi', *EI*, II, 1894, pp. 366-402.
Chakladar, H.C., *The Aryan Occupation of Eastern India*, rpt., Calcutta, 1962.
———, *Social Life in Ancient India: Studies in Vātsyāyana's Kāmasūtra*, Delhi, 1976.
Chakrabarti, Dilip K., 'Beginning of Iron and Social Change in India', *Indian Studies: Past and Present*, XIV, no. 4, 1973, pp. 329-38.
———, 'The Beginning of Iron in India', *Ant.*, 1, 1976, pp. 114-24.
———, 'Some Theoretical Aspects of Early Indian Urban Growth', *Puratattva*, no. 7, 1974, pp. 87-109.
Chakrabarti, Kanchan, *Society, Religion and Art of the Kusana India: A Historico Symbiosis*, Calcutta, 1981.
Chakraborty, Chhanda, *Common Life in the Ṛgveda and Atharvaveda*, Calcutta, 1977.
Chakraborty, H., *Asceticism in Ancient India*, Calcutta, 1973.
———, *Early Brahmi Records in India*, Calcutta, 1974.
———, *Trade and Commerce of Ancient India*, Calcutta, 1967.
Chanana, D.R., *Slavery in Ancient India: As Depicted in Pāli and Sanskrit Texts*, Delhi, 1960.
Chandra, A., 'Professions and Occupation in the Mahabharata', *JOIB*, XII, 1962-3, pp. 59-68.
———, Treasury and Principles of Taxation in the Mahabharata', *JOIB*, XI, 1961-2, pp. 371-84.
Chatterjee, A.K., *Ancient Indian Literary and Cultural Tradition*, Calcutta, 1974.
Chatterjee, Bhaskar, 'Religion and Policy in the Kushana Age', *JIH*, LIV, 1976, pp. 511-15.
Chatterjee, Heramba, *Studies in Some Aspects of Hindu Saṁskāras in Ancient India*, Calcutta, 1965.
Chattopadhyay, B., *Kushana State and Indian Society*, Calcutta, 1975.
Chattopadhyaya, D.P. et al., *Buddhism: The Marxist Approach*, rpt., Delhi, 1978.
———, *Lokayata: A Study in Ancient Indian Materialism*, Delhi, 1978.

———, 'Sources of Indian Idealism', *History and Society: Essays in Honour of Professor Niharranjan Ray*, Calcutta, 1978, pp. 239-70.

Chattopadhyaya, S., *Bimbisāra to Aśoka*, Calcutta, 1977.

———, *Social Life in Ancient India* (in the background of the *Yājñavalkya-Smṛti*), Calcutta, 1965.

Childe, G., *Bronze Age*, Cambridge, 1930.

———, *What Happened in History?*, London, 1942.

Choudhary, R.K., *Kauṭilya's Political Ideas and Institutions*, Varanasi, 1971.

———, 'Iron and Urbanisation in Ancient India', *JBPP*, I, 1977, pp. 127-32.

———, 'Ownership of the Land in Ancient India', *JBRS*, LIII, 1967, pp. 27-52.

———, 'Position of the Brāhmaṇas in Ancient India', *Professor P.K. Gode Commemoration Volume*, ed. H.L. Hariyappa and M.M. Patkar, Poona, 1960, pp. 43-9.

———, 'Some Aspects of Feudalism in South India', *JIH*, LIII, 1975, pp. 63-100.

———, '*Jaiminīya Grihyasūtra:* Some Aspects of Social History', *JOIB*, III, 1953-4, pp. 391-402.

Chowdhury, K.A., K.S. Saraswat and G.M. Ruth, *Ancient Agriculture and Forestry in North India*, Bombay, 1977.

Crawford, S. Cromwell, *Evolution of Hindu Ethical Ideas*, Calcutta, 1974.

Cunningham, A., *Coins of Ancient India*, Delhi, 1971.

Daftari, K.L., *The Social Institutions in Ancient India*, Nagpur, 1947.

Dange, S.A., *India From Primitive Communism to Slavery: A Marxist Study of Ancient History in Outline*, Delhi, 1979.

Darian, S.G., 'The Economic History of the Ganges to the End of Gupta Times', *JESHO*, XIII, I, 1970, pp. 62-87.

Das, D.N., *The Early History of Kalinga*, Calcutta, 1977.

Das, D.R., *Economic History of the Deccan: From the First to the Sixth Century* AD, Delhi, 1969.

Das, S.K., 'A Study of Folk-Cattle Rites', *MI*, XXXIII, 1953, pp. 232-41.

Dasgupta, M., '*Sraddha* and *Bhakti* in Vedic Literature', *IHQ*, VI, 1930, pp. 315-33, 487-513.

Dasgupta, Surama, *Development of Moral Philosophy in India*, Bombay, 1961.

Datta, B.N., 'Brahmanical Counter Revolution', *JBORS*, XXVII, 1941, pp. 369-75.

———, 'Origin and Development of Indian Social Polity', *MI*, XXII, 1942, pp. 22-63.

Datta, J.M., 'Influence of Religious Beliefs in the Geographical Distribution of Brahmanas in Bengal', *MI*, XIII, 1962, pp. 277-91.

De, Gokuldas, *Democracy in Early Buddhist Samgha*, Calcutta, 1955.

———, *Significance and Importance of Jatakas (with Special Reference to Bharhut)*, Calcutta, 1951.

Deo, S.B., 'Some Social Impacts on Jaina Monastic Life', *Indica*, Bombay, 1953, p. 77.

Derrett, John Duncan M., *Introduction to Modern Hindu Law*, Oxford, 1963.

———, *Religion, Law and the State in India*, London, 1968.

Deshmukh, P.S., *Religion in Vedic Literature*, Bombay, 1933.

Dharma, P.C., 'Some Customs and Beliefs from the *Rāmāyaṇa*', *PO*, II, 1937-8, pt. 2.

Divatia, H.V., 'Hindu Law, "Ancient and Modern"', *BV*, I, 1940, pt. II, pp. 120-3.

Dixit, V.V., 'Relations of Epics to Brāhmaṇa Literatures', *PO*, VI, 1941, pp. 1-32.

Dogra, S.D., 'Horse in Ancient India', *JOIB*, XXIII, 1973, pp. 54-8.

Douglas, M., ed., *Man in Society: Patterns of Human Organisation*, VI, London, 1964.

Drekmeier, C., *Kingship and Community in Early India*, Bombay, 1962.

Dubois, A.J.A., *Description of the Character, Manners and Customs of the People of India and of Their Institutions, Religious and Civil*, London, 1817.

———, *Hindu Manners Customs and Ceremonies*, tr. H.K. Beauchhamp, Delhi, 1978.

Durkheim, E., *The Elementary Forms of Religious Life*, London, 1915.

Dutt, N., *Aspects of Mahayana Buddhism and its Relation to Hinayana*, London, 1930.

Dutt, N.K., *Origin and Growth of Caste in India*, vol. I, Calcutta, 1968.

Dutt, S., *Buddhist Monks and Monasteries of India: Their History and Their Contribution to Indian Culture*, London, 1962.

———, *Early Buddhist Monachism*, rev. edn., Bombay, 1960.

Dutta, B.N., *Dialectics of Hindu Ritualism*, Calcutta, 1952.

Dwivedi, R.C., ed., *Contribution of Jainism to Indian Culture*, Varanasi, 1975.

Edgerton, F., *The Beginnings of Indian Philosophy: Selections from the Rigveda, Atharva Veda, Upanisads and Mahabharata*, London, 1965.

Eichler, Lillian, *The Customs of Mankind*, London, 1924.

Ekeh, Peter, *Social Exchange Theory: The Two Traditions*, London, 1974.

Emerson, Ralph Waldo, *Essays: First and Second Series*, Delhi, 1965.

Engels, F., *The Origin of the Family, Private Property and the State: In the Light of the Researches of Lewis H. Morgan*, Moscow, 1948.

Fairservis, W.A., *The Roots of Ancient India: The Archaeology of Early Indian Civilization*, London, 1971.

Fick, Richard, *The Social Organisation in North-India in Buddha's Time*, tr. S.K. Maitra, Delhi, 1972.

Filliozat, J., *India: The Country and its Traditions*, tr. Margaret Ledesert, London, 1962.

———, *Political History of India: From the Earliest Times to the 7th Century* AD, tr. Philip Spratt, Calcutta, 1957.

———, 'Les doctrines indiennes de la charite', *Annuaire du College de France*, Paris, 1955, pp. 229-35.

Firth, R., ed., *Man and Culture: Evaluation of the Work of Bronislaw Malinowski*, London, 1960.

———, *Primitive Polynesian Economy*, London, 1939.

Fiser, Ivo, 'The Problem of the Setthi in the Buddhist Jatakas', *AO*, XXII, 1954, pp. 238-66.

Fox, Robin, *Kinship and Marriage: An Anthropological Perspective*, London, 1967.

Frazer, J.G., *The Golden Bough: A Study in Magic and Religion*, abridged edn., London, 1954.

Fromm, Erich, *The Anatomy of Human Destructiveness*, New York, 1975.

Fuchs, Stephen, *The Origin of Man and his Culture*, Bombay, 1963.

Gajendragadkar, S.N., 'The Roving Mendicants in the *Mahābhārata* and their Teaching', *JASB* (Bombay), XXX, 1955, pp. 43-51.

Ganguly, D.K., *Aspects of Ancient Indian Administration*, Delhi, 1979.

Ganguly, R., 'Cattle and Cattle-rearing in Ancient India', *ABORI*, XII, 1931, pp. 216-30.

Ghosh, A., *The City in Early Historical India*, Simla, 1973.

Ghoshal, U.N., *The Agrarian System in Ancient India*, Calcutta, 1973.

———, *Contributions to the History of the Hindu Revenue System*, Calcutta, 1972.

———, 'The Status of the Brāhmaṇas in the *Dharmasūtras*', *IHQ*, XXIII, 1947, pp. 83-92.

———, 'The Status of the Śūdras in the *Dharmasūtras*', *IC*, XIV, 1947-8, pp. 21-7.

Ghurye, G.S., *Caste and Class in India*, Bombay, 1957.

———, *Vedic India*, Bombay, 1979.

Gluckman, Max, *Politics, Law and Ritual in Tribal Societies*, Oxford, 1977.

Gokhale, B.G., 'Brahmanas in Early Buddhist Literature', *JIH*, XLVIII, 1970, pp. 51-61.

———, 'Buddhist Social Ideal's', *IHQ*, XXXII, 1956, pp. 141-7.

Gombrich, Richard F., ed., *The Perfect Generosity of Prince Vessantara*, Oxford, 1977.

———, *Percept and Practice*, Oxford, 1971.

Gonda, J., *Aspects of Early Viṣṇuism*, rpt., Delhi, 1969.

———, *Change and Continuity in Indian Religion*, rpt., New Delhi, 1985.

———, '"Gifts and Giving" in the *Ṛgveda*', *Selected Studies*, vol. IV, pp. 122-43.

Gopal, Lallanji, *Aspects of History of Agriculture in Ancient India*, Varanasi, 1980.

———, 'India's Foreign Trade in the Ancient Period: Its Impact on Society', *QRHS*, V, 1965-6, pp. 186-93.

———, 'Ownership of Agricultural Land in Ancient India', *JBRS*, XLVI, 1960, pp. 27-44.

———, 'Proprietary Rights of the Village Community in Northern India', *S.K. De Memorial Volume*, ed. R.C. Hazra and S.C. Banerji, Calcutta, 1972, pp. 145-55.

———, 'Some Terms of Ancient Land-grants', *JIH*, XXXVIII, 1960, pp. 587-92.

Gopal, M.H., *Mauryan Public Finance*, London, 1935.

Gopal, Ram, *India of Vedic Kalpasūtras*, Delhi, 1959.

Goswami, K.G., 'Buddhism in the Śuṅga Period', *IHQ*, XXXII, 1956, pp. 211-22.

Gouldner, S.W., 'The Norm of Reciprocity', *ASR*, XXV, 1960, pp. 161-78.

Gregory, C.A., *Gifts and Commodities*, London, 1983.

Griswold, H.D., *The Religion of Rigveda*, rpt., Delhi, 1971.

Gupta, B.A., 'Folklore in Caste Proverbs', *JASB*, NS, XIII, 1917, pp. 1-12.

Handiqui, K.K., *Yaśastilaka and Indian Culture*, Jivaraja Jaina Granthamala, no. 2, Sholapur, 1949.

Hands, A.R., *Charities and Social Aid in Greece and Rome*, London, 1968.

Hardy, Spence, *Eastern Monachism*, London, 1850.

Hazra, R.C., *Studies in the Puranic Records on Hindu Rites and Customs*, rpt., Delhi, 1975.

———, 'Pre-Puranic Society before 200 AD', *IHQ*, XV, 1939, pp. 403-31.

Heesterman, J.C., *The Ancient Indian Royal Consecration*, The Hague, 1957.

———, 'Reflections on the Significance of the *Dakṣiṇā*', *Indo-Iran. Journal*, III, 1959, pp. 241-58.

———, 'Brahmin, Ritual and Renounce', *Wien. Z. Kunde Sud-Ostasien's*, 1964, pp. 1-31.

Herskovits, M.J., *Cultural Anthropology*, rpt., Delhi, 1969.

———, *Economic Anthropology*, 1952.

Hindery, R., *Comparative Ethics in Hindu and Buddhist Traditions*, Delhi, 1978.

Hoebel, E. Adamson, *Man in the Primitive World: An Introduction to Anthropology*, New York, 1958.

Hoebel, E. Adamson and Everett L. Frost, *Cultural and Social Anthropology*, New Delhi, 1976.

Hopkins, E.W., *The Mutual Relations of the Four Castes According to the Mānavadharmaśāstram*, Delhi, 1976.

———, *The Social and Military Position of the Ruling Caste in Ancient India as Represented by the Sanskrit Epic*, rpt., Delhi, 1972.

Hutchinson, W., ed., *Customs of the World*, vol. I, London, n.d.

Hyde, L., *The Gift: Imagination and the Erotic Life of Property*, New York, 1979.

Jain, J.C., *Life in Ancient India as Described in the Jain Canons*, Bombay, 1947.

Jain, J.P., *The Jaina Sources of the History of Ancient India (100 BC-AD 900)*, Delhi, 1964.

———, *Religion and Culture of the Jains*, Delhi, 1975.

Jain, K.C., *Lord Mahavira and His Times*, Bikaner, 1974.

Jain, R.C., *The Most Ancient Aryan Society*, Sri Ganganagar, 1964.

Jaiswal, Suvira, *The Origin and Development of Vaisnavism*, Delhi, 1967.

———, 'Studies in Early Indian Social History: Trends and Possibilities', *IHR*, VI, 1979-80, pp. 1-63.

Jayasundere, A.D., 'Why is *Dāna* not Included in the Noble Eightfold Path', *MB*, 1947, pp. 80-1.

Jayaswal, K.P., *Manu and Yājñavalkya*, Calcutta, 1930.

Jha, D.N., *Revenue System in Post-Maurya and Gupta Times*, Calcutta, 1967.

———, *Studies in Early Indian Economic History*, Delhi, 1980.

———, 'Early Indian Feudalism: A Historiographical Critique', Presidential Address, Section I, Ancient India, *Pro. IHC*, 1979, pp. 15-45.

Jha, H.N., *The Licchavis (of Vaiśālī)*, Varanasi, 1970.

Jha, M., *The Beggars of a Pilgrims City*, Varanasi, 1979.

———, *Dimensions of Indian Civilization*, Delhi, 1979.

Joshi, M.C., 'Early Historical Urban Growth in India: Some Observations', *Puratattva*, no. 7, 1974, pp. 90-1.

Joshi, N.P., *Life in Ancient Uttarapatha*, Varanasi, 1967.

Jung, G.C., *Psychology and Religion: West and East*, vol. II, tr. R.F.C. Hull, London, 1958.

Kaegi, Adolf, *Life in Ancient India: Studies in Rig Vedic India*, tr. R. Arrowsmith, rpt., Calcutta, 1950.

———, *The Rigveda*, tr. R. Arrowsmith, rpt., Delhi, 1972.

Kanal, P.V., *Altruism*, Delhi, 1956.

Kane, P.V., *History of Dharmaśāstra*, vols. I-V, Poona, 1930-74.

———, *Kātyāyanasmṛti on Vyavahāra (Law and Procedure)*, Bombay, 1933.

Kangle, R.P., *The Kauṭilya Arthaśāstra*, 3 pts., Bombay, 1965.

Kapadia, K.M., *Marriage and Family in India*, Bombay, 1966.

Karambelkar, V.W., *The Atharvavedic Civilization: Its Place in the Indo-Aryan Culture*, Nagpur, 1959.

Karve, I., *Kinship Organization in India*, Bombay, 1965.

Keith, A.B., *The Religion and Philosophy of the Veda and Upanishads*, 2 pts., rpt., Delhi, 1970.

Keny, L.B., *Agrarian and Fiscal Economy in the Mauryan and Post-Mauryan Age (c. 324 BC-AD 320)*, Delhi, 1973.

———, 'Land Sale in Ancient India (321 BC-AD 320)', *JOIB*, XII, 1962-3, pp. 259-63.

———, 'Public Expenditure in Ancient India (324 BC-AD 300)', *JIH*, XLII, 1964, pp. 809-21.

Koller, John M., 'Ritual and World View in the *Ṛg-Veda*', *Religion and Society in Ancient India, Sudhakar Chattopadhyaya Commemoration Volume*, Calcutta, 1984, pp. 109-19.

Kosambi, D.D., *The Culture and Civilization of Ancient India in Historical Outline*, rpt., Delhi, 1976.

———, *An Introduction to the Study of Indian History*, Bombay, 1975.

———, *Myth and Reality: Studies in the Formation of Indian Culture*, Bombay, 1962.

———, 'Dhenukakata', *JASB* (Bombay), NS, XXX, 1955, pp. 50-71.

———, 'Marxism and Ancient Indian Culture', *ABORI*, XXIX, 1948, pp. 271-7.

———, 'Marxist Approach to Indian Chronology', *ABORI*, XXXI, 1950, pp. 258-66.

———, 'On the Development of Feudalism in India', *ABORI*, XXXVI, 1955, pp. 258-69.

Krause, C., *An Introduction of Jaina Ethics*, 1929.

Krishna, Y., 'Decline of Buddhism in India', *VIJ*, II, 1964, pp. 264-97.

———, 'Was There Any Conflict between the Brahmins and the Buddhists', *IHQ*, XXX, 1954, pp. 167-77.

Kropotkin, Petr, *Mutual Aid: A Factor of Evolution*, New York, 1904.

Kulkarni, C., *Vedic Foundations of Indian Culture*, Bombay, 1973.

Kunte, M.M., *The Vicissitudes of Aryan Civilization in India*, Bombay, 1880.

Kushner, Gilbert, 'Hindu *Jajmānī* System', *MI*, XLVII, 1967, pp. 35-60.

Law, B.C., *Geography of Early Buddhism*, rpt., New Delhi, 1979.

———, *India as Described in Early Taxes of Buddhism and Jainism*, Delhi, 1980.

———, 'Bhikshunis in Indian Inscriptions', *EI*, XXV, 1939-40, pp. 31-4.

———, 'A Short Account of the Wandering Ascetics (*Parivrajakas*) in India in the Sixth Century BC', *JBRS*, LIII, 1967, pp. 17-26.

———, 'Social, Economic and Religious Conditions of Ancient India: According to the Buddhist Texts', *Commemorative Essays Presented to K.B. Pathak*, Poona, 1934, pp. 68-79.

———, *A Study of the Mahāvastu*, Delhi, 1978.

Lowie, R.H., *Primitive Society*, London, 1921.

———, *Social Organization*, New York, 1960.

MacCormack, G., 'Mauss and the Spirit of the Gift', *Oceania*, LII, 1982, pp. 286-93.

———, 'Reciprocity', *Man*, XI, pp. 89-103.

Macdonell, A.A., 'The Principles to be followed in Translating the *Ṛgveda*', *R.G. Bhandarkar Commemoration Volume*, rpt., Delhi, 1977, pp. 3-19.

Macnicot, Nicol, *Indian Theism*, rpt., Delhi, 1968.

Madan, T.N., 'The Gift of Food', *Culture and Society: A Festschrift to Dr. A. Aiyappan*, Delhi, 1975.

Mahadevan, T.M.P., 'Social, Ethical and Spiritual Values in Indian Philosophy', *The Indian Mind: Essentials of Indian Philosophy and Culture*, ed. Charles A. Moore, Honolulu, 1967, pp. 152-72.

Mairy, Lucy, *An Introduction to Social Anthropology*, Oxford, 1972.

Maity, S.K., *Early Indian Coins and Currency System*, Delhi, 1970.

Maitra, S.K., *The Ethics of the Hindus*, rpt., Delhi, 1978.

Majumdar, A.K., *Economic Background of the Epic Society*, Calcutta, 1977.

Majumdar, D.N., 'Disease, Death and Divination in Certain Primitive Societies in India, *MI*, XIII, 1933, pp. 115-49.

———, Tribal Cultures and Acculturation', *MI*, XIX, 1939, pp. 99-172.

Majumdar, R.C., *Corporate Life in Ancient India*, Calcutta, 1969.

Malefift, A.W., *Religion and Culture: An Introduction to Anthropology of Religion*, New Delhi, 1968.

Malik, S.C., *Indian Civilization: The Formative Period*, Simla, 1968.

Malinowski, B., *Argonauts of the Western Pacific*, London, 1922.

Mallik, M.S., 'Brahmanas as Depicted in Pāli Canon', *Religion and Society in Ancient India, S.C. Chattopadhyaya Commemorative Volume*, Calcutta, 1984, pp. 287-305.

Mandelbaum, D.G., *Society in India*, 2 vols., Bombay, 1970.

Marshall, John and Alfred Foucher, *The Monuments of Sanchi*, 3 vols., London, 1940.

Mauss, Marcel, *The Gift*, tr. I.A.N. Cunnison, London, 1954.

McCrindle, J.W., *Ancient India as Described by Megasthenes and Arrian*, Calcutta, 1960.

———, *Ancient India as Described in Classical Literature*, rpt., New Delhi, 1979.

Mckenzie, J., *Hindu Ethics: A Historical and Critical Essay*, rpt., New Delhi, 1971.

Mees, G.H., *Dharma and Society*, The Hague, 1935.

Metraux, Guy S. and Francois Crouzet, ed., *Studies in the Cultural History of India*, Unesco, Agra, 1965.

Michael, Aloysius, *Radhakrishnan on Hindu Moral Life and Action*, Delhi, 1979.

Mishra, G.S.P., *The Age of Vinaya*, New Delhi, 1972.

———, 'A Study of Philanthropy in Early Buddhist Ethics', *Indica*, XVIII, no. 2, 1981, pp. 73-81.

Mishra, Padma, *Evolution of Brāhmaṇa Class (In the Perspective of Vedic Priesthood)*, Varanasi, 1978.

Mishra, V.B., *Religious Beliefs and Practices of North India during the Early Medieval Period*, Leiden, 1973.

Mishra, Y., *An Early History of Vaiśālī*, Delhi, 1962.

Mitra, Priti, *Life and Society in the Vedic Age*, Calcutta, 1966.

Mitra, S.C., 'On Some Indian Ceremonies for Disease Transference', *JASB*, NS, XIII, 1917, pp. 13-21.

Mitra, Veda, *India of Dharma Sūtras*, Delhi, 1969.

Mitter, Dwarka Nath, *Position of Women in Hindu Law*, Calcutta, 1913.

Mookerji, R.K., *Ancient Indian Education* (*Brahmanical and Buddhist*), Delhi, 1969.

Mookerji, Sandhya, *Some Aspects of Social Life in Ancient India* (*325 BC-AD 200*), Allahabad, 1976.

Morgan, L.H., *Ancient Society*, rpt., Calcutta, 1958.

Moti Chandra, *Trade and Trade Routes in Ancient India*, Delhi, 1977.

———, *The World of Courtesans*, Delhi, 1973.

Motwani, K., *Manu Dharmaśāstra: A Sociological and Historical Study*, Madras, 1958.

Muir, J., 'On the Relations of the Priests to the other Classes of Indian Society in the Vedic Age', *JRAS*, II, 1866, pp. 257-302.

Mukherjee, B.N., *The Disintegration of the Kushana Empire*, Varanasi, 1976.

Mulla, D.F., *Principles of Hindu Law*, Bombay, 1960.

Nag, D.S., *Tribal Economy*, Delhi, 1958.

Nair, B.N., *The Dynamic Brahmin*, Bombay, 1959.

Nanda, Serena, *Cultural Anthropology*, New York, 1980.

Nandi, R.N., *Religious Institutions and Cults in the Deccan* (*c.* AD *600-1000*), Delhi, 1973.

———, *Social Roots of Religion in Ancient India*, Calcutta, 1986.

———, 'Client Ritual and Conflict in Early Brahmanical Order', *IHR*, V, nos. 1-2, pp. 64-118.

———, 'Land Grant, Colonization and Food Production *c.* AD 600-1000', *Pro IHC*, 1969, pp. 117-19.

———, 'Some Social Aspects of the Grihyasutras', *Pro. IHC*, 1977, pp. 167-77.

Narain, A.K., *The Indo-Greeks*, Oxford, 1957.

Nash, Manning, *Primitive and Peasant Economic Systems*, New York, 1966.

Nath, Vijay, 'Continuity and Change in the Institution of Dāna', *JASB* (Bombay), NS, LIV-LV, 1979-80, pp. 95-102.

———, 'Dāna in the Context of Commerce and Urbanisation in Kuṣāṇa Times', *JBRS*, LXV-LXVI, pts. 1-4, 1979-80, pp. 166-77.

Neale, Walter C., 'Reciprocity and Redistribution', *Cultural and Social Anthropology: Selected Readings*, ed. R.B. Hammond, London, 1964.

Nigam, S.S., *Economic Organisation in Ancient India (200 BC-AD 200)*, New Delhi, 1975.

Niyogi, Pushpa, *Contributions to the Economic History of Northern India: From the Tenth to the Twelfth Century AD*, Calcutta, 1962.

———, 'Organisation of Buddhist Monasteries in Ancient Bengal and Bihar', *JIH*, II, 1973, pt. III, pp. 531-57.

Norbeck, E., *Religion in Primitive Society*, New York, 1961.

O'Malley, L.S.S., *Indian Caste Customs*, rpt., Delhi, 1974.

———, *Popular Hinduism*, Cambridge, 1935.

Oman, J.C., *Cults, Customs and Superstitions of India*, rpt., Delhi, 1972.

———, *The Mystics, Ascetics and Saints of India*, London, 1903.

Pal, Radhabinod, *The History of Hindu Law in the Vedic Age and in Post-Vedic Times down to the Institutes of Manu*, Calcutta, 1958.

Palmer, G.H., *Altruism: Its Nature and Varieties*, New York, 1919.

Pargiter, F.E., 'Verses Relating to Gifts of Land cited in Indian Land Grants', *JRAS*, 1912, pp. 248-54.

Parry, J., 'The Gift, the Indian Gift and the Indian Gift', *Man*, XXI, 1986, pp. 453-73.

———, 'The Moral Parts of Exchange in a Hindu Pilgrimage City', *The Symbolism of Money and the Morality of Exchange*, ed. M. Bloch and J. Parry.

Patel, Manilal, 'The Ninth *Maṇḍala* of the *Ṛgveda*', *BV*, I, 1940, pt. II, pp. 17-27.

Prasad, Kameshwar, *Cities, Crafts and Commerce under the Kuṣāṇas*, Delhi, 1984.

———, 'Urban Occupations and Crafts in the Kuṣāṇa Period', *Pro. IHC*, 1977, pp. 107-17.

Prasad, Narmadeshwar, *The Myth of the Caste System*, Patna, 1957.

Prasad, P.C., *Foreign Trade and Commerce in Ancient India*, Delhi, 1977.

Przyluski, J., *The Legend of Emperor Aśoka in Indian and Chinese Texts*, tr. D.K. Biswas, Calcutta, 1967.

Puri, B.N., *India in the Time of Patañjali*, Bombay, 1968.

———, *India under the Kushans*, Bombay, 1965.

———, 'Some Aspects of Social Life in Kushana Period', *IC*, XVI, 1949.

Radcliffe Brown, A.R., *Structure and Function in Primitive Society*, London, 1952.

Radin, Paul, *Primitive Religion: Its Nature and Origin*, New York, 1957.

Raftis, J.A.,'Western Monasticism and Economic Organisation', *Comparative Study of East and West*, vol. 3, 1960-1.

Raghunathji, K., 'Bombay Beggars and Criers', *IA*, XI, 1882, pp. 14, 22, 44, 172.

Ragozin, Z.A., *Vedic India (As embodied principally in the Rig-Veda)*, rpt., Delhi, 1961.

Rahul, W.I., *What the Buddha Taught*, Bedford, 1959.

Rahurkar, Y.G., *The Seers of the Rigveda*, Poona, 1964.

Rai, Jaimal, *The Rural-Urban Economy and Social Changes in Ancient India (300 BC-AD 600)*, Varanasi, 1974.

Ranade, R.K., 'Indian Charity', *PO*, VI, 1941, pp. 37-42.

Rao, K.L.S., *The Concept of Shraddha (in the Brāhmaṇas, Upaniṣads and the Gītā)*, Delhi, 1974.

Rapson, E.J., ed., *The Cambridge History of India*, vol. 1, *Ancient India*, rpt., Delhi, 1955.

Rawlinson, H.G., *Intercourse Between India and the Western World: From the Earliest Times to the Fall of Rome*, rpt., Delhi, 1977.

Ray, J.C., 'Food and Drink in Ancient India', *MI*, XIV, 1934, pp. 15-35.

Ray, Niharranjan, *Maurya and Post-Maurya Art*, Delhi, 1975.

Redfield, Robert, *Peasant Society and Culture: An Anthropological Approach to Civilization*, Chicago, 1956.

Renou, L., *The Civilization in Ancient India*, tr. P. Spratt, Calcutta, 1954.

———, *Vedic India*, tr. P. Spratt, Calcutta, 1957.

Rice, Stanley, *Hindu Customs and Their Origins*, London, 1937.

Risley, H., *The People of India*, ed. W. Crooke, rpt., Delhi, 1969.

Roy, Brajdeo Prasad, *The Later Vedic Economy*, Delhi, 1984.

———, *Political Ideas and Institutions in the Mahabharata*, Calcutta, 1975.

Roy, T.N., *A Study of Northern Black Polished Ware Culture: An Iron Age Culture in India*, Delhi, 1986.

Ruben, W., 'The Development of Town in Ancient India', *History and Society: Essays in Honour of Professor Niharranjan Ray*, ed. D.P. Chattopadhyaya, Calcutta, 1978, pp. 229-37.

Russel, Bertrand, *Human Society in Ethics and Politics*, London, 1954.

Saddhatissa, H., *Buddhist Ethics: Essence of Buddhism*, London, 1970.

Sahi, M.D.N., 'Stratigraphical Position of the NBP Ware in the Upper Ganga Basin and Its Date', *Puratattva*, no. 7, 1974, pp. 91-4.

Saraswati, B.N., *Brahmanic Ritual Tradition*, Simla, 1977.

Sarkar, Benoy Kumar, *The Positive Background of Hindu Sociology*, bk. I, *Introduction to Hindu Legal History*, Hoshiarpur, 1958.

Sasaki, G.H., *Social and Humanistic Life in India*, Delhi, 1971.

Sastri, K.A.N., *Aspects of India's History and Culture*, Delhi, 1974.

———, ed., *A Comprehensive History of India*, vol. II, *The Mauryas and Satavahanas*, Bombay, 1957.

Satyarthi, H.C., 'Some Aspects of Group-consciousness among the Brahmanas of Northern India 185 BC-AD 319', *Pro. IHC*, 1969, pp. 98-104.

———, 'Some Aspects of the Problem of Insecurity Among the Higher Brahmanas during the Post-Maurya Period of North India (*c.* 2000 BC-AD 300)', *Pro. IHC*, 1978, pp. 296-304.

———, 'Some Aspects of the Social Position of the Brahmanas 185 BC-AD 319', *Pro. IHC*, 1970, pp. 93-101.

———, 'Some Aspects of the Vaisyas during the Post-Maurya Period of Northern India *c.* 185 BC-AD 319', *Pro. IHC*, 1972, pp. 86-91.

———, 'Some Aspects of the *Stridhana* in Post Maurya North India (*c.* 2000 BC-AD 300)', *Pro IHC*, 1973, pp. 114-19.

Satyavrat, 'Bhoodan in Ancient India', *BV*, XVII, 1957, pp. 143-7.

Schubring, W., *The Doctrine of the Jainas: Described After the Old Sources*, tr. W. Beurlen, Delhi, 1962.

Schwimmer, Erik, 'Reciprocity and Structure: A Semiotic Analysis of Some Orokaiva Exchange Data', *Man*, XIV, 1979, no. 2, pp. 271-85.

Sen, B.C., *Economics in Kautilya*, Calcutta, 1967.

Sengupta, Padmini, *Everyday Life in Ancient India*, Bombay, 1955.

Shah, C.J., *Jainism in Northern India (c. 800 BC-AD 526)*, Bombay, 1932.

Shamashastry, R., 'Economical Philosophy of Ancient India', *ABORI*, XII, 1930-1, pp. 25-39.

Sharma, Hardutt, 'Contributions to the History of Brahmanical Asceticism', *PO*, II, 1938-9.

Sharma, Ramashraya, *A Socio-Political Study of the Valmiki Ramayana*, Delhi, 1971.

Sharma, R.N., *Ancient India According to Manu*, Delhi, 1980.

———, *Brahmins Through the Ages: A Study of Their Social, Cultural, Political, Religious and Economic Life*, Delhi, 1977.

———, *Culture and Civilization as Revealed in Śrautasūtras*, Delhi, 1977.

Sharma, R.S., *Ancient India*, New Delhi, 1980.

———, *Aspects of Political Ideas and Institutions in Ancient India*, Delhi, 1968.

———, *Indian Feudalism: c. 300-1200*, Calcutta, 1965.

———, *Light on Early Indian Society and Economy*, Bombay, 1966; rev. edn., *Perspectives in Social and Economic History of Early India*, New Delhi, 1983.

———, *Material Culture and Social Formations in Ancient India*, Delhi, 1983.

———, 'Social Changes in Early Medieval India (*c.* AD 500-1200)', *The First Devraj Chanana Memorial Lecture*, Delhi, 1969.

———, *Sudras in Ancient India*, Delhi, 1958.

———, ed., *Indian Society: Historical Probings*, in Memory of D.D. Kosambi, Delhi, 1974.

———, 'Forms of Property in the Early Portions of *Rig Veda*', *Essays in Honour of Professor S.C. Sarkar*, Delhi, 1976.

———, 'Conflict Distribution and Differentiation in Ṛg-Vedic Society', *Pro. IHC*, 1977, pp. 177-91.

———, 'Class Formation and its Material Basis in the Upper Gangetic Basin (*c*. 1000-500 BC)', *IHR*, II, 1975, pp. 1-13.

———, 'The Later Vedic Phase and the Painted Grey Ware Culture', *History and Society: Essays in Honour of Professor Niharranjan Ray*, ed. D.P. Chattopadhyaya, Calcutta, 1978, pp. 133-41.

———, 'Stages in Social Evolution in Ancient India', *Ancient Indian Culture and Literature, Pt. Ganga Ram Commemoration Volume*, ed. Mohan Chand, Delhi, 1980.

———, 'Iron and Urbanisation in the Ganga Basin', *IHR*, I, 1974, no. 1, pp. 98-103.

———, 'Problems of Social Formations in Early India', General Presidential Address, *Pro. IHC*, 1975, pp. 1-14.

Shastri, Ajay Mitra, *An Outline of Early Buddhism*, Varanasi, 1965.

Sherring, M.A., *Benaras: The Sacred City of the Hindus: Past and Present*, Delhi, 1975.

———, *Hindu Tribes and Castes*, 3 vols., rpt., New Delhi, 1974.

Sidhanta, N.K., *The Heroic Age of India*, rpt., New Delhi, 1977.

Sikdar, J.C., *Studies in the Bhagwati Sutra*, Muzaffarpur, 1964.

Singh, J.P., *Aspects of Early Jainism (As known from the Epigraphs)*, Varanasi, 1972.

Singh, M.M., *Life in North-Eastern India in Pre-Mauryan Times*, Delhi, 1967.

———, 'Dhamma of the *Jātakas*', *JBRS*, 1963, pp. 43-7.

———, 'The Early Jain Monastic Life', *IHQ*, XXXVI, 1960, pp. 171-6.

———, 'Life in the Buddhist Monastery During the Sixth Century BC', *JBRS*, XI, 1954, pp. 131-54.

Singh, R.P., 'Artisans in Manu', *Pro. IHC*, 1970, 102-17.

Singh, S.D., 'Iron in Ancient India', *JESHO*, V, 1962, pp. 212-16.

Singh, S.P., 'Metal, Technology During the Kushana Period', *Pro. IHC*, 1977, pp. 736-41.

Singh, Shivaji, *Evolution of the Smṛti Law*, Varanasi, 1972.

Sinha, B.P., *Readings in Kauṭilya's Arthaśāstra*, Delhi, 1976.

Sinha, N.K.P., *Political Ideas and Ideals in the Mahabharata*, Delhi, 1976.

Sinha, Prabhavati, *Smṛti, Political and Legal System: A Socio-Economic Study*, New Delhi, 1982.

Sircar, D.C., *Landlordism and Tenancy in Ancient and Medieval India as Revealed by Epigraphical Records*, Lucknow, 1969.
———, ed., *Early Indian Indigenous Coins*, Calcutta, 1970.
———, *Some Problems Concerning the Kushanas*, Dharwar, 1971.
———, *Studies in the Political and Administrative Systems in Ancient and Medieval India*, Delhi, 1974.
———, 'Some Epithets of Brāhmaṇa Donees in South Indian Characters', *JIH*, LI, 1973, pt. I, pp. 289-92.
———, *Social Life in Ancient India*, Calcutta, 1971.
Siri, Perera, 'Charity or Dana in Buddhism', *MB*, 1973, pp. 172-4.
Sogani, K.C., *Ethical Doctrines in Jainism*, Jivaraja Jaina Granthamala, no. 19, Sholapur, 1967.
Somasundaram, A.M., 'Glimpses into Primitive Culture of India', *MI*, XXX, 1950, pp. 28-45.
Soni, R.L., 'Aspects of Dāna', *MB*, 1957, no. 65, pp. 427-32, 462-70.
Sofokin, Pitiram A., *The Reconstruction of Humanity*, Bombay, 1958.
Spratt, P., *Hindu Culture and Personality: A Pyscho-Analytic Study*, Bombay, 1966.
Sramanera Jivaka, 'The Art of Giving', *MB*, 1959, pp. 279-83.
Srivastava, Balram, *Trade and Commerce in Ancient India: From the Earliest Times to c.* AD *300*, Varanasi, 1968.
Srivastava, S.L., *Folk Culture and Oral Tradition*, Delhi, 1974.
Sternbach, Ludwik, 'Law and Economic Conditions', *ABORI*, XXIII, 1952, pp. 528-48.
Stevenson, Sinclair, *The Rites of the Twice Born*, rpt., New Delhi, 1971.
Subbarao, B., 'Rise of Magadha in Indian History and Archaeology', *JOIB*, X, 1960-1, pp. 365-73.
Subrahmanyam, B.R., 'Appearance and Spread of Iron in India', *JOIB*, XIII, 1963-4, pp. 349-59.
Tachibana, S., *The Ethics of Buddhism*, rpt., London, 1975.
Thakur, S.C., *Christian and Hindu Ethics*, London, 1969.
Thakur, Upendra, 'Religion and Culture: A Study in Hindu Ethics', *Religion and Society in Ancient India, S. Chattopahdyaya Commemoration Volume*, Calcutta, 1984, pp. 333-43.
———, 'Economic Data from the Early Coins of India', *JESHO*, XIV, 1971, pp. 269-85.
———, 'A Study in Barter and Exchange in Ancient India, *JESHO*, XV, 1972, pp. 297-315.
Thapar, Romila, *Ancient Indian Social History: Some Interpretations*, Delhi, 1978.
———, 'Ethics, Religion and Social Protest in the First Millennium BC in

Northern India', *Dissent Protest and Reform in Indian Civilisation*, ed. S.C. Malik, Simla, 1977, pp. 115-30.

———, 'The Impact of Trade *c.* 100 BC-AD 300 in India', H. Kruger, ed., *Kunwar Mohammad Ashraf Volume*, Delhi, 1969, pp. 30-8.

———, 'Some Aspects of the Economic Data in the *Mahābhārata*', *ABORI*, Diamond Jubilee Volume, 1978, pp. 993-1007.

Thapar, Romesh, ed., *Tribe, Caste and Religion in India*, New Delhi, 1977.

Thomas, P., *Festivals and Holidays of India*, Bombay, 1971.

———, *Hindu Religion, Customs and Manners*, Bombay, n.d.

Thompson, E.P., 'Folklore Anthropology and Social History', *IHR*, III, 1977, no. 2, pp. 247-66.

Trautmann, T., 'The Gift in India', paper delivered before the Eleventh Annual Conference on South Asia, University of Wisconsin, November 1982.

Tripathi, Vibha, *The Painted Grey Ware: An Iron Age Culture of Northern India*, Delhi, 1976.

Upadhyaya, B., 'Indian Society in Post-Aśokan Age', *JBRS*, 1, 1964, pp. 27-31.

———, 'The Monastic Economy and Eradication of Beggary in Ancient India', *JBRS*, LIV, 1968, pp. 45-50.

Upadhyay, G.P., *Brahmanas in Ancient India*, Delhi, 1979.

Varma, V.P., *Early Buddhism and its Origins*, Delhi, 1973.

Vidyarthi, L.P., *The Sacred Complex in Hindu Gaya*, Bombay, 1961.

Vidyarthi, L.P. and B.K. Rai, *The Tribal Culture of India*, Delhi, 1977.

Vigasin, A.A. and A.M. Samozvantsev, *Society, State and Law in Ancient India*, New Delhi, 1985.

Vora, D.P., *Evolution of Morals in the Epics (Mahābhārata and Rāmāyaṇa)*, Bombay, 1959.

Vyas, S.N., *India in the Rāmāyaṇa Age*, Delhi, 1967.

———, 'Religious Beliefs in the *Rāmāyaṇa*', *JOIB*, VII, 1957-8, pp. 125-34.

———, 'Some Religious Practices of the *Rāmāyaṇa* Age', *JOIB*, V, 1956, pp. 217-33.

———, 'Minor Rites and Rituals Attributed to the Brahmanas in the *Nikāya* Texts of Pāli Canon', *JOIB*, XVII, 1967-8, pp. 363-72.

———, 'Social Groups and Ranking: An Aspect of Ancient Indian Social Life Deprived from the Pāli Canonical Texts', *JESHO*, X, 1967, pp. 278-316.

Wagle, N., *Society at the Time of Buddha*, Bombay, 1966.

Walker, Benjamin, *Hindu World*, 2 vols., rpt., New Delhi, 1984.

Warder, A.K., *Indian Buddhism*, Varanasi, 1970.

Warmington, E.H., *The Commerce Between the Roman Empire and India*, Cambridge, 1974.
Weber, Max, *The Sociology of Religion*, rpt., London, 1965.
Westermarck, E., *Christianity and Morals*, London, 1939.
———, *Origin and Development of Moral Ideas*, London, 1924.

Index